149.2
H 631

CRITICAL REALISM

CRITICAL REALISM

STUDIES IN THE PHILOSOPHY OF
MIND AND NATURE

BY

G. DAWES HICKS

M.A. (CANTAB.) ; PH.D. (LEIPZIG) ; LITT.D. (MANCHESTER)

FELLOW OF THE BRITISH ACADEMY
AND EMERITUS PROFESSOR OF PHILOSOPHY IN THE UNIVERSITY OF LONDON

MACMILLAN AND CO., LIMITED
ST. MARTIN'S STREET, LONDON
1938

PRINTED IN GREAT BRITAIN

PREFACE

THE papers contained in the present volume have been written at various times during the last twenty years, and are concerned with different aspects of one fundamental philosophical issue. I have selected them from a number of others because I find that together they form a coherent whole, and may be regarded as the working out in detail of a point of view respecting the relation of mind to nature to which I have gradually attained, by surveying the matter in the light of the history of thought and by grappling with the specific problems which the view in question at once raises.

I am, of course, aware that the term " critical realism " has been adopted by a group of seven distinguished American philosophers to denote a theory which they hold in common and which they sharply distinguish from that of the so-called " neo-realists ". But, in the first place, I had used the term long prior to their adoption of it. The first essay in this volume was published originally in 1917, three years before the appearance of the *Essays in Critical Realism*. And, in the second place, while there are many things in their book with which I am in thorough accord, there are also not a few from which I strongly dissent, some of which latter seem to me to give their case away. Moreover, while they disclaim any reference to the Kantian philosophy in their use of the word " critical ", I claim to be using it in what may legitimately be said to be the Kantian sense. It was, I take it, the essence of Kant's critical method that it should put as the first question to be faced in philosophical inquiry, what are the conditions of knowledge of objects ? For, in answering that question, there must come to light such explanation

v

as is possible of the range and validity of the notions which in knowing we necessarily employ in determining the nature of the objects known.

Probably the analysis of sense-perception which at the present day stands in most direct antithesis to the analysis which in these essays I am trying to develop is that known as the " sensum theory " ; and, accordingly, I have examined it at some length. The writers who adopt it fall, I think, into the cardinal error of regarding an " appearance " as an existent entity, a *tertium quid*, between the real object and the perceiving mind.

For a long while I was perplexed with the phenomena of imagination. So-called " images " did seem to present a character which it was difficult to reconcile with the results of the analysis one was offering of the facts of perception. I was, indeed, all along persuaded that the process of imagining is of one piece, so to speak, with the process of perceiving, on the one hand, and with that of conceptual thinking, on the other. In the end, however, I reached the view which is tentatively set forth in the fourth essay, and subsequent reflexion has strengthened my conviction that it is, in the main, on the right lines, and is psychologically justified.

Obviously, if the interpretation of cognitive processes here offered be well founded, it entails a conception of physical nature and of mental lives strikingly at variance with those frequently maintained. And in the later essays I have tried to bring out some of the chief points on which, as it seems to me, much current theorising will have to undergo modification. Let me only add that the tenth essay, which was originally written to open a discussion at the Jowett Society in Oxford, is reproduced here, not so much on account of its criticism of a doctrine which in 1934 was inciting a considerable amount of interest, as on account of the argument presented in its concluding paragraphs.

It may be thought, perhaps, that the last two essays in this volume are here somewhat out of place. But it appeared

to me that an account of Meinong's researches, which have
been to me extremely suggestive, would be helpful in following the lines of argument I have been pursuing. And the
examination of the doctrines of the relation between mind
and matter inculcated by Spinoza and Leibniz respectively
will be seen, I think, to be not irrelevant to the issues
handled in the preceding portions of this work.

I have to express my indebtedness to the following for
permission to republish articles : to the Secretary of the
Aristotelian Society for I, II, VII, VIII, IX, and XII, which
originally appeared in the Society's *Proceedings* ; to the
Editor of the *British Journal of Psychology* for IV ; to the
Editor of *Mind* for VI and XI ; to the Editor of the *Hibbert
Journal* for X ; and to the Editor of the *Proceedings of the
Sixth International Congress of Philosophy*, held at Harvard
University, Cambridge, Mass., for III. These essays are, in
the main, reproduced as they at first appeared, but I have
made some, and not unimportant, corrections. The fifth
essay has not hitherto been published. It formed originally
one of the Upton Lectures in Philosophy, delivered at Manchester College, Oxford, 1933-34, which I have, however,
revised and expanded.

G. DAWES HICKS

October 1937

CONTENTS

PAGE

INTRODUCTION - - - - - - - - **xiii**

   1. *The Term " Critical Realism "*   *xiii*

   2. *Can Realism Dispense with a Theory of Knowledge?*   *xviii*

I. THE BASIS OF CRITICAL REALISM (1917) - - - 1

   1. *The Nature of Cognition* - - - - - - *1*

   2. *The Two-fold Character of the Act of Perceiving* - - *8*

   3. *" Acquaintance and " Description "* - - - - *17*

   4. *Minds and Things* - - - - - - *26*

   5. *Concluding Considerations* - - - - - *43*

II. THE SENSUM THEORY (1916) - - - - - 48

   1. *Perceptual Situations of ordinary Experience* - - *49*

   2. *Broad's Reasons for rejecting the Common-sense View* - *51*

   3. *Can " Sensa " be " Appearances of " Physical Objects?* - *53*

   4. *" Sensa " may appear to be different from what they actually are* - - - - - - - - - *58*

   5. *The Theory of a general process of Sensing* - - - *60*

   6. *Perception and Introspection* - - - - - *66*

III. SENSIBLE APPEARANCES AND MATERIAL THINGS (1922) 68

IV. ON THE NATURE OF IMAGES (1924) - - - - 85

   Retention or Revival, an ultimate fact for psychology. Impossibility of " presentations " persisting in a region of sub-consciousness - - - - - - *85*

   1. *Imagination continuous with Perception. Nature of Perception. What it is that is revived or reproduced. Influence of Revival in the field of Perception* - - *89*

   2. *Transition from Perception to Imagination. Ambiguity of the term " image ". " Images " in the strict sense. Instances of the presence of a nucleus of perceived fact in " images " that appear as objective* - - - - *97*

   3. *Imagery in Dreams. Evidence of the presence of a nucleus of perceived fact as the basis of dream-imagery. The effect of Attention upon an " image "* - - - - *109*

   4. *The problem as to how subjective factors can affect the character of the content apprehended. What occurs in Einfühlung analogous to what occurs in imaging. Subjective factors do not necessarily vitiate the act of perception* - - - - - - - *116*

PAGE

V. CONCEPTUAL THOUGHT AND REAL EXISTENCE (1933) 121

1. *The Reflective Character of Conceptual Thinking* - *122*
2. *Analytic and Synthetic Nature of the Process of Judging* *124*
3. *The Objective Reference involved in Conceptual Thinking* *130*
4. *The Three-fold Distinction of Act, Content and Objective Reality* - - - - - - - - *134*
5. *Existence and Subsistence* - - - - - *135*
6. *Bergson's View of Conceptual Thinking* - - - *143*
7. *Bradley's Theory of the Nature of Judgment* - - *148*
8. *Subjectivity of the knowing process* not *a vitiating influence in respect to Knowledge* - - - - *152*

VI. F. H. BRADLEY'S TREATMENT OF NATURE (1925) - **156**

1. *What Bradley meant by " Nature "* - - - - *157*
2. *The Dictum that " to be real is to be indissolubly one with sentience "* - - - - - - - *157*
3. *Physical Nature and Finite Organisms* - - - *162*
4. *Bradley's Theory of Experience* - - - - *164*
5. *His View of Appearance and Reality* - - - *169*
6. *Absolute and Relative Truth* - - - - *172*

VII. THE DYNAMIC ASPECT OF NATURE (1925) - - **175**

1. *Force, in the popular acceptation of the term, not a subjective phenomenon* - - - - - *175*
2. *Nor exclusively based upon physiological conditions* - *184*
3. *Force and Energy in the physical world. Matter and Force inseparable* - - - - - - *187*
4. *Modern Atomic Theories and the Concept of Energy* - *193*
5. *General Theory of Relativity and the Forces of Nature* - *199*

VIII. PROFESSOR EDDINGTON'S PHILOSOPHY OF NATURE (1929) - - - - - - - - **204**

IX. IS THE MIND A COMPOUND SUBSTANCE? (1926) - **229**

1. *Nature of the Theory to be discussed* - - - *229*
2. *Comparison of it with Kant's theory of the " empirical subject "* - - - - - - - *231*
3. *The Nature of " Emergence "* - - - - *232*
4. *The " bodily " and the " psychic " factors* - - - *233*
5. *The Hypothesis of a universal " psychic factor "* - *237*
6. *What is meant by the term " Mind "* - - *239*
7. *The Unity and Continuity of the Conscious Subject* - *240*
8. *The Doctrine of " Traces "* - - - - - *243*
9. *" Entelechies " and " Psychic Factors "* - - - *249*

X. THE REFUTATION OF SUBJECTIVISM (1934) - - **251**

PAGE

XI. THE PHILOSOPHICAL RESEARCHES OF MEINONG (1922) 268

   1. *The Nature and Aims of Philosophical Inquiry* - - 272
   2. *The Hume-Studien. Abstract Ideas and the Theory of Relations* - - - - - - - 275
   3. *" Object " and " Content ". The Subjectivist Interpretation of Relations* - - - - - - 287
   4. *Gegenstandstheorie* - - - - - - 293

XII. THE " MODES " OF SPINOZA AND THE " MONADS " OF LEIBNIZ (1918) - - - - - - 305

   1. Esse essentiae *and* esse existentiae - - - - 308
   2. *Activity as the Principle of Individuality* - - - 319
   3. *Stages in the Development of Individual Things* - - 325
   4. *The Relation of Finite Individuals to God* - - - 329
   5. *Conclusion* - - - - - - - 335

INDEX - - - - - - - - 339

INTRODUCTION

1. *The Term "Critical Realism".*
2. *Can Realism Dispense with a Theory of Knowledge?*

1. *The Term " Critical Realism "*

THE term " realism " has become sufficiently current in recent philosophical discussion. It has attached itself, with or without their concurrence, to the lines of thought that are being developed by Mr. Bertrand Russell and Professor Moore ; it has been deliberately adopted by Professor Alexander for the strikingly original metaphysical theory he has expounded in his Gifford Lectures on *Space, Time and Deity* ; and the so-called " neo-realism " of the six American essayists has occasioned no inconsiderable amount of interest on this as on the other side of the Atlantic. I have no fondness for the term. Like all such labels in philosophy it seems to me often more misleading than helpful ; but I make use of it here as perhaps, on the whole, best adapted to indicate briefly the tendency of the set of considerations I am concerned to bring forward in the present work.

Realism, as Professor Perry has defined it, stands for the principle that " things may be, and are, directly experienced without owing either their being or their nature to that circumstance ". [1] Provided no special interpretation be put on the phrase " directly experienced ", I am prepared to accept this statement as a general description of the standpoint I wish to maintain ; or, more accurately, of the result towards which various paths of reflexion seem to me to lead.

At the outset, it is worth while to remind ourselves that realism, in the sense indicated, is no novelty or new departure

[1] *Present Philosophical Tendencies*, p. 315.

xiii

in philosophical speculation. Long prior to the writings of
any of the authors to whom I have alluded, there had been
coming to light a steadily increasing recognition of the inadequacy of the central thought of the earlier idealist systems
and of the *impasse* in front of which they appeared to be at a
stand. I am not now referring to Thomas Reid and his
followers. The so-called " natural realism " of the Scotch
Common-sense School, with its reiterated appeals to the
instinctive belief of the unsophisticated intelligence, disposed
of the " way of ideas " in far too rough-and-ready a fashion
to satisfy the demands of exact and methodical inquiry, although it is not to be forgotten that the acute and critical
mind of Henry Sidgwick found in the philosophical work of
Reid many features that seemed to him of enduring value. I
am thinking rather of a number of patient investigators who,
whilst imbued with the lesson of Kant and Hegel, came to
see that the place assigned to Nature in the idealist systems
of the nineteenth century was unsatisfactory and impossible.
The discrepancy between the large conceptions of the
idealist systems and the important results which the special
sciences were accumulating in such abundance came perhaps
first into due prominence through the labours of Lotze. It
has been said of Lotze's philosophical views as a whole that
his is, after all, only a half-philosophy, and the estimate is
doubtless a true estimate. But Lotze combined in singular
measure the speculative instinct of the constructive metaphysician with the cautious attitude of the trained scientific
inquirer, and the numerous detailed researches undertaken
by him prepared the way for a more radical change in the
interpretation of experience than he himself discerned. If,
in the long run, he offered a final reading of the universe in
terms of ethical idealism, yet " it is ", he was convinced,
" only inquiries conducted in the spirit of realism that will
satisfy the wishes of idealism ". The estimate I have just
quoted of Lotze's philosophy as a whole is that of Professor
Adamson, and Adamson may not unfairly be said to have

remodelled and carried on much of Lotze's work.[1] Like
Lotze, he brought to the treatment of philosophical problems a profound and intimate acquaintance with the entire
history of speculation and a critical faculty of rare power and
depth. He had thought through every detail of the Kantian
and post-Kantian systems, and, although he never had complete confidence in the Hegelian metaphysic, he certainly,
at one time, approached the questions of philosophy with more
than " the companionable feeling ", which he acknowledged
to be his later, towards idealism.   " For him," as Professor
Sorley put it, " the Copernican change consisted in displacing
self-consciousness from the position it occupies in every
system of idealism." Nothing in its way is more significant
in the history of recent thought than the set of reasons that
gradually led to that change. Adamson came to see, for
example, that it was only in so far as the distinction marked
by space and its absence was recognised by consciousness
that a conscious subject, in any intelligible sense of the word,
was possible at all ; that it was, therefore, reversing the real
order of development to regard space as in any way a condition imposed by the conscious subject on the contents of
his experience. He came to see that, since the time-relation
applied not merely to the contents supposed to be arranged
by the conscious subject but to the successive processes of
the conscious subject's own mental life whereby those
contents are apprehended, it must be pronounced an inconceivable thought that the conscious subject invests the contents of his experience with time as a form which has only
subjective significance. He came to see that it was the con-
stancy of connexion exhibited amongst the elements of
experience which first suggests the notion of cause ; that it
could not, therefore, be the notion of cause which first
makes objective experience possible. In short, Adamson
was driven to the conclusion that throughout what the

---

[1] See especially the two posthumous volumes entitled *The Development of
Modern Philospohy*, edited by W. R. Sorley, Edinburgh and London, 1903.

idealists had been taking to be the logical conditions of
experience—viz., the general and abstract—are, in point of
fact, the late results of experience—our interpretations, in
other words, of those constancies of conjunction in the
material of experience which constitute what we call the
laws of real fact. And, in the long run, it seemed to him, the
basis of all logical necessity is the necessity of fact. A somewhat similar line of reflexion was pursued by Professor
Hobhouse in his careful and suggestive book on *The Theory
of Knowledge*.[1] Quite in accordance with the thought of
Adamson, Professor Hobhouse contended that the mistake of
natural or intuitive realism was to start with the assumption
that the independence of the object is immediately given,
whilst the mistake of any subjective idealism was to assume
that the object is first given as inward. In truth, he argued,
it is not given as either. It is given as a content present to
an inward state, but the distinction between inner and outer,
or between subject and object, gradually comes to recognition
in the course of mental evolution. At no point in the development of knowledge do we discover thought as such determining the nature of the reality which it thinks. Each judgment
claims to be true *of* reality, and makes that claim on the
ground of its special relation to the given. " The understanding makes knowledge, but it does not make nature."
So, too, the various writings of Professor Fullerton, particularly his exhaustive work entitled *A System of Metaphysics*, were devoted to the task of unfolding a view of
nature and mind that is, in general, in conformity with the
trend of thought I have been indicating. And I think it may
be claimed that much of Shadworth Hodgson's *Metaphysic
of Experience* tended in the same direction. Nor should
one neglect to mention the name of Professor Lossky,
whose valuable analysis of the nature of judgment makes
unmistakably for epistemological conclusions of a like
import.

[1] First published in 1896.

The movement I have thus rapidly traced is a distinctive movement in philosophy—a movement that for nearly half a century has been consistently progressing and maturing, and before which " the long and difficult path of facts ", that Adamson declared to be the only road to philosophic truth, lies open instead of being more or less closed as, I think, it came to be for the earlier idealism.[1] Nevertheless, the movement in question may be looked upon as a perfectly legitimate development of what is contained in the " constructive speculation " of the period immediately preceding its own. Unlike the American " neo-realism ", it was no reversion to pre-Kantian modes of philosophising, but was carrying on the traditions of the critical method. To a large extent, the very premisses upon which it was proceeding were an inheritance from the long labour of the post-Kantian idealists. For one thing, the old arguments advanced by Berkeley in favour of idealism had been thoroughly sifted by Hegel and by such thinkers as T. H. Green ; and the " objective idealism " of the nineteenth century had aimed, at all events, to free itself from the subjectivism that dogged the footsteps even of Kant. Nor would it require any long search in the recent literature of idealism to come across lines of reflexion from which a transition to realism of the type I have been depicting would be but a short advance. " Idealism," wrote one of its most distinguished representatives, " in dealing with the higher life of reason, has been intent merely upon the affinity of all objects with spirit. It is still occupied in endeavouring to reduce all things into spirit : it is trying to show that every natural object, and every atomic part of every natural object, and, I suppose, every point in space and every instant of time, if they are real, must be spiritual realities—that is, conscious or feeling centres. It is *assumed* that only in this way can the world be proved to be spiritual and the last dualism be over-

[1] I mean that the subordination of all fact to the conditions of thought tended so to emphasise the importance of the latter as to make it appear as though the detailed investigation of particular kinds of fact were of comparatively slight philosophical significance.

come. And it is certainly not realised that if idealism suc-ceeded in this enterprise and reduced all things into feeling, it would then be obliged either to content itself with a world without distinctions, or to evolve out of feeling the differences it had deleted. In fact, this abstract idealism is not explain-ing the world of objects, but explaining it away." [1] And he went on to argue that its spiritualisation of the world will re-main barren until it reinstates the variety of real being and recognises that space, time, matter and natural objects has each a real nature of its own. " Every object, in the degree in which it is known, is found ", he added, " to possess quali-ties of its own ; and, in the degree in which it is understood, takes its place in a necessary order."

I have, then, I hope, sufficiently indicated the trend of thought towards which this volume is a contribution, and I need offer no further explanation of the term " critical " than the foregoing remarks and those that follow will provide. In many crucial respects, what is currently called the " new realism " seems to me to be drifting into the very subjectivism it was intended to avoid, and I shall now try to bring out the significance of certain positions I hold to be essential by contrasting them with those taken by the writers who have associated themselves with the " new realism ".

2. *Can Realism Dispense with a Theory of Knowledge?*

Professor Marvin, the author of the opening essay in the volume entitled *The New Realism*, strenuously insists that the movement in question is " a return to dog-matism ", and even suggests that its more appropriate title would be "neo-dogmatism ". " Metaphysics should be emancipated from epistemology "—such is the thesis which he endeavours at some length to substantiate. A theory of knowledge is, he argues, no more logically fundamental to metaphysics than it is to the other sciences, for the

---

[1] Sir Henry Jones, *The Working Faith of the Social Reformer*, pp. 77-8.

actual conditions of valid knowledge can only be determined
on the basis of data furnished by logic, physics, psychology
and metaphysics. Only inductively and empirically can it be
shown either what knowledge is possible, or how it is possible,
or what are the limits of our knowledge ; only from the
vantage ground of actual scientific achievement can we
scrutinise the truth of our positive knowledge. Furthermore,
no light can be thrown by epistemology upon the nature of
the existent world or upon the fundamental postulates and
generalisations of science, except in so far as the knowledge of
one natural event or object enables us at times to make
inferences regarding certain others ; instead of furnishing the
basis for a theory of reality, epistemology always presupposes
some theory of reality in order to make headway at all. The
source of any genuine theory of reality is positive science, and
the business of the metaphysician is to think through, to
make explicit, and to organise the theory of reality which the
scientists are implicitly entertaining.

Now, if epistemology be supposed to have for its subject-
matter knowledge or ideas as distinct from reality, and to
have as its problem to inquire whether and how far from these
assumed entities a transition can be made to things as actual
existents, then I readily admit not only that such an inquiry
is not " fundamental ", but that it has no claim whatsoever
to rank as a science. It would, however, be a sheer blunder
to identify the critical method with an " epistemology " of
that description. The contrast drawn by Kant between his
own method and that of the empirical school ought in itself
to be sufficient to guard against such a misinterpretation.

Not only so. Kant neither raised any doubt as to whether
knowledge is possible nor instituted any inquiry designed to
test the legitimacy of such doubt.[1] The problem with which

[1] Dr. Bosanquet seemed rather to countenance this misconception when,
in describing the change in spirit which had come about with the development
of post-Kantian speculative philosophy, he wrote : " All difficulties about
the general possibility—the possibility in principle—of apprehending
reality in knowledge and perception were flung aside as antiquated lumber.

the Kantian philosophy took its start was not *whether* knowledge is possible, but *how* knowledge is possible. The idea
that the critical method, as Kant conceived it, was necessary
in order " to show that we can know the trees, the birds, the
rocks, the earth and the stars " [1] is such an extraordinary
caricature of the critical standpoint that it leaves one gasping
in a vain attempt to imagine what unhappy phrase in the
Kritik can be responsible for it. Our ordinary common-
sense experience of the world of nature and the world of mind,
the systematised bodies of knowledge represented by the
mathematical and physical sciences—these were assumed by
Kant as data that everyone admits, and he never dreamed of
undertaking to demonstrate *that* they were possible.[2] What
he proposed to do was to inspect knowledge in its character
as apprehensive of fact, and to determine not the laws under
which it is gradually attained, but the conditions implied in
its nature. The " dogmatism " to which he objected was not
the naïve dogmatism, if the expression be permissible, inci-
dent to experiencing or knowing as such, but the metaphysical
dogmatism which consisted in abstracting notions from the
context in which their use is quite unimpeachable and apply-
ing them, without prior investigation, to a subject-matter in
regard to which they may become wholly unintelligible and
meaningless. The conceptions of substance and attribute, of
ground and consequent, of cause and effect, and the like, had
justified their position in the realm of experience by the
functions they there perform, but, until their precise import
and significance are determined, to employ them as likewise
unconditionally valid in dealing with the universe in its
totality seemed to Kant both unscientific and unphilosophical.

What was undertaken was the direct adventure of knowing; of shaping a
view of the universe which would include and express reality in its completeness." (*Phil. R.*, January, 1917, p. 8.)

[1] *New Realism*, p. 62.

[2] Respecting pure mathematics and natural science, Kant wrote:
" Von diesen Wissenschaften, da sie wirklich gegeben sind, lässt sich nun
wohl geziemend fragen : Wie sie möglich sind ; denn *dass* sie möglich sein
müssen, wird durch ihre Wirklichkeit bewiesen." (*Kritik*, B. 20.)

Professor Marvin's polemic against the critical method appears to me, therefore, misdirected. Kant did not claim that a theory of knowledge is " fundamental " in the sense in which his critic represents him as doing so. " A science of the mere criticism of pure reason, its sources and limits," was a propædeutic not to the special sciences, but to metaphysics, and explicitly to the metaphysics which was then prevalent. Thus, for example, when it was attempted to prove that the soul is immortal since it is a simple entity ; and, therefore, irresolvable into a plurality of elements, the argument must remain an airy fabric without solidity or foundation, because the prior question had been left out of consideration, whether, namely, such a notion as substance can have any meaning except as applied to a composite object in space. Or, when Locke attempted to establish the existence of God by the " evident demonstration that from eternity there has been something ", he was interpreting the relation between God and the universe in terms of causality, without having previously asked himself whether the conception of cause is a legitimate conception in a context beyond the range of sense-experience ; and, consequently, his reasoning evinces itself as barren. In the most explicit terms, Kant points out that *for their own* safety and certainty, neither mathematics nor natural science had any occasion for such a critical investigation as he desiderated, seeing that the former rests upon its own evidence and the latter upon experience and its thorough confirmation. It was not for themselves, but for the sake of another science, viz., metaphysics, that both these sciences stood in need of the inquiry in question.[1] Doubtless he did mean to assert that *ultimately* the special sciences are dependent for their truth upon the logical conditions which knowledge itself implies, but this assertion relates not to the specific truths which form the body of these sciences ; it relates to the fundamental principles which they rightly take for granted, and which it is the business of philosophy to justify.

[1] *Prolegomena*, § 40.

The question, then, is whether Kant was right in insisting upon the *philosophical* importance of a theory of knowledge, and in assigning to it, so far as philosophy is concerned, the fundamental position he did. Let it be noted that the question does not at all relate, as apparently Professor Marvin takes it to relate, to the temporal order in which the various branches of philosophy may best be pursued, but solely to the systematic order—an order, that is to say, corresponding to the nature of the subject-matter under investigation. And in respect to the systematic order, there is, it seems to me, but one principle of distribution which can be legitimately followed—the fundamental department of philosophy must be that which involves the relatively least complex conceptions, and which handles what all the other departments of philosophy of necessity involve. Now, in the philosophical treatment of any order of facts—whether those of outer nature or those of the mental life—the thinker employs notions and depends upon general principles the consideration of which, while naturally of the most abstract character, must, nevertheless, in strict logical sequence, precede the more concrete studies. Epistemology most assuredly cannot " give a theory of reality ", but any " theory of reality " will certainly remain a dubious structure, until the conceptions that have been used in framing it have been examined and tested.[1]

Nothing, I think, can be clearer than that the whole fabric of " neo-realism ", as a metaphysical theory, rests upon and presupposes certain definite conceptions as to the nature of knowledge ; and it is, in itself, a noteworthy circumstance that a volume which starts with demanding " the emancipation of metaphysics from epistemology " should, in the sequel, be mainly composed of efforts to provide an epistemological basis for the metaphysical doctrine it is written to expound. Even though the " ultimate crucial test " of all our theories,

---

[1] In a footnote (p. 45) Professor Marvin tells us that under the term metaphysics he includes two subjects : (*a*) the study of the logical foundations of the sciences ; (*b*) the theory of reality. I fail to see what the former of these subjects can consist of, if not of the problems I have been indicating.

metaphysical and other, be, as Professor Marvin believes, " perception ", and even though it be granted that " perception ", as he contends, " simply is "—that is to say, is *ipso facto* an apprehension of reality—yet that assumption does not exonerate us from the task of inquiring how the act of perceiving is related to the object perceived and what is involved in such relation. If logical, mathematical and physical complexes are independent of consciousness, that " independence " is just as much in need of the epistemological proof which Professor Perry, for instance, tries to give [1] as is the opposite contention of idealism. And if these complexes, despite their independence, may become objects of knowledge, this means, as Professor Perry further recognises, that in being known any such complex " enters into a system which is internally determined ", and must conform to " the conditions which knowledge imposes ".[2] Is it not obvious, then, that a " realistic theory of independence " will be left hanging in the air, until those conditions have been ascertained and their compatibility with the theory made manifest ? So, again, even though, on the ground that " cognition is not the universal condition of being ", it be allowed that " cognition must take its place within being, on the same plane as space, or number, or physical nature ",[3] yet our only approach to " being " is through the avenue of cognition, and the fact, if fact it be, that cognition is on the same plane with other things that are, or have being, does not absolve us from the necessity of inquiring into its nature, as an essential preliminary to the philosophical account we may have to offer of those other things. The very circumstance that, within the sphere of ordinary experience, the distinction between true and false plays the part it does is surely in itself a sufficient warrant for the contention that until the significance of that distinction has been made the subject of investigation, it is vain to speculate upon what is called the " ultimate truth of things ". And the very circumstance that,

[1] *New Realism*, p. 126 *sqq.*   [2] *ibid.*, p. 133.   [3] *ibid.*, p. 33.

within the sphere of natural science, it is possible to apply categories wrongly is surely in itself a sufficient warrant for insisting that a metaphysical employment of those categories needs some justification for their extended use.

I conclude, therefore, that an analysis of knowledge in its widest sense, a critical examination of the conceptions by which we endeavour to interpret the world, is in no way rendered superfluous for philosophy because we see reason for thinking that " the nature of things is not to be sought primarily in the nature of knowledge ". Whether the group of problems which thus arise be described as epistemological, logical or metaphysical, is a matter of small import ; the important thing is to recognise that they have got to be faced, if we are to understand, so far as may be given to us, the nature and significance of the universe in which we find ourselves.

I

THE BASIS OF CRITICAL REALISM

1. *The Nature of Cognition.*
2. *The Two-fold Character of the Act of Perceiving.*
3. *" Acquaintance " and " Description ".*
4. *Minds and Things.*
5. *Concluding Considerations.*

1. *The Nature of Cognition*

PERHAPS no feature in Kant's analysis of experience was more distinctly a new departure than his singling out the characteristic of objectivity as that which presented the central problem for the theory of knowledge. Why was it that that which is known *stands over against* the knowing subject, and is recognised as other than and distinct from the act of knowing? How came it that a subjective activity, be it produced or not produced by the influence of some external reality, should carry with it the unique characteristic—reference to an object?

It will be sufficient to recall very briefly the Kantian solution of this problem. Sense-data, received into the pure *a priori* forms of intuition, Space and Time, are apprehended as constituents of objects in consequence of being wrought into the texture of experience through means of the categories, or pure notions of the understanding. The object cognised is, that is to say, essentially a complex of heterogeneous factors ; and, in and by the process of cognising, a conjunction or synthesis of these factors is effected. The process involves, in the first place, the manifold of sense-material—sense-presentations, or impressions, not *as such* cognisable, and devoid of any power to group or arrange themselves. These particular *a posteriori* elements Kant

A   1

seemed often inclined to say are given through the action of
real things upon the faculty of sensibility. The process involves, in the second place, two general forms into which the
manifold of sense-data is received. As universal conditions
of sense-perception, the forms of Space and Time, although
sensuous in character, do not belong to any sense, nor are
they, although general, concepts or notions. They are pure
a priori forms of intuition—ways in which any intelligence
that is, like ours, sensuously affected *must* receive what is thus
given. The process involves, in the third place, the rules or
principles according to which the given elements of sense are
combined, and, in being combined, are cognised. The manifold of sense-material is, in itself, a mere ἄπειρον, a merely indifferent mass of disjointed particulars ; it can become content of knowledge only through being brought into relation
with the unity of consciousness, the one identity in the midst
of difference. The supreme unity in experience is the unity of
self-consciousness; and, as referred to this unity, the data of
sense have imposed upon them systematic order and connectedness. The categories are just the ways in which the
unity of self-consciousness expresses itself in relation to the
empirical elements, or plants itself out, so to speak, in the
given material. And the gist of Kant's contention is that it
is precisely the function of the act of synthesis to give to
sense-presentations that centre of reference, that unity in
difference, which is what we mean by their objectivity—it is
precisely its function, in other words, to be productive of the
peculiar component in the object which constitutes it, apart
from its special concrete clothing, an object at all. A contention of this sort would, indeed, have been paradoxical,
had Kant meant to identify the unity of self-consciousness
with the individuality of the finite subject. Such, however,
was not his meaning. The unity of self-consciousness was
not the unity of a finite individual—which, as Kant viewed
it, was the specific unity of an object, an " inner " object, it is
true, as contrasted with an " outer " object—but the unity

which is implied as a prior condition in making even the inner life matter of contemplation. As distinguished from the unity of the finite subject, the " transcendental " unity was the common element in all consciousness, that by which consciousness is what it is. Whilst actualised, if the expression may be permitted, in each concrete centre of consciousness, " consciousness in general " yet transcended the latter in the aspect of what Windelband has described as a " super-individual function ". In every act of knowing, the individual mind *must* conform to the conditions imposed by consciousness as such ; the object is apprehended by the individual knower as standing over against himself, because the categories—the ways in which " consciousness in general " functions in relation to empirical data—are not his private property, but the common property of every self-conscious mind. As an individual knower, he is constrained to conform to the conditions of *Bewusstsein überhaupt* ; and it is that very constraint which evinces itself in the characteristic of objectivity.

The analysis thus rapidly sketched raises at once several issues, upon some of which it is important for my present purpose to dwell. (*a*) There is a loss of continuity in the working out of the position owing to the circumstance that Kant proceeds by severing what he takes to be the two components of experiencing, sensibility and understanding, in order to discover in what way and to what extent *a priori* knowledge is possible in either. When it is said that " by sensibility objects are given to us, by understanding they are thought ", it is hard to see from what point of view the first of these assertions has been framed. So far as Kant is concerned, it must, however, be taken to imply at least two things—(i) that stimulation of the faculty of sense is an esential condition in the process of coming to know; and (ii) that only on occasion of, and in reference to, the sense-presentations resulting from such stimulation is there apprehension of objects on our part. Furthermore, the generic difference constituted between sensibility and understanding—a difference expressed in one of its aspects by the opposing terms, receptive and active—leads inevitably to the supposition that each of these is regarded as furnishing, taken separately, a special kind of knowing, somewhat after the manner in which " knowledge by acquaintance " and " knowledge by description " have been contrasted in recent discussion. But, as the analysis proceeds, it becomes very evident that such was not Kant's real view. Understanding cannot, we find, produce for itself the content of objects, sensibility cannot itself give rise to awareness of the content it receives. The former without the latter is empty ; the latter without the former is blind. " In no other way than through the combination of these two can knowledge arise." (b) The assumed heterogeneity in nature of sense and thought—the one characterised by receptivity, the other by spontaneity—creates for Kant many perplexing difficulties, of which the artificial contrivance of the schemata is no real solution, when he has to face the problem as to the manner of their co-operation. Leaving, however, these difficulties on one side, the point I am more concerned to emphasise is the following. The particular generic difference upon which Kant insists obscures altogether from his view the genetic difference that does unquestionably present itself as we survey the various stages in the history of conscious experience. In a certain sense, the terms sense-apprehension, perception, imagination and thought may be said roughly to describe successive phases in the development of intelligence. The crude primitive awareness of things, " the experience of the first look," prepares the way for the more accurate discernment of common-sense knowledge, and for that differentiation of " sensuous universals " by means of which things are grouped in classes and inferences are drawn " from particulars to particulars ", until finally, through a reflective interpretation of what is offered in ordinary experience, objects are construed in terms of atoms and ions, forces or modes of energy, laws and relations of various kinds, the terms differing according to the special science concerned. A sharp antithesis, such as Kant repeatedly works with, between the pure generality of thought and the indeterminate particulars of sense allows no room for this progressive development. What he virtually did was to take scientific experience as typical of all experience, and with that alone before him no doubt the severance in question appeared plausible enough. No sooner, however, is experience inspected in its entire range than the antithesis breaks down hopelessly, for it is just as impossible to imagine that the highly generalised notions unfolded in the table of categories are operative, even implicitly, in the primitive consciousness as it is to suppose that the primitive consciousness is condemned to the " blindness " of mere sense receptivity.[1] (c) It is certainly not unfair to say that the antithesis alluded to is mainly responsible for the subjective character which is by Kant assigned to knowledge as a whole. There undoubtedly clings to his entire mode of exposition the view that cognition is brought about through a mechanical affection of the mind by a real agent, the result of such affection being the empirical elements of experience, and that a sufficient criterion of what in the complex cognised is due solely to the mind is furnished by the marks of universality and necessity. Thought is thus conceived as an instrument by means of which the crude materials given are worked up into the form of knowledge, and so to conceive it is at once to imply that the outcome of such work stands as a kind of intermediary, a *tertium quid*, between the cognising mind and the world of real existence. The object known must accordingly be a *construction* on the part of the mind itself, a *product* of the mind's own making, and as such lie within the limits of the mental life of the conscious subject. And so the awkward predicament confronts us of having, on the one hand, to

[1] " The common root," from which Kant himself, in one place, suggests that the two contrasted stems may have sprung, was only " hidden " from him through the unfortunately narrow sphere to which he confined attention.

admit that what is experienced is constituted exclusively of mental elements, whilst, on the other hand, it has all along been recognised as the core of the whole problem, that the very essence of an act of knowing what we call " things " consists in a "reference" to that which is other than and distinct from the finite knower.

A violent contradiction of this sort clearly indicates the necessity of a return to the premises from which the start was made for the purpose of ascertaining in what respect they stand in need of revision. Where the initial false step was taken can hardly be a matter of controversy. Kant had accepted, apparently without scruple, the view of sense-data which he found in the writings of Hume—that is to say, a thoroughly atomistic view. As " affections " or " impressions ", sensations could be no other than discrete units, constituting in and for themselves no more than an aggregate. And the unity, which Hume searched for in vain, Kant believed he had discovered in the general notion. The essence of an act of cognition was the reduction of the manifold to the unity of consciousness through general notions. Every apprehended content thus consisted of a plurality, combined into a whole. For knowledge, then, a synthesis or combination of the manifold was necessary ; and the cardinal principle of the Kantian theory may be said to be that *the act of synthesising or combining is the very act of knowing.*

Now, precisely at this juncture it can be clearly seen where the roads divide—the one leading to a phenomenalism that will with difficulty be distinguishable from the subjectivism of Berkeley's earlier period, the other to a realism of the type I have been depicting. For let it be granted, meanwhile, for the sake of argument, that the doctrine of sensations which Kant borrowed from Hume is an erroneous doctrine ; let it be granted that the conception of sense-data as " impressions " received into the mind through a process of stimulation, or in any other way, is a mistaken interpretation of the facts, and that secondary qualities are no more mental

" affections " than are spatial relations, according to Kant's account of them ; let it be granted, in short, that sense-qualities are, what they purport to be, veritable properties of external things—entities which, as Kant himself had agreed, stand over against the conscious subject as the objects of his cognitive states. Then, obviously, the act of knowing will no longer be an act of synthesising, in Kant's sense : the act of knowing will, in that case, necessarily be an act of *discriminating*, of *distinguishing*, of *comparing*, features which, as presented, are already synthesised. The object, in other words, will need no construction ; as already fashioned and constructed, it will present itself to the conscious subject, and to become aware of it the latter will need to discriminate its features, to distinguish it from its surroundings, to recognise, to some extent, its relations.[1] Kant's problem in regard to objectivity will, it is true, still remain on our hands, for the mere circumstance that what is apprehended does, as a matter of fact, stand over against the conscious subject will not in itself explain his coming to be aware of that fact. But the chief difficulty of this problem, as it framed itself for Kant, will have been removed. We shall no longer need to inquire how features which are in fact subjective come to appear as just the opposite ; we shall be left rather with the psychological task of tracing the way in which the distinction between inner and outer, or between self and not-self, attains gradually to recognition.

On what, then, does a decision between the two positions I have contrasted mainly depend? Clearly, I think, upon the answer given to the question as to the nature of so-called " sense-data "—whether they, or their causes, are to be conceived as wandering detached elements (' *heimatlose Gegenstände* " as Meinong expressed it), affecting the mind, or as

---

[1] I am not saying, of course, that no synthesis will be involved in the act of knowing. Synthetic, in a certain sense, I should say every cognitive act undoubtedly is. But the synthesis will not be a putting together of the parts of an object. It will consist in holding together different items of awareness. *Cf. infra*, p. 126 *sqq.*

qualities or properties of physical things. To that question I now turn.

2. *The Two-fold Character of the Act of Perceiving*

" That there cannot be an act of knowing without something to know ; or, more generally, that there cannot be an act of judging, even an act of apprehending at all, without something to judge, something to apprehend, is ", declared Meinong, " one of the most self-evident propositions yielded by a quite elementary consideration of these processes ". And, with the doubtful exception of certain feelings and desires, he laid it down as a characteristic feature of the psychical, in contradistinction to the non-psychical, that it is directed upon something (*auf etwas gerichtet*), and that this " something " is neither identical with, nor partially identical with, the psychical act directed upon it. A mental act is not, in other words, an event which is complete in itself. In a sense the same is, no doubt, true of every event. A physical event is dependent for its occurrence upon what is other than itself. But the dependence here in question is a dependence of a totally different order. A physical event can be described in and for itself. Not so a mental event. To speak of an act of awareness simply would be to speak of that which is never met with. Awareness in and for itself has no existence, and, indeed, no meaning ; a " something " of which there is awareness is its indispensable correlative.

The " something " upon which the act of awareness is directed Meinong called its object (*Gegenstand*) ; and to the term " object " he gave a very wide significance. As is well known, what he has called *Gegendstandstheorie* is an attempt to distinguish, differentiate and classify the various objects of apprehension, and to determine what can be known *a priori* about them. Under the general term, he included such differing entities as sense-data—colours, tones, temperatures, etc. —the " things " of perception, qualitative differences, relations, numbers, propositions, scientific hypotheses, philo-

sophical theories. All these entities are—they have being;
but they fall into the three great classes of objects which
exist, objects which do not exist but which subsist (*bestehen*),
and objects, such as a false proposition, which neither exist
nor subsist.

I am not now going to raise the question whether this
comprehensive use of the term *Gegenstand* was a wise procedure on Meinong's part. To me there seem to be serious
objections to it. It gives countenance, for one thing, to the
tacit assumption that a universal in being known *stands over
against* the act of thought in a manner similar to that in
which a " thing ", in being known, *stands over against* the act
of perceiving—an assumption for which I, at any rate, can
find no justification.[1] But, meanwhile, I can avail myself of
what Meinong has named " the prejudice in favour of the
actual " (*das Vorurteil zugunsten des Wirklichen*) and confine
attention to the case where the " something " we are concerned with is an existent fact of the kind usually described
as physical. And, so far, the term " object " need signify for
us no more than what it signified for Kant—namely, a specific
and definite centre of reference for distinguishable predicates.

As referring to perception, no one, I take it, will challenge
Meinong's assertion that the cognitive act is neither identical
with, nor partially identical with, the entity upon which it is
directed. So much even Berkeley allowed when he insisted
that the qualities of bodies (extension, figure, etc.) are in the
mind " not by way of mode or attribute ", as the act of perceiving is, but " only by way of *idea* " (*Principles*, § 49). I
pass, then, at once, to what I conceive is further involved in
Meinong's contention, although I do not know to what extent
he would have accepted the following analysis. A physical
thing is related to the perceiving act by which it is apprehended in more ways than one. In particular, there are two

---

[1] I think it also tends to obscure the very important fact that whilst in
the earlier stages of cognitive experience the act of apprehension has still
the characteristic of being directed upon something (*das auf etwas Gerichtet-
sein*), it has not there that characteristic *for the consciousness in question*.

relations which it is of the utmost importance clearly to distinguish. These are : (a) the relation, whatever it be, whether causal or otherwise, which is expressed by saying that the physical thing occasions, or gives rise to, the occurrence of the cognitive act ; and (b) the relation between the physical thing and the cognitive act which is involved in the knowledge or awareness of the former by the latter—a relation which, when we are dealing with consciousness that has reached a certain stage of development, may be expressed by saying that the physical thing is the object of the cognitive act. The distinction coincides very largely with that which Shadworth Hodgson was accustomed to draw between " consciousness as an existent " and " consciousness as a knowing ". Consciousness taken in the former sense, he used to argue, is dependent upon neuro-cerebral processes which go on concomitantly with it, and to the question why it is that such and such an act of perception occurs at such and such a time it is legitimate to answer because such and such a neuro-cerebral process has just taken place, or is taking place, at that time. But, on the other hand, consciousness taken as a knowing—the nature of consciousness, that is to say, which, however, he regarded as made up of qualities that, for the most part, do not seem to me to belong to it—can in no wise be said to be dependent upon the processes mentioned ; we are wholly incapable of conceiving the character of consciousness *quâ* character as caused in any way whatsoever. When we attempt to do so, we are really conceiving not the cause of the conscious state being *what* it is, but the cause of its happening or existence. Let us, then, look more closely at the two relations I have thus contrasted.

(a) In treating of the first, we labour under the difficulty that any theory we can frame concerning the connexion between body and mind must be of an extremely hypothetical nature. But, without touching that controversy, I emphasise certain general considerations with respect to the matter before us. One can proceed best by means of a concrete instance. I am observing (say) a yellow primrose. On scientific grounds, it is certain that a complicated network of physical and physiological events has been instrumental in bringing about that mental state of mine. From the primrose there have probably emanated modes of energy—be they of the form of transverse vibratory motions propagated longitudinally through the ether conceived according to the undulatory theory, or of the form of the electromagnetic waves conceived by Clerk Maxwell and Hertz—and through them my visual organ has undergone impression or stimulation. In consequence of that stimulation, delicate changes, probably chemical in character, occur in the cones of the retina, the fibres of the optic nerve have been thereby affected, and the influence, whatever it is, is conveyed by the optic-nerve fibres to the cerebral centres in the cortex with which the optic nerve is connected. What happens then? What is the next link in this chain of events? Commonly it is supposed that then, in some way admittedly mysterious, a transition is made, either in the brain or in the mind, from molecular motion to a so-called secondary quality. Under cover of the ambiguous term " sensation " there is supposed, then, to be produced both the yellow and the awareness of it, though why, in that case, the yellow should be projected into an object (say) " by the river's brim " is confessedly no less an enigma than its mode of production. As a matter of fact, however, this supposed final stage in the sequence of events is a gratuitous assumption which solves no difficulty but creates difficulties out of all proportion more serious than any which it finds. All we are justified in asserting is that either concomitantly with, or in consequence of, the cerebral change there arises, not a brand new quality nor the awareness of one, but a mental state or activity, in and through which, *when a certain other set of conditions has been fulfilled, and not until*, there ensues awareness of a definitely coloured object. The entire sequence of physical and physiological events might have occurred as in this instance, and even have incited a mental act, but unless that mental act had been, as Meinong put it, " directed upon something ", the awareness in question would not have happened. In short, when we are inquiring about what I am going to call the content of the completed act of perception, wave-motions, retinal changes, nerve currents, cerebral disturbances become totally irrelevant. They have been instrumental in awakening, if that term be appropriate, the incipient act of perception ; it is, therefore, related to them, but it is not related to them as a knowing is related to things known. Our knowledge of them is based upon inferences drawn from different facts than the act of perception itself. And, in consequence, in describing the relation of the act of knowing to its occasioning conditions, our attitude must necessarily be that of an external spectator ; we are then endeavouring, that is to say, to take up, in regard to the act of apprehension, the position of an onlooker, and to observe the way in which that act comes into being.

(b) Leaving now its mode of occurrence, consider the cognitive act itself. Any accurate description of its nature can be obtained only by adopting an attitude which is the reverse of that just characterised. In other words, we must attempt to describe it not as it might conceivably present itself to an observer surveying it from the outside, but as it reveals itself to us conducting our analysis, so to speak, from within. We have got to dismiss, in making that attempt, all reference to the ways in which the cognitive act in question has come about, for, as we have seen, the cognitive act tells us not the tale of its own manner of origin. Now, a self-conscious subject is able, more or less, to take up this reflective attitude ; it is possible for him to turn his attention upon his own mode of procedure in the act of knowing, and to convince himself as to how it is that the state of mind in which he finds himself achieves its end and becomes a definite act of awareness. What report, then, does the cognitive act give of itself when thus reflectively treated? Not at all, I venture to urge, the report which Kant conceived it to yield. It does not reveal itself as an act of building up or of putting together the parts of that of which it comes to be aware. That description of it is a result not of scrutinising it from within but of attempting to inspect it from without. Kant was really taking up in regard to it the attitude of one who, having followed some such sequence of events as we were considering a moment ago, proceeds to ask : What, now, should I further observe if I went on inspecting this series of events in its later stages? [1] And it seemed to him, naturally from his point of view, that what, in that case, he would observe would be the gradual emergence of a unified object from the data which he supposed the events up to that point had been the means of supplying. But a self-conscious subject, who has not thus been contemplating the mechanism that has been working behind the scenes, but who has been trying to discover what he has been doing, so to speak, in the act of perceiving, will have a very different story to relate. A concrete illustration will, perhaps, most clearly bring out what I mean, and I do not know that I can select a better than that used by Professor Lossky in a paper of his read before the Aristotelian Society in 1914. It is a summer's day, and I am walking on a river bank covered with vegetation, but instead of noticing the details around me I am losing myself in and becoming one, so to speak, with the life of nature. In such a condition, nothing distinctive will manifest itself to me ; all things will appear to be merged in one confused stream of life. There occurs, however, a sudden splash in the water, and thereby my attention is, as we may say, aroused. Forthwith the scene becomes *for me* entirely changed. The mirror-like surface of the water, the green banks, the reeds near the shore—these gradually stand out as distinct from one another. And, as the cognitive process continues, the growth near the banks, which before had appeared like a confused uniform

---

[1] This external attitude is, I need hardly say, especially prominent in the " Deduction of the Categories " of the first edition of the *Kritik*.

mass, breaks up into the dark green of the reeds contrasted with the lighter green of the sweet sedge, and even in the dark mass of the reeds their stems, leaves and dark brown brushes can be distinguished from one another by their colour, shape and position. We have here, no doubt, an extremely complicated act, or succession of acts, of perception ; but, so far as the general nature of the process is concerned, it is typical of perception in all the forms in which we are familiar with it. Whoever endeavours faithfully to describe, as he has lived through it, a perceptive act of his own will describe it in some such manner as that here exemplified. Viewed from within, it will invariably evince itself as a process, not of constructing an object, but of differentiating the features of an object, of gradually discerning distinctions which were not at first noticed, and of tracing connexions which were not at first discerned. It is perfectly true that in the instance I have been using the mind at work was a mind capable of bringing to bear in its procedure the results of a long prior experience—green banks, reeds, sedges, stems, leaves, etc. were all for it familiar objects, and hence the task of distinguishing them in the situation depicted was comparatively easy. I am prepared, nevertheless, to carry the main principle the example illustrates right down the scale of conscious existence, and to maintain that wherever cognitive activity is exercised it is essentially a process *generically* the same as that which we thus find the process to be in our own mental lives. The mistake psychologists have too often made is to suppose that discrimination necessarily involves the abstract ideas of comparison and relation which it does unquestionably involve in its higher forms. There is, in truth, no ground for such a supposition ; but, on the contrary, every ground for urging that " things " may be crudely discriminated from one another without the faintest recognition of either the relation of difference or of the differences as aspects distinguishable from the facts that differ.

The act of cognition, then, is no sooner called into being

than it is "directed upon something", and evinces its
character as an act of discriminating. Through such discrimination, the conscious subject gradually attains to
recognition of the various features or characteristics of the
object ; the act of cognition gradually becomes the state of
being aware of the object. What precisely does this phrase
" aware *of* the object " imply? It does not imply that the
object or any part of it is existentially contained in the act of
being conscious ; still less does it imply, as Professor Holt
contends, that consciousness is " out there " where the object
is. It implies that the cognitive act has now acquired a
specific definite character ; it has become awareness *of
something,* of a more or less distinct and definite something.
The awareness of a water-drop differs, for example, *as an
awareness,* from the awareness of a primrose. Neither the
water-drop nor the primrose, as existing entities, are in any
way part of, or contained in, the awareness ; the object of an
act of awareness is always other than, and distinct from, the
act of being aware of it. But, although act of awareness and
object are essentially separate entities—the former being
always mental ; the latter, in the case we are considering,
being physical—yet it is not indifferent to the nature of an
act of awareness whether it is an act of being aware of a water-
drop or of a primrose. Both acts are alike in being acts, and
in being acts of discriminating ; but they differ in so far as
the discrimination has resulted in the one case in producing
the awareness of a water-drop, and in the other case in producing the awareness of a primrose. Cognition, in other
words, is not a bare activity that remains entirely untouched
by the attributes of the things which it discriminates ; there
is no such thing as awareness in general, just as there is no
such thing as feeling in general or willing in general. Every
act of awareness is a specific concrete act, and its specific
character is determined, or partially so, by what it is awareness of. It has become customary to denote this specific
character of an act of awareness by the term content, and

what I am now desirous of doing is to make clear, if I can, the significance one would attach to this term. In the first place, it does not signify a part of the act of cognition that can stand over against the other part, so to speak, and be itself cognised as an object. Rather is it an inseparable aspect of the whole act, as, for example, extendedness is an inseparable aspect of a material body. In the second place, it is not a " representation ", or copy, or picture of the object. That was the cardinal error of those who spoke of " presentations " or " ideas " as contents of the act of cognition. The " idea of blue " was taken to be itself " blue ", the " idea of extension " to be " extended ".[1] And thus " ideas " as mental entities, although characterised by non-mental properties, came to be regarded as standing between the mind and things. Both these errors I believe to be due to the false severance that has been instituted between the content of a cognitive act and the act—a severance as false as that between the nature of a thing and the thing. Once conceive of the content as a separate entity, and the step is inevitable to regarding it as the immediate object of apprehension. The content is, however, a " what " that is inseparable from its " that ". The content of the act of cognising blue is not blue, but the *awareness of blue*, just as the content of the act of perceiving a primrose is not a primrose but the awareness of one. And when I am apprehending blue, I am not apprehending my awareness of blue, but the blue. The content apprehended, that is to say, is *not* the content of the act by which it is apprehended.

I can perhaps make my meaning clearer by reference to a well-known doctrine of F. H. Bradley's. Bradley maintained that whenever I apprehend anything as having a certain quality, that quality is always present in its entirety as a content of my own psychical existence. And in the act of

---

[1] " Psychologists must admit," says Professor Holt, " that a sensation of red is a red sensation, and the perception of a landscape is as big as the landscape."—*The Concept of Consciousness*, p. 148.

apprehension this quality is divorced from the mental state of which it was a content and attached to another existent external to the mental state. Now, this account of the matter seems to me impossible precisely on the ground I have just been urging. In the concrete situation of my affirming hardness of the table in front of me, I can discern myself as being in a certain state—in the state, namely, of being aware of this hard table. And I, as being in this state, am an existent reality of a certain definite content or character. I can likewise discern the table, as another existent reality also with a certain character or content, part of which I am discriminating as belonging to the table. But the content of my mental state is neither the table nor the hardness which I predicate of the table. Part, at any rate, of the content of my mental state is no doubt awareness of the hardness which I have discriminated. I am not, however, ascribing awareness of hardness, in any sense, to the table. Analyse the character of the mental state as completely as you may, you will never find hardness as part of that character. Hardness is a content which I discover as belonging to existents other than myself, as, for example, tables and chairs. It is not a content of mind but a content of matter. Awareness of hardness is, on the other hand, a content of mind, but awareness of hardness is not a compound made up of the constituents, awareness and hardness.

3. *"Acquaintance" and "Description"*

I have been confining attention to the concrete process of perception, and I am convinced that only in doing so is one, in reference to the main problem before us, on secure ground. In actual experience, our perceptual apprehension of the external world is always apprehension of individual concrete things and of their relations to one another. It is, however, natural to reflect that perception is a complex process, and to insist that the right method of procedure is first to analyse the complex process into its constituents and then to deal

B

with these separately. In ordinary experience, it will be admitted, we are rarely or never concerned with the factors in isolation. Colours as seen are the colours of things ; tones as heard are elements in voices or other complex sounds and are recognised as coming from a certain distance ; temperatures as felt are the temperatures of warm or cold things, etc. But we may, by careful analysis, single out the elements that go, for instance, to constitute the perception of a brown table, and attend merely to the apprehension of the colour. And, by such means, we may observe the characteristics of the sense quality itself and determine the manner in which it stands related to the cognitive act.

That this mode of procedure is, within certain limits, legitimate, it would, of course, be absurd to question. But it is peculiarly liable, unless sufficiently safeguarded, to lead the inquirer astray. In the first place, it tends inevitably to suggest that the concrete process of perception itself is an aggregate made up of the factors into which it has thus been, by artificial means, analysed. Then readily enough we are led to imagine that we have on hand, as the result of our analysis, simple processes, each of which may be regarded as separately a specific kind of knowing, precisely as we have seen Kant was tempted to do in regard to sensibility and thought. It very soon evinces itself that the object apprehended in sense-perception cannot be treated as a mere complex of sense-qualities. That which makes it a whole and gives it meaning is quite inexplicable on such a supposition. So a process of thinking or judging is called in to do that which cannot be accomplished by any combination of acts of sensing. The consequence is that perceiving appears to be a sort of mongrel, in which thought loses part of its pure nature as concerned with universals and relations, and sense is raised above its crudeness in merely accepting the given. And, in the second place, the procedure is apt to conceal from us the important consideration that the analytically simple is not necessarily the genetically prior, and that it may be wholly erroneous to suppose that the elements reached by analysis of developed experience, or some of them, are the genetic elements with which experience began. " It is," a recent writer has declared, " almost a universal belief (among psychologists) that the child experiences colours, hears sounds, feels pressures, long before he sees balls, hears voices, or feels solid objects " [1]—a belief which, as the writer shows, is wholly without justification.

Now, I venture to submit that the distinction, which has of late been so much in vogue, between " acquaintance " and " description " illustrates the dangers just mentioned. Mr. Russell conceives that there are two main cognitive relations with which a theory of knowledge has to do, radically contrasted by the fact that the one, presentation or knowledge by acquaintance, is a two-term relation of a cognitive act to a single (simple or complex) object ; whilst the other, judgment or description, is a multiple relation of a cognitive act to the several objects concerned in the judgment. Amongst the objects of which there can be " acquaintance " are those of the kind in which the presentation is a sensible presentation, and it is to this mode of " acquaintance " that I here confine attention. Obviously, Mr. Russell does not intend to identify sense " acquaintance " with the mere receptivity, nor judgment with the mere spontaneity, of Kant ; but he does suppose that these are two specific kinds of knowing, and that there can, at least, be the former without the latter. And in this respect we have, I would urge, essentially a repetition of Kant's mistake, with the result that difficulties similar to those of the Kantian theory at once arise.

Mr. Russell does not, I have said, take " acquaintance " of the sensuous kind to be equivalent to mere receptivity of impressions. For knowledge at all, be it no more than simply awareness of a sense-particular, there is requisite, in his view, a cognitive act on the one hand and an object on the other ;

[1] Grace A. de Laguna, " Sensation and Perception," *Journal of Phil.*, xiii, p. 534 (1916).

consequently, we are not entitled to say that what is sensuously apprehended is an affection of the mind. Yet when we scrutinise more closely the account offered of sensuous " acquaintance ", its difference from the Kantian doctrine of sensibility tends, even in this respect, to disappear. There is involved, so it is maintained, an act of sensing that is totally distinct from the *sensibile* which is sensed and which may exist when it is not sensed. But, if one tries to form a conception of what an " act " in the situation depicted can really signify, the effort will end in failure. In the complex act-acquainted-with-object, the two terms, act and object, have to be so inseparably " married " that the independence of the " act " is reduced to a vanishing point. No error must be allowed to enter into this fast and imperturbable wedlock ; the wife has it all her own way ; the husband pays the piper but she calls the tune. " Objects of sense, even when they occur in dreams ", must be " the most indubitable real objects known to us ".[1] One asks, then, in perplexity, what the term " act ", under such circumstances, can possibly be supposed to indicate. An " act " implies ordinarily the exercise of some function, some mode of " doing " ; but here it seems to imply exactly the reverse—a purely static condition of acquiescence in what is given—indeed, Mr. Russell expressly sanctions the belief that " we feel passive in sensation ".[2] I am bound, therefore, to confess that in these *sensibilia*, pictured as wives, entering into questionable " relations " with the shadowy entities called " acts ", pictured as husbands,[3] I can discover little else than the disjointed fragmentary " impressions " of former days, that

---

[1] *Our Knowledge of the External World*, 1914, p. 85.

[2] *ibid.*, p. 75.

[3] It ought to be mentioned that later Mr. Russell abandons, as was to be anticipated, the notion of " act " as " unnecessary and fictitious ". For instance, he writes : " The occurrence of the content of a thought constitutes the occurrence of the thought. Empirically, I cannot discover anything corresponding to the supposed act ; and theoretically I cannot see that it is indispensable." (*The Analysis of Mind*, 1921, pp. 17 and 18.)

made, however, less pretence to be things of importance. For, now, they are declared to be themselves " objects "— " objects " possessing " the highest degree of certainty "— and, needless to say, Kant's problem concerning the way in which knowledge of an object is possible is silently passed over as though it were no problem at all.

If, however, Mr. Russell should ever undertake the task, which he more than once hints at, of showing how, from " a world of helter-skelter sense-data ",[1] there has actually been derived " the common-sense world " of ordinary experience, he would assuredly find Kant's problem confronting him with all its old persistency. As it is, one of the puzzles which baffle the reader of Mr. Russell's writings is that of determining the denotation of the term " sensible object ", as employed by him. It is true, he explicitly informs us, in the *Lowell Lectures*, that when he speaks of a sensible object he does not mean such a thing as a table, but " just that patch of colour which is momentarily seen when we look at the table, or just that particular hardness which is felt when we press it, or just that particular sound which is heard when we rap it." [2] Yet, throughout the subsequent discussion, he is repeatedly meaning by " sensible object " precisely what he has told us he does not mean by it. It will not do to dismiss this as a pedantic objection, and to retort that the language of common-sense is only resorted to for the sake of brevity and convenience of exposition. Not one argument merely but a number of arguments would collapse utterly were the phrase " sensible object " understood in the way we have been bidden to understand it. Take, for instance, the argument about the " objects of sense " which occur in dreams, and which it is contended are, as such, " indubitably real ". If Mr. Russell dreams that he is in America, but wakes up and finds himself in England, his dream may or may not have been an " insubstantial pageant ", but it certainly did not consist simply of patches of colour and snatches of

[1] *Our Knowledge of the External World*, p. 107.   [2] *ibid.*, p. 76.

sound, or assemblages of these. Or, again, when it is maintained that if, while walking round a table, we press one eye
and, in consequence, see two tables, " then there *are* two
visual tables ",[1] is it not manifest that the whole point of the
argument would be lost unless the two visual objects are
understood to be unified wholes of a distinct and definite
kind? As Professor Whitehead puts it, " a single sense-object
is a complex unity ", and, as Mr. Russell himself admits,
" each mind sees at each moment an immensely complex
three-dimensional world ". " We imagine ", writes Professor Whitehead, " that we have immediate experience of a
world of perfectly defined objects implicated in perfectly
defined events, which, as known to us by the direct deliver-
ance of our senses, happen at exact instants of time, in a
space formed by exact points, without parts and without
magnitude " ;[2] and, although perhaps too much is here
credited to our imagination, even as " moulded by science ",
I am not concerned at present to raise any question on that
score. What I am concerned to urge is that ordinary common-sense experience, however crude and fragmentary it
may be, is never made up of " wandering adjectives ", which
may be christened *sensibilia* ; but that, at the stage of
common-sense experience, sense-qualities are invariably
apprehended, and directly apprehended, as belonging to
" things " (hard though it is to interpret philosophically the
term " belonging to "), and that the directly apprehended
" things " invariably contain factors which cannot be described as *sensibilia*. Mr. Russell acknowledges that " the
world of pure sense has become strange and difficult to rediscover ". I ask, then, what has happened to " the world of
pure sense ", or " the world of helter-skelter sense-data "—
which, be it remembered, is yet, according to the theory we
are considering, the real world, or part of it—that it should
have come to assume for us unsuspecting mortals the form

[1] *Our Knowledge of the External World*, p. 86.
[2] *The Organisation of Thought*, p. 110.

of " the neat, trim, tidy world " in which we imagine ourselves to live and move and have our being?

It is one of the merits of Professor Whitehead's treatment
of the subject that he fully realises the importance of this
question. The kind of answer he would give to it he indicates
by calling to his aid " the whole apparatus of common-sense
thought ". He speaks unhesitatingly of " the thought-
objects of perception ". " The material universe is largely ",
he insists, " a concept of the imagination which rests on a
slender basis of direct sense-presentation. But none the less
it is a fact ; for it is a fact that actually we imagine it. Thus
it is actual in our consciousness just as a sense-presentation is
actual there." [1] And I take it that when Mr. Russell talks of
" common-sense belief ", and describes it as " a piece of
audacious metaphysical theorising ", he means very much
what Professor Whitehead means by " common-sense
thought ", and that it fulfils, according to his view, very much
the same function. Yet, no sooner has this result been reached
than it becomes evident that an object, as actually apprehended in common-sense experience, is taken to be largely
composed of conceptual elements—elements, that is, which
are in no way given, but which are introduced into the given
by the apprehending mind. We have here, so far, a " return
to Kant " in a more literal sense than even Otto Liebmann,
who originally raised that cry, had intended. Once again,
thought is conceived as an instrument by means of which the
crude data of sense are worked up into the form of knowledge ; and, as in the Kantian system, the known object
turns out to be a product of the mind's making—a construction which possesses, as such, no claim to independent
existence. Man weaves a web of his own and calls it " nature " ; but according, at any rate, to this new Kantianism,
the web is a fictitious artifice, and there is, in truth, no
" nature " at all. Nor does there appear to be any reason
why there should not be any number of such artificial crea-

[1] *ibid.*, p. 155.

tions. Indeed, the amazing thing is how the apparent world of " fairly permanent and fairly rigid bodies " should ever have come to be for human intelligences the one common world. For precisely at this crucial stage of the speculation the " return to Kant " is arrested. Kant, as I have already pointed out, sought to make good the position that the thought relations which he took to be essential components of any fact of experience of which we could become aware were in no sense accidents of the particular mechanism of thinking in the finite subject, but were relatively thereto objective— that is to say, universal and necessary. Finite subjects, as he viewed them, all belonged to one world, of which a unifying self-consciousness was the organising principle, so that the ways in which the manifold of intuition was combined were not at the mercy of individual caprice. Mr. Russell, on the contrary, conceives of " common-sense " as a process of imaginative invention set going by " our savage ancestors in some very remote prehistoric epoch ". These " prehistoric metaphysicians " accomplished the marvellous feat not only of devising the belief in so-called " things "—" stones, mountains, the earth and moon and sun," etc.—but of somehow, without any of the modern means of propaganda, so impregnating with their theory the minds of their fellows that it has been for countless ages the universal belief of mankind. Verily, the achievements of historic metaphysicians pale into insignificance in comparison with theirs!

Reverting now to the antithesis between " knowledge by acquaintance " and " knowledge by description ", my contention, then, is that it calls to be rejected. There is no such relation as that which Mr. Russell would denote by the phrase " knowledge by acquaintance "—no cognitive relation, that is to say, in regard to which the question of truth or error cannot arise. The crudest act of sense-apprehension is still an act of discriminating and comparing, an act involving, therefore, the characteristic that, in a highly developed form, is fundamental in an act of judging. And the presence of discrimination and comparison implies at once the possibility of error ; indeed, the more purely sensuous the cognitive act, so much greater the liability to mistake and illusion. The capacity of discerning separately the sense-particulars, of which an object, that is always complex, consists, increases as discrimination proceeds. But to suppose that the primitive mind starts with clear and definite apprehension of such particulars is to set at defiance some of the best attested results of psychological inquiry. It is, however, easy to see why the tendency thus violently to separate sense-apprehension from the process of thinking or judging asserts itself so persistently in epistemological reflexion. All too readily it is taken for granted that the factors which by analysis may be detected in the contents of our knowledge *must be* the factors that have gradually been brought together in the process of its development. Yet you might as well suppose that the fragments into which you can pulverise a picture must have been the fragments which the artist used in its construction. For, if the " things " of common-sense experience—" tables and chairs, stones, mountains, the earth and moon and sun "—be veritable existents ; and if, through a process of perception progressing in trustworthiness, our apprehension of those things has come to be more and more in accordance with fact, then it would still be possible to take such perception in one of its later stages, and by analysis, to " bifurcate " it into what would *seem*, from an external point of view, to be two distinct modes of being aware. Only, in that case, these would be artificial severances made by our abstracting thought, not actual mental states or activities, and even farther removed from the concrete life of mind than the corresponding *abstracta* of Kant, because he *did* see that, if taken to operate in isolation, the one would be blind and the other empty.

4. *Minds and Things*

It is intelligible that, following the line of thought he does, the existence of physical objects, conceived as they had been conceived in *The Problems of Philosophy*, should have come to seem to Mr. Russell dubious. To infer the existence of " matter " (possessing the properties only, so far as science is concerned, of position in space and the power of motion according to the laws of motion) from " sense-data " by the aid of some *a priori* principle such as " that our sense-data have causes other than ourselves ",[1] must inevitably evince itself as a precarious mode of argument, which, at the best, could only lead to a doctrine of things-in-themselves of the very type against which Kant directed his polemic. Accordingly, Mr. Russell contends that, if the " class of appearances " will fulfil the purposes for the sake of which the " thing " of common-sense and the " physical thing " of science were invented, then, by the principle of Occam's razor, we are justified in identifying the " thing " with the " class of its appearances ". In that case, the " thing " may be regarded as the system of its aspects or appearances. All the aspects or appearances of a " thing " will be existents, whereas the " thing " will be a " logical construction " or a " symbolic fiction ". Here, again, an interesting parallel is to be found in Kant's proposal to treat the " thing-in-itself " as a *Grenzbegriff*, a limiting notion, to which reflexion on the entire system of phenomena seemed to him to constrain us.

Mr. Russell has worked out his theory with great skill, and has certainly succeeded in presenting an atomistic philosophy more thorough-going than any which had previously seen the light. At present, however, I wish only to lay stress upon two considerations in regard to it.

In the first place, I do not understand how it can be claimed that the procedure adopted by Mr. Russell enables him to dispense with the notion it was expressly devised to

[1] *Scientia*, vol. xvi, 1914, p. 2.

avoid—the notion, namely, of unknowable things-in-themselves, wholly remote from the data of sense. He thinks it
probable—indeed, he sometimes speaks as though it were
proved—that sense-data " depend for their existence upon
physiological conditions in ourselves "—that, for example,
" what we see is causally dependent upon our body and is
not, as crude common-sense would suppose, something which
would exist if our eyes and nerves and brain were absent ".[1]
Now, it has to be remembered that, in accordance with the
general principle laid down, eyes and nerves and brain, conceived as " things ", are themselves " logical constructions ",
and that we have got to express them as functions of sense-
data. In other words, eyes and nerves and brain are to be
regarded as assemblages of momentary particulars. When,
then—to take a concrete instance—we see, as we say, the
sun, what we really see are groups of appearances that owe
their existence to the physiological assemblages of particulars
in relation, I suppose, to certain of the particulars that form
the solar assemblage. The sun itself is declared to be " a
whole assemblage of particulars, existing at different times,
spreading out from a centre with the velocity of light and
containing among their number all those which are seen by
people who are looking at the sun ".[2] I waive the question
as to the legitimacy of including within the " whole assemblage " the last named despite the fact that their existence is
causally dependent upon other " assemblages ". My concern is with the vastly greater number of the particulars that
go to constitute the sun on the one hand, and eyes and nerves
and brain on the other. These are not and can never become
sense-data, simply because they are not dependent for their
existence upon physiological conditions in ourselves. I ask,
then, on what ground it is assumed that *they* either are or can
be particulars " of the same sort " as our momentary visual
objects? So far as I can discover, the only ground offered is
that of the principle of continuity. " We have not ", writes

[1] *Monist*, vol. xxv, 1915, p. 407. [2] *ibid.*, p. 410.

Mr. Russell, " the means of ascertaining how things appear from places not surrounded by brain and nerves and sense-organs, because we cannot leave the body ; but continuity makes it not unreasonable to suppose that they present *some* appearances at such places ".[1] But surely the appeal to continuity suggests precisely the opposite conclusion. Does not the very absence of conditions such as those to which our sense-data owe their existence indicate in itself a breach of continuity between the particulars in question and the data of sense? These particulars, if not intrinsically incapable of being sensed, are, at any rate, *ex hypothesi*, precluded from being sensed ; they are as rigidly prohibited from entering the sphere of experience as either the atoms of the physicist or the *Dinge an sich* of Kant. To christen them *sensibilia* seems, therefore, purely arbitrary. A *sensibile*, we are told, is an entity which may become a sense-datum by entering into the relation of acquaintance. That, however, is just what *these* unfortunate particulars are debarred from doing, unless, indeed, disembodied spirits frequent the universe, in which case, however, to speak of sense-data as their objects of apprehension is, to say the least, embarrassing.

In the second place, I urge that the use Mr. Russell makes of the term " appearance " is fatally misleading, and tends to slur over the vital distinction between " apparent " and " real "—a distinction which, nevertheless, the course of his own argument compels him to recognise. A " thing " may be regarded, it is contended, as " a certain series of appearances ". And by " appearance " Mr. Russell desires to have consistently understood an existing entity—in other words, a *sensibile*, as he has defined it. Now, it would not be denied that the substitution of " a certain series of appearances " for the " thing " of common-sense experience violently contradicts the deliverances of common-sense experience itself. Certainly, no unsophisticated person ever supposes a " thing " to consist of " a series of appearances ". When common-

[1] *Scientia*, vol. xvi, 1914, p. 5.

sense contrasts a " thing " with its " appearances ", it takes
the " appearances " to be not existing entities, not constituent
parts of the ' thing ", but ways in which the " thing " presents itself to a percipient, ways in which the " thing " is
apprehended. I hold that, in this respect, common-sense is,
in the main, right ; but the point is that, whether right or
wrong, the common-sense distinction re-asserts itself in Mr.
Russell's novel rendering of the facts. For, what this novel
rendering virtually comes to is that " appearances ", now
regarded as existent entities, assume the rôle of newly invented " things " which usurp the place of the old. And, in
reference to these newly invented " things ", there breaks
out again the familiar antithesis. Take, once more, a concrete illustration. The table in front of me is " to be regarded, not as one single persistent entity, but as a series of
entities succeeding each other in time, each lasting for a very
brief period, though probably not for a mere mathematical
instant ".[1] That is the table's real nature. But the table of
which in perception I am immediately aware appears to be
of a very different nature ; it appears to me one single persistent entity, lasting certainly for the considerable interval
during which my act of perception may be directed upon it.
And, be it noted, I am not now referring to my " belief " that
the table is still there when I am not perceiving it ; I am
referring to its at least apparent persistence whilst I am perceiving it. To retort that the table appears to me different
from what it is because I make false judgments about it is
surely to give the whole case of immediate acquaintance, as
contrasted with judgment, away. Here am I in immediate
relation to that complex of sense-data which, ex hypothesi,
constitute what I call the table. This complex seems to me
to persist. If the persistence be an illusion, due to false
judgments on my part, then I ask, where in the world do I
ever get the undiluted " acquaintance " with sense-data that
is free from such illusion? Where do I ever contrive to be-

[1] Monist, vol. xxv, 1915, p. 403.

come " acquainted " with *sensibilia* as they really are, namely, as " entities succeeding each other in time, each lasting for a very brief period, though probably not for a mere mathematical instant "? If the cinematographic deception is everywhere prevalent, what becomes of that infallible " knowledge by acquaintance ", the objects of which are so indubitable as to be " the ultimate certainty on which all knowledge of what exists must be based "? [1] In treating of the theory of continuity, Mr. Russell himself supplies an instance of the antithesis in question manifesting itself in regard to what he calls " immediate data ". We may, he there urges, " suppose a single sense-datum, *e.g.*, in sight, to be a finite surface, enclosing other surfaces which are also single sense-data ". A single sense-datum may enclose (say) the coloured surfaces A and B. And the colour A may, as a matter of fact, differ from the colour B, although the difference between the surfaces as directly sensed is indiscernible.[2] In respect to the matter under discussion, it is irrelevant to maintain that " the indistinguishability is a purely negative fact ". Be the fact negative or positive, what it involves is that the single sense-datum enclosing A and B appears in the act of sensing to be different from what it actually is—it appears, namely, to be all of one colour, whereas in reality it is not all of one colour.

In criticising this theory of momentary *sensibilia*, and in maintaining, as against it, the opposite position that the material world is made up of more or less permanent "things", I have no intention, it need hardly be remarked, of coming to the rescue of the doctrine of the " physical object " as an entity *in toto* distinct from the " sensible object ". Far from it. My contention, of course, is that the " sensible object " is not one thing and the " physical object " another. To put the matter broadly, any real object, such as we are in the habit of describing as a single " thing ", is, I should say,

[1] *Mind*, N.S., vol. xxii, 1913, p. 79.
[2] *Our Knowledge of the External World*, pp. 148-9.

enormously complex—a combined whole, comprising a manifold of parts and possessing a variety of properties or attributes. Many of these characteristics we are enabled, through
the process of perceiving, to discriminate and to apprehend.
Our apprehension is, however, never infallible ; it is always
liable to error. Through the effects of contrast, or what not,
the red colour of a heated poker, for example, may appear to
us otherwise than it would appear were the disturbing influences absent. And although, by the advance of science,
numerous empirical means are at our disposal for distinguishing true " appearances " from false, yet, in the end, we may
have to admit that we have no absolute criterion. Yet this is
a practical difficulty : it is not a theoretical difficulty in the
way of the contention I am urging. It affords not the smallest
presumption that the real poker is colourless, or even that its
actual colour deviates to any appreciable extent from what,
under the normal conditions of vision, it appears to us to be.
Further, in the real object there is obviously vastly more than
our limited powers of perceptual discrimination enable us to
discern. Nevertheless, there is no ground for supposing that
the " more " in the object is inconsistent with the features
that are perceptible. Under the " more " may quite well be
included the elements which the physicist has good reason
for thinking go to constitute the " matter " of the object. A
luminous body may *both* shine with a red light *and* consist of
particles vibrating at the rate, roughly, of four hundred
billion times a second. Probably the chief obstacle to conceiving how a quality such as red can be a property of a
physical object is due to prejudice. We have become so
inured to the physicist's account of light as a " mode of
motion " that we are constrained to think the wave-motions
must be the physical equivalent of the red colour, or the
cause of the red colour. For that assumption there is, however, no scientific warrant. M. Bergson, for instance, speaks
of the consciousness of a flash of light as being the condensation, into one simultaneously apprehended whole, of billions

of successive vibrations. Thus, in one place, he tells us that a sensation of red light, experienced by us in the course of a second, corresponds in itself to a succession of vibrations which, if separately distinguished by us, with the greatest possible economy of time, would occupy more than two hundred and fifty centuries of our history.[1] And, in another place, he affirms that any one quality, such as a colour, " resolves itself, on analysis, into an enormous number of elementary movements ".[2] But a red colour is simply *not* a mode of wave-motion ; and no explanation of its character whatsoever is afforded by taking it to be " the condensation into one second of duration of four hundred billions of successive vibrations ". On the other hand, I can find no valid reason for denying that *both* the colour *and* the vibratory motions may be present in the luminous body, that these may be specifically related the one to the other, and that thus the wave-motions, although not the cause of the colour, are the cause of the stimulation of the sense-organ which occasions the act of apprehending the colour. Why should not the particles of a red-hot body be red? Or, if not that, why should we refuse to allow that the body as a whole may have qualities which its parts have not? As Dr. Broad once admirably stated it, " you cannot be sure that the perception of red is not caused by events in what is red until you know that they are events in what has *merely* primary qualities, and, therefore, you cannot use the scientific theory of the causation of perception to disprove the reality of colour ".[3]

I turn, now, to neo-realistic conceptions of the mind or mental life. Sense-qualities, we are agreed, form no part of the mind's structure. Just as ether-tremors or wave-motions throw no light on the coming to be of such a sense-quality as red, so the latter's mode of origin is left equally in the dark by appeal to a " re-action " of the mind upon stimu-

[1] *Matière et Mémoire*, p. 229 *sqq.*

[2] *L'Évolution Créatrice*, p. 325.

[3] *Perception, Physics and Reality*, 1914, p. 224.

lation. There is as little in the notion of mental " re-action " as in the notion of mechanical energy to render explicable the qualitative differences of nature. In fact, the two notions are by no means so widely divergent as they have usually been taken to be. For, after all, " re-action upon stimulation " is a " mode of motion " ; and it is scarcely an effective way of disposing of materialism to transport into the " mind ", and when there to use as your principle of explanation, the very mechanism you have shown to be un-availing in the domain of " matter ". So far, at any rate, the " new realism " has helped to clear the ground of lingering fictions. But its doctrine of sense-data, which, except that they are no longer held to be mental in character, are pre-cisely the " presentations " or " ideas " of the old subjectiv-ism, precludes it from advancing to anything like an adequate account of the nature and functions of mind.

Mr. Russell, as we have seen, is content to leave the charac-ter of a " mental act " in total obscurity. On the other hand, Professor Alexander, whose general philosophical view is, if I mistake not, far nearer in accord than Mr. Russell's is with that which I am trying to delineate, has been wrestling long and resolutely with the task which evidently devolves upon a realist who is not speedily to find himself at a stand-still. Yet I am bound to confess that the attempt to reduce the life of mind to a system of " conations " strikes me as the least satisfactory part of a way of thinking with which, as a whole, I feel considerable sympathy. There is, Professor Alexander maintains, no difference of quality between cona-tions of any order. They have, all of them, the single quality of consciousness, and the only difference they exhibit is a " difference of direction ". But, if that were the case, I fail to see what could be meant by talking about " the riches " of mind and its " hoarded wealth of mental suggestion ". A man revisits, let us say, the place of his childhood, and gazes, after years of absence, upon the house and garden that was once his home. There it stands, the familiar object, as

c

though he had left it but yesterday. Certainly, his act of perception is directed upon it. Instantly, however, a crowd of memories, ideas, thoughts—using the ordinary phraseology—occupy his mind, reminiscences of former days, recollections of youthful ambitions, reflexions on the contrast between early dreams and actual achievements, and so on. These are not, I agree, elements of the object, not features he is discerning in it. But how can the theory of consciousness as possessing only the single quality of consciousness be reconciled with inner experiences of this kind? We " live through " or " enjoy " our own minds, Professor Alexander has been labouring to teach us ; we do not " contemplate " them. Be it so ; but what would there be to " enjoy " or to " live through ", if our minds were simply complexes of activities that differed from one another *merely* in their modes of " direction "? Professor Alexander gives, I venture to urge, the case away when he admits that the mind may intrude itself upon the objects of its perception, that, for example, an aesthetic object is neither wholly physical nor wholly mental, but a form of existence in which both these kinds are blended—for obviously what is thus " imputed " to the object is not the bare quality of consciousness. And when he describes an act of willing as the taking up of the willed object into the self—a mode of expression, be it said, I should be pedantic enough to object to—he is virtually recognising what I have been calling the " content " of a mental act. In short, empty consciousness of everything that gives it concreteness and determinateness and you have deprived yourself of the right to speak, as Professor Alexander does, of the mind's intellectual, moral and spiritual "endowments ".

" ' Consciousness ' ", said William James, " when once it has evaporated to the estate of pure diaphaneity, is on the point of disappearing altogether ". Professor Alexander will not countenance its dismissal ; but the adherents of the " new realism " have not his scruples, and, according to the

" relational theory " of consciousness, to which most of them are committed, what alone survives is the name. Professor Holt's volume on *The Concept of Consciousness* embodies an able attempt to work out this theory in detail, and I can perhaps best proceed by setting forth my case in opposition to his.

We are, so Professor Holt conceives, in the midst of a universe in which all things—physical, mental and logical, propositions and terms, existent and non-existent, false and true, good and evil, real and unreal—subsist or have being. Concerning these entities, there is no question of substances, for, if we are to speak of substance at all, they must all be said to be of one substance—a substance which is " neutral ". These " neutral entities " form a system ; they are graded in a strict order of complexities. As primary or fundamental entities are to be recognised the relatively simple—the concepts of identity, of difference, of number and of the negative. Then follow the logical and mathematical entities—the forms of order, the innumerable algebras which are elaborated cases of order. Next in this hierarchy of being come the " secondary " qualities, or, more properly, the qualities, and with them the concept, of intensity. Upon these supervene geometry, the higher mathematics, space, time, motion (depending on purely mathematical change), mass, the subject-matter of mechanics, of physics, of chemistry, the larger material aggregates, vegetable and animal life, consciousness or mind, and, with the last named, the sciences of anthropology, psychology, history, etc. Finally, we reach the realm of values—the least fundamental, but for us human beings the most important, of entities. Admittedly, at certain stages of this curious simple-to-complex series, entities appear which do not seem to consist of what is simpler and more fundamental. Each one of the qualities is a case in point. And yet, it is contended, there is no improbability involved in supposing that qualities may some day be seen to develop deductively from systems which, at the outset, do not contain these qualities. For, with the advance of knowledge, the tendency has been for entities, once taken to be unresolvable into simpler components, to turn out to be resolvable after all. Thus the " vital force ", which to former generations of scientists presented the aspect of being quite distinct from the entities of the inorganic world, is now generally acknowledged to be explicable in chemical terms. It is, then, Professor Holt's contention that a " mind " or " consciousness " may likewise be interpreted as a complex or collection of more fundamental " neutral entities ". Steering his course at night with the help of a searchlight, the navigator illuminates now this object and now that, and thus defines a new collection of objects, all of which, except occasionally the bow and foremast of the ship itself, are integral parts of the region through which the ship is passing (and remain so), although they have thus gained membership in another manifold—the class of all objects on which the illumination falls. A mind or consciousness may be regarded as just such a manifold—a cross-section of the universe, selected by the nervous system in any one of its responses to the influences of the environment. So conceived, a mind or consciousness would be a class or group of entities within the subsisting universe. If, now, we are ready to recognise with Aristotle that thought and its object are one, why should we hesitate to recognise that sensations and perceptions and ideas are likewise one with their " objects "? What reason is there for believing in the existence of *both* sensations or perceptions or ideas or thoughts *and* their objects? Objects there are, and these, when included in the particular manifold or cross-section which you call consciousness, may be described as sensations and perceptions and ideas and thoughts, whilst when included in the particular manifold or cross-section you call a room they may be described as material things.

Here, undisguisedly, the wheel has come full circle! A line of reflexion which took for its point of departure the necessity of distinguishing the act of consciousness from its object, and which emphasised the duality between sensing and *sensum*, between perceiving and percept, between thinking and thought,[1] ends by reaching the conclusion that there is no such distinction, that seeing just means colours occurring, that hearing means sounds occurring, that thinking means thoughts occurring—all these in a certain context entitled a " psychic cross-section ". Troubles and predicaments innumerable strew the ground at once. I confine attention to a few. In the first place, the " cross-section " which *is* consciousness is alleged to be defined by the responses of the nervous system. And the human being is asserted to be conscious of that to which his nervous system responds. But can any such principle as that be seriously maintained? Is it not manifest that a human being is conscious of countless things—of Prospero's enchanted isle, of the binomial theorem, of the law of gravitation—to which his nervous system would seem to be profoundly indifferent, whereas the things to which his nervous system does respond—ether-tremors, air-vibrations, and the like—make, at the time, no appearance in consciousness at all? To reply to an objection of this sort that whilst " the nervous system is nothing but a physical mechanism acted on by physical forces ", yet these physical entities are seen on analysis to be " aggregates of logical or neutral entities ", would surely be futile. For, on the one hand, be they aggregates of the alleged kind or not, it is, in any case, *motions* to which the nervous system responds, and not to their assumed logical components ; and, on the other hand, in such instances as those just cited, it is certainly not *the* " neutral entities " of which the physical forces may be supposed to consist that form the constituents of the " psychic cross-section ". In truth, it is only because " consciousness " is surreptitiously introduced into the nervous response on which it is declared to depend that the account given of the nervous response as selecting and defining the contents of consciousness wears even a semblance of

[1] *Cf.* Perry, *Present Philosophical Tendencies*, pp. 274–5.

plausibility. The contradiction comes plainly enough to the surface. On the one hand, in the simile I have mentioned, the nervous system is represented by the searchlight and consciousness by the totality of objects illuminated (and not by the light which illuminates them) [1] ; on the other hand, it is insisted that " no neutral responses are unconscious, or subconscious, unless this is meant as sub-selfconscious ".[2] Now, granting, for the sake of the argument, the identity of consciousness with its objects, it is clear, at any rate, that the objects are not identical with the nervous response, so that if the latter is conscious, its consciousness cannot consist of the objects responded to. In the second place, so far from consciousness being dependent on nervous response, Professor Holt's reasoning would rather make for the opposite conclusion. For he vigorously enforces the doctrine that the component elements of a whole retain their distinct self-identity, whatever be the context into which they enter. Grouped together in one context, tables and chairs and books form contents of consciousness, and may be called percepts ; grouped together in another context, they form contents of a room, and may be called material things ; in both contexts, however, they remain the same identical tables and chairs and books. And, similarly, in regard to the simple entities of which they are complexes. Being experienced, therefore, makes no difference to the facts ; the individual items of the universe do not change their character when taken into the web of an experience ; new combinations arise, but the elements in themselves are what they previously were. Nevertheless, we are explicitly told that any term or proposition of the hierarchy of being included in the conscious cross-section is itself conscious [3]—that is to say, not merely is the totality of the objects in the cross-section conscious, but each one of these objects singly is likewise conscious. If, then, the circumstance of constituting an element of the cross-section

[1] *Concept of Consciousness*, p. 209 *et passim*.
[2] *ibid.*, p. 206.   [3] *ibid.*, p. 207.

affects in no way the nature of the element itself, does it not follow that an object which is conscious in a cross-section is equally conscious outside that context? I do not suggest that Professor Holt intends this consequence to be drawn. All the same, it would be in accord with various subsidiary contentions of his to which otherwise it is difficult to attach a meaning. For example, pains and pleasures, or, at all events, large numbers of them, are declared to be not in us but " in the outer world " ; and, generally, " emotions and feelings " are said to be " neutral entities, or groups of these, precisely as objective as the other components of being " [1]; so that, presumably, whether within or without a psychic cross-section, the entities in question " enjoy the air they breathe ". This leads me to note, in the third place, that whoever insists upon identifying knowing and the known virtually cuts the ground from under the doctrine of mind as being *restricted* to certain cross-sections of the universe. Or, changing the metaphor, he thereby opens the door through which the waters of Hegelian idealism, rushing in, will overflow the house. For a cross-section selected out of a wider whole of objective reality is only another way of expressing what idealist writers have meant in speaking of a *finite* mind as " a partial world ". Only they would go on to say, and surely not without justification, that it is impossible, at this point, to call " halt ". A finite mind that is able to recognise itself as but a section of a wider world, and to interpret what is outside that section, has, they would urge, already transcended the limits of its sectional character, and must be thought of as possessing within itself " the principle of infinity taken in the sense of the nisus towards unity and self-completion ".[2] In other words, the whole of which the finite mind is a fragment would itself be Mind or Consciousness ; the " single, infinite, deductive system in which the entire variety develops deductively from a relatively small number of fundamental

[1] *ibid.*, pp. 110 and 292.
[2] *Cf.* Bosanquet, *The Value and Destiny of the Individual*, p. 4.

propositions " [1] would only be another name for Hegel's Absolute.

There is no other basis upon which a realistic theory of knowledge can rest than the distinction between the act of knowing and the object known. The distinction requires, however, if its real meaning is to be grasped, that we should be in earnest with it and recognise that it throws upon us the task of offering some intelligible account of the " act " in and through which knowledge of an object is possible. In perception, the mind is unquestionably directed upon an object. But to suppose that the specific character of the mental activity involved consists merely in such " direction " seems to me an error arising from the attempt to inspect that activity from the outside—as a part, so to speak, of the whole objective situation—instead of from within as a mode of the conscious subject's own life. Take up in regard to it the position of an external spectator, and its difference from any other mental activity may well seem expressible in terms of " direction ". And from " direction " it is but a short step to " nervous response ", and to the substitution of the latter in the place of the activity originally described as " mental ". Scrutinise, on the contrary, the cognitive act from the point of view of the conscious subject whose act it is, and, as I have tried to show, it evinces itself as neither the source of what is " constitutive ", in the Kantian sense, on the one hand, nor as " diaphanous " on the other, but as consisting essentially in discriminating what is presented to it, and as thus acquiring the definite content of awareness of certain features or characteristics. Nothing is easier than to fall into the blunder of abstracting the contents of such mental acts from the mental acts whose contents they are and of ascribing to them a fictitious mode of independent existence. From that to the " representative theory " is no far cry. We first speak, for example, of " the idea of red " instead of " the awareness of red ", and then, by a further transition, we go on to substitute

[1] *Concept of Consciousness*, p. 164.

" red " for " the idea of red "—that is to say, the content
cognised for the content of the act of cognising it, or what is
present *to* the mind for what is present *in* it—and all the
paradoxes of subjectivism are upon our hands. Now, there
is no getting out of this quagmire by following the path prescribed by the " new realism "—namely, by accepting
Berkeley's identification of " idea " with " object ", whilst
rejecting his dictum that the *esse* of the " object " or " idea "
is *percipi* and insisting that the term " idea " indicates no
more than that the " object " is related to the mind that
knows it. To cut the Gordian knot in this fashion, by brush-
ing aside the crucial difficulty of the problem, is more
dazzling than helpful. I agree in unreservedly rejecting the
" representative theory ", but I urge that its rejection forces
upon us in no way the conclusion that " knowledge and the
object of knowledge are identical ".[1] It is just because the
content of the act of knowing never is the object of that act,
never is, in fact, an object at all, and, therefore, never can
stand in the way of that upon which the act is directed, that
the act of knowing is not disqualified for the discharge of its
function. Were the awareness of shape not shapeless, the
awareness of motion not motionless, and the awareness of
colour not colourless,[2] apprehension of the shape, motion and
colour of things *would* be precarious indeed.

If, now, a perceiving act only acquires its specific content
through being directed upon an object, and if that acquisition
does not imply that any quality of the object has been transported into the act, or that the content of the act is, in any
sense, an intermediary object (a " nearer object ", as Dr.
Bosanquet called it), the *specific* character of the act is no
impediment to adequate apprehension of the object. We
need not assume, that is to say, that consciousness must be
" diaphanous ", if its report of what is other than itself is to
be trusted. But the way in which the notion of its " diaphanous " character has arisen is not hard to trace. Try, as

[1] *ibid.*, p. 223.   [2] *ibid.*, p. 142.

an onlooker, to observe the two states, the act of being aware of red and the act of being aware of blue, and almost inevitably the former will appear to be made up of " awareness " *and* " red ", and the latter of " awareness " *and* " blue ". The " red " and the " blue " will appear to be readily distinguishable, while the " awareness " in the one case will appear to be indistinguishable from the " awareness in the other, and each to be just something that can be looked through and nothing seen but the red or the blue. One reason for this is obvious. " Awareness ", so regarded, has become a universal—just exactly the " I think " which Kant affirmed " must be capable of accompanying all my presentations "—and naturally it will elude detection as a particular. Similarly, *in this respect*, take a " red colour " to be made up of " red " *and* " colour ", and a " blue colour " to be made up of " blue " *and* " colour ", and the " colour " will be no less difficult to detect ; it, too, will seem to be " diaphanous ". More important is it, however, to insist that, viewed from within, the act of being aware of red *is*, for the conscious subject, a specific act clearly distinguishable from the act of being aware of blue, and that, in the relation of perception, it is *this* act, with its definite content, " awareness of red ", and not merely " awareness " *simpliciter*, over against which the " red " which is a quality of the object stands.

A continuum of such specific acts, along with those conditions of feeling-tone which seem to be their invariable accompaniments, is, I take it, essentially what we mean by a mind. The continuum involves certainly, and only becomes possible through, the retention and revival into subsequent moments of consciousness of the contents of previous states. I find not in conation but in knowing the fundamental characteristic of mental life. Doubtless, in psychology it is advisable to restrict the use of the term " knowledge " to cognition that has reached a certain level of psychical development ; but the main principle is not thereby affected.

A human mind, at any rate, depends for its very being upon knowledge ; its place in the scheme of existence is determined by and through its capacity of knowing. But let us beware of demanding of knowing that it should do more than enable us to know—a demand the fulfilment of which, if it *could* be fulfilled, would prove destructive of knowledge, and of all that depends upon it. Even in perfectly completed knowledge the antithesis between knowing and that which is known would remain, for it is an antithesis implied in the very notion of knowledge itself.

5. *Concluding Considerations*

My object in the foregoing discussion has not been to propound a metaphysical theory. The problem with which I have been concerned is essentially an epistemological problem, and I have striven to confine the consideration of it, so far as possible, within the sphere of epistemology. It may, however, conduce to clearness to add, in conclusion, one or two observations of a more general kind. And, first of all, let me guard against misunderstanding by disowning any attempt that may be made to see in what I have written a defence of the doctrine commonly called " dualism ". That material things and mental lives are fundamentally disparate entities I have certainly tried to show reason for holding. But to me it seems that the world is full of entities, or modes of being, which are, in their way, no less disparate in character than mind and matter. Nor am I in the least concerned to deny that absolute independence cannot be claimed for any of the concrete particulars of the universe, or that ultimately they must form an interconnected system. So much I am, on the contrary, quite willing to grant. Yet a bare statement of that sort amounts in itself to little. The question for metaphysics to answer, if it can, is as to the kind of system that would be compatible with what we know of the contents of reality. I may be blind, but I fail to see why, in order to constitute a system, there must needs be one matrix from which all qualitative differences have arisen—one ultimate being of which everything else is a partial manifestation.

To come back, however, to the themes we have been handling. More than one writer has observed that the " new realism ", notwithstanding its avowedly polemical attitude towards idealism, is, in truth, separated from the latter only by the thinnest of lines. The considerations I have been pressing amply bear out that contention.

When, for example, it is maintained that sense-data are physical and not mental, and when the term " physical " is defined as meaning " what is dealt with by physics ", while a particular is called " mental " if " it is aware of something ",[1] there is plainly, so far, nothing to distinguish the point of view in question from subjective idealism of the most thorough-going type. Berkeley, at any rate, had no intention of asserting that the *esse* of sensible things was *percipere*, nor would he have considered it worth his while to protest that the *esse* of " what is dealt with by physics " might quite well be *percipi*. Underlying Berkeley's reasoning throughout there lies the conviction that the " mental " is not exhausted in what he called the " modes " or " attributes " of mind, but that " qualities " may be " mental " in the sense that they *are* only as perceived by a mind. It is true that Berkeley was disposed to regard pleasure and pain as allied in this respect to " ideas ", whereas Mr. Russell conceives pleasurableness and painfulness to belong to the act of being aware, and that, on the latter supposition, one of Berkeley's arguments in support of his position falls to the ground. But, even on this point, the " new realists " are by no means unanimous and Professor Holt, as we have seen, advances a view of pleasure and pain which, if admitted, would make the argument in question relevant enough.

A more fundamental basis of agreement is, however, this. Both the " new realism " and the idealism it would displace interpret a " thing " as made up of its " appearances ". Mr.

[1] Russell, *Scientia*, vol. xvi, 1914, p. 5.

Russell would have us free our minds from the " assumption "
of permanent " things " with changing appearances.   A
" thing " he takes to be a certain series of appearances, connected with each other by continuity and by certain causal
laws.   Leaving, for the moment, on one side the atomism
that is bound up with Mr. Russell's conception, this contention is in strict accordance with the view of nature with which
the post-Kantian idealism has made us familiar.   In an able
paper read before the Aristotelian Society in 1915, Professor
J. W. Scott was proceeding on true Hegelian lines in maintaining that a sensible object is some kind of concretion of the
entirety of its appearances into one appearance, that what is
called the " real thing " may be said to be that " appearance "
which contains the rest as its content, and generally that
appearances constitute the content of reality.[1]   No doubt the
two writers would differ radically in regard to the ultimate
meaning to be assigned to what they both call "appearances" ;
but they are at one in refusing to recognise in the physical
universe as such any particulars other than those which are
expressible in terms of " appearances ".

Now the " realism " for which I have been seeking to offer
justification joins issue with idealism in respect to each of the
positions just indicated.   On the one hand, it meets the
contention that the *esse* of sensible objects is *percipi* by laying
stress upon the fact that the occurrence of an act of perception involves conditions which are not, and never can be,
perceptible, and by showing that there is nothing in the
notion of perception which at all implies restriction of the
object perceived to the type of concrete existence called
mental rather than to any other.   And, on the other hand, it
meets the contention that " things " are groups or complexes
of " appearances " by calling in question the whole conception of " appearance " which lies at the root of that contention.
" Appearances," according to the view I am taking, are not
themselves existing entities, but ways in which existing

[1] *Proceedings of Arist. Soc.*, N.S., vol. xvi, 1916, p. 63 *sqq.*

entities are apprehended. In other words, the distinction
between a " thing " and its " appearances " is *not* a distinction between the " thing " as a whole and its constituents.
A " thing " is made up of parts and of qualities, and any one
of its qualities may " appear " in a countless number of
ways. But this quality is not resolvable into its ways of
appearing ; it remains one, though its appearances vary, and
is, as such, a quality of the " real thing ", while the appearances of it are not. The appearances are no more than the
orderly manner in which the quality is apprehended by a
finite mind under the conditions and limitations imposed by
sense intuition.

A " crude brickbat notion of physical object " [1] is about as
far removed from the notion of " thing " to which the course
of reflexion we have been following would point as any notion
could well be. How the different parts (" atoms," if you
will) and qualities of what we name a " thing " are combined
in one whole, and how they are related there to one another,
are metaphysical questions with which I have not attempted
to deal. But nothing could be more remote from my purpose
than to suggest that " any and every property of the object
can under any and all circumstances be predicated ", or that
" all its properties can be predicated of each of its parts ".
Absurdities of that order merit not serious refutation. On
the other hand, certain propositions respecting the nature of a
" thing " we are, I think, entitled, on empirical grounds, to
lay down. The brown-shiny-oblong which I apprehend by
sight and the hard-solid-oblong which I discern by touch I
am entitled, it seems to me, to assert is a single thing—the
table, namely, in front of me at which I am at this moment
sitting. And, further, that these properties of the table are
on a different footing from the parts of it which are co-
existent in space, because *their* co-existence is of a peculiar
kind, for they jointly occupy the same portion of space,
whereas the parts do not. And a " brickbat " notion of a

[1] *New Realism*, p. 371.

physical object is disposed of, once for all, by that consideration alone.

In like manner, the notion of a " soul-substance ", which
subsists in " awful isolation " and " receives its own unique
sensations ",[1] is utterly foreign to the notion of mind which
the considerations I have been urging would lead us to adopt.
The mind, from the point of view I have been regarding it,
receives nothing ; it is essentially an activity that finds and
discovers, and whose being is constituted by the awareness of
what it finds and discovers.   Whether, and, if so, in what
sense, the stream of psychical activity is rightly conceived as
constituting a substantial identity of existence is again a
metaphysical question upon which, for our present purpose,
it was not necessary to discuss.   But, as outcome of our
inquiry, this much, at least, can be said.   Substance or no
substance, the mind is certainly not one entity, and its states,
or modes of activity, something else.   The mind is its states ;
but these are connected together in a manner as little analogous to a series of beads upon a string as they are to a succession of films in a cinema entertainment.   A mental life has
not parts analogous to the atoms of physical things.

[1] Holt, *Concept of Consciousness*, p. 110.

II

THE SENSUM THEORY

1. *Perceptual Situations of ordinary Experience.*
2. *Broad's Reasons for rejecting the Common-sense View.*
3. *Can " Sensa " be " Appearances of " Physical Objects ?*
4. *" Sensa " may appear to be different from what they actually are.*
5. *The Theory of a general process of Sensing.*
6. *Perception and Introspection.*

I PROPOSE to confine myself here to a discussion of the theory of sensa in the form in which it has been presented by Dr. C. D. Broad in two of his well-known treatises.[1] It is a great gain to have the theory exhaustively worked out in detail ; and, although I am destined to play the somewhat ungrateful *rôle* of a critic, I have no other feeling than that of unreserved admiration of the extraordinary care and thoroughness with which Dr. Broad has fulfilled his task.

The volumes I have referred to will be sufficiently familiar. It will, therefore, suffice to indicate very briefly, at the outset, the essential features of the theory, as elaborated by Dr. Broad. In every perceptual situation there are involved, it is contended, states of mind which may be designated "sensations ". By the term " sensation ", when employed in this context, we are to understand a complex whole that is analysable into an act of sensing directed upon an object, which may here be called a sensum. The sensum is a particular *existent*, but a particular existent of a peculiar kind. It is not a physical existent ; and there is no reason for supposing that it is a mental existent, in the sense of being either a state of mind or existentially dependent on mind. It re-

---

[1] *Scientific Thought*, 1923, and *The Mind and its Place in Nature*, 1925. I use the abbreviation *S.T.* when referring to the former ; in other cases the references are to the latter.

sembles physical entities, as ordinarily conceived, in having spatial and other characteristics usually ascribed to physical entities ; it resembles mental entities in being private to the individual percipient. But, on the one hand, it is not, in any plain straightforward sense, in the one " physical space " in which physical things are supposed to be ; and, on the other hand, although not existentially dependent on mind, it may, to some extent, be qualitatively so dependent, and strong grounds can be furnished for taking it to be existentially partly dependent on the position, internal states and struc- ture of the body. Furthermore, our apprehension of sensa is intuitive, immediate ; we may make judgments about them, but the act of sensing them is not itself an act of judging. And, finally, it is by the existence of sensa and their presence to our minds in sensation that we are led to believe that physical objects exist and are present to our senses. Whatever properties we ascribe to physical objects we ascribe to them in consequence of the properties that actually characterise our sensa. So that sensa may be said to be in some way the *ratio cognoscendi* of the physical world, while the physical world would appear to be in some way the *ratio essendi* of sensa.

1. In dealing with the problem of sense-apprehension, Dr. Broad is obviously pursuing the right method in starting from " perceptual situations ", as in ordinary experience we are familiar with them, and not from the fragmentary " data ' which sensa have sometimes been taken to be. Whether or not it be true that for primitive experience the world con- sisted of " helter-skelter sense-data ", which " our savage ancestors in some very remote prehistoric epoch " gradually learnt to collect into series, and to regard each series as con- sisting of successive appearances of one " thing ", certain it is that *for us* mere sensa (*e.g.*, a patch of colour or a particular hardness) are not given at all, but are, at the best, entities which we can only " rediscover " by an arduous process of abstraction. When I look at the table in front of me, how-

D

ever momentary the glance may be, I simply do not *see*
merely a ' patch of colour ". With some little effort, I may
limit what I am aware of to a patch of colour of more or less
definite extent, which is continuous with what surrounds it,
and which consists of parts related to and distinguished
from one another. But notoriously the vast number of
sensible objects are not of this meagre character. Pre-
eminently in visual perception we seem, practically at every
moment of our waking lives, to be apprehending *intuitively*
and *directly* physical things, each with a variety of properties
and of inter-related parts or constituents, and each connected in manifold ways with other things. This " immediate
intercourse between the mind and its object ", as Hume
styled it, seems unquestionably *the* outstanding feature in
what we take to be our awareness of external nature. Call
it " belief ", or a " universal and primary opinion of all men ",
or what you will, our ordinary thought and conduct are
absolutely dominated by it, and were we to begin to distrust
it in the practical affairs of life the consequences would soon
prove disastrous. Hume thought that the " belief " was
" soon destroyed by the slightest philosophy ", Dr. Broad
thinks that it needs " careful and critical reflexion " to
realise that it is philosophically unjustified, but both agree
that such doubts " vanish at once when we again begin to
perceive ", and " that then the naïvely realistic view is
reinstated as if it had never been questioned " (p. 242). Now,
I am thoroughly at one with Dr. Broad in refusing to recognise that there is anything sacred about " common-sense ",
and I am far from wishing to imply that a philosophical
theory is in any way invalidated simply because it deviates
widely from " common-sense " views. Yet, in regard to an
overwhelming assurance of ordinary experience such as that
in question, I do say, firstly, that we require very strong evidence indeed of its erroneousness to entitle us to reject it as
unfounded ; and, secondly, that no theory which involves
its rejection can be satisfactory unless it enables us to account

for the fact that plain men and philosophers in ordinary life invariably think and act on the basis of a " belief " violently out of keeping with the theory. It will not do, therefore, to dispose of the latter problem in the cavalier fashion it has sometimes been disposed of by describing the common-sense view either as " a piece of audacious metaphysical theorising " which has come down to us from primitive ages, or as due to a " blind and powerful instinct of nature " ! And one of the many merits of Dr. Broad's work is that he does not do so. He recognises to the full that we have got to start from the fact that the perceptual situations of ordinary experience do carry with them the claim that their " objective constituents " are spatio-temporal parts of the physical objects which we are said to be perceiving, and that since, as he thinks, this claim cannot be substantiated, the problem has to be faced of trying to explain how it comes to be made and trust in its credentials so perfectly adapted to the practical purposes of human life.

2. Dr. Broad's main reason for holding that what, as he says, " we all believe except when we are philosophising " (p. 249) is to a very large extent false may be stated in a few words. He maintains that although every perceptual situation does claim that its " objective constituent " is a spatio-temporal part of a physical object, yet this claim is certainly false in some cases and extremely hard to justify in any. It is certainly false in delusive perceptual situations. And certain well-established facts render it highly dubious in respect to perceptual situations that are not delusive. Of such facts the following are instances. The " objective constituents " of a visual perceptual situation will seem to be of different shapes and sizes to an observer who changes his position in regard to what he takes to be a physical object ; while, if two observers, one standing and the other moving about, are looking at what they take to be the same object, the " objective constituent " of the former's perceptual situation will seem constant in size and shape, and the " objective con-

stituents " of the latter's successive perceptual situations will seem to differ in size and shape. And so on. Now, he allows that on what he calls the " multiple relation theory of appearing ", it is possible to account for these and similar facts without relinquishing the position that the " objective constituent " is literally a spatio-temporal part of the physical object. I will not go here into the details of this theory. I should need to state it in a way somewhat different from the way in which Dr. Broad states it, if I were trying to defend what seems to me a tenable view. I want, however, in passing to refer to the reason which he gives for believing that the balance of advantage inclines " slightly on the side of the sensum theory " (p. 195). The latter does not, he argues, require us to assume absolute space-time as a pre-existing matrix, while the former does. The argument, if I rightly understand it, amounts to this. In view of mirror-images, aberration, etc., those who hold the " multiple relation theory " must, it is contended, assert *either* that a single extended particular can appear to be two distinct extended particulars at a distance apart from each other, *or* that sensible qualities and forms appear to inhere not in physical objects but in regions of space. I am far from thinking that these alternatives are exhaustive, nor do I know why the first of them is pronounced to be incredible. But, with respect specially to the second, I would ask, is it, in truth, necessary to assume that a mirror-image appears to inhere in a space which is physically empty? No space with which we are familiar is physically empty, nor does it even appear to us to be physically empty. The space behind the mirror is filled at least with air and with the innumerable particles which the air always contains, and surely this would provide substance enough for sensible qualities to inhere in or to appear to inhere in. I fail, therefore, to see that the theory in question does presuppose absolute space-time ; and, if it does not, Dr. Broad should be willing to concede that it possesses, at any rate, a degree of probability equal to that of the sensum theory.

3. I want next to raise the question whether sensa, conceived as Dr. Broad conceives them, can rightly be said to be " appearances of " physical objects. A sensum *s* may, we are told, be said to be an " appearance of " a physical object *o* if *s* has to *o* a certain relation *R* which it has to no other physical object. And, when several persons are said to perceive *o*, what is meant is that their several perceptual situations contain the sensa s_1, s_2, s_3, . . . etc., and that all these have to *o* the relation *R*. Moreover, of the relation *R* we can say (*a*) that it is not *ex hypothesi* the relation of spatio-temporal part to spatio-temporal whole, and (*b*) that it is a many-one relation—that is to say, a relation which many different sensa can have to one physical object, but not a relation which one sensum can have to several physical objects. Further, it is asserted that, on Russell's theory, the relation *R* is that of class-membership, while on such a theory as Berkeley's it is that of one part of a total effect to the cause of this total effect (pp. 182-3). Analogously, one would suppose that, on the theory before us, the relation would be that of one part of a total effect to one of the joint causes of this effect, although in this case the effect is not, as Berkeley maintained, a mental entity, nor the partial cause, as he thought, a certain volition in God's mind. But that a sensum is related as an effect to something else as a partial cause would surely not in itself justify the description of it as an " appearance of " that something else (and, unless my memory is at fault, Berkeley nowhere speaks of " ideas " as " appearances of " anything). In describing sensa as " appearances of " physical objects, Dr. Broad wishes, I should gather, to imply that physical objects, or the qualities of physical objects, either are or seem to be manifested to us by sensa (*see, e.g.*, pp. 242, 250, 296 and 304). And the point I desire to press is that if the " objective constituents " of perceptual situations be taken to be concrete, particular existents, such as coloured or hot patches, noises, etc., which are distinct and separate from physical existents, it is

utterly misleading to speak of them as manifestations or appearances *of* the latter.

The sensa which it is claimed are " appearances of " physical objects are, *ex hypothesi*, products generated by special occurrent conditions, *i.e.*, stimulations that originate from extra-organic sources, affect the sense-organs and are transmitted by specific nerves to the brain. All this is, on the theory in question, admittedly purely hypothetical—for if there be no way of proving the existence of physical entities (*S.T.*, p. 269) there is, *a fortiori*, no way of proving the existence of sense-organs, nerve-fibres and brains—but, meanwhile, let the assumption stand. In what sense, then, can these products be said to manifest or reveal to us physical objects? Clearly not in the sense that they disclose to us *the properties or characteristics* of such objects. The sensa manifest such and such qualities, physical objects have altogether other qualities (p. 152) ; it is the sensa alone that are coloured or hot or cold or hard or soft ; there is " not the slightest reason " to ascribe so-called secondary qualities to physical things (p. 206). So far, therefore, instead of manifesting to us the properties of physical objects, sensa very effectively delude us as to those properties and hide them from us. And even though we grant Dr. Broad's contention, which I am far from thinking he has successfully sustained, that what he calls the " persistent and neutral conditions " of sensa *must* be interpreted by analogy with visual sensa and their relations in the visual field (p. 204), still there is equally not the slightest reason for believing that sensa disclose to us the shapes, sizes and positions of physical entities. How could they? Even if it be possible, as Dr. Broad thinks it is possible, to construct a single, neutral, public Space-Time of physical entities and events on the analogy of the many private space-times of various observers' sense-histories,[1] yet clearly the shapes, sizes and positions of visual or tactual sensa, as they occur in visible or tactual space, could in no

[1] See *infra*, p. 60 *sqq.*

way exhibit the shapes, sizes and positions of things that are not in visible or tactual space, and whose structure is confessedly totally different from the structure of sensa. Nor do I see in what way sensa, interpreted as the theory requires them to be interpreted, could so much as indicate to us the bare *existence* of such physical entities. Assuming that sensa are, as a matter of fact, caused or generated by the action of physical things upon the bodily organism, yet the sensa would carry with them no tidings that they were effects of certain causes. And, even assuming that any particular sensum s has, as a matter of fact, to a particular entity o a relation R which it has to no other physical entity, by what conceivable means could a percipient mind be made aware of the fact? Why, indeed, should a sensum not, in truth, stand in a like relation to several physical entities, for evidently several might co-operate in producing it? And, furthermore, if it is to be called an " appearance of " something, why should it not be pronounced an " appearance of " a part of the brain or nervous system, which, according to the theory, would have at least an equal claim with the extra-organic physical entity to be " manifested " by it, in whatever sense it can be said to " manifest " or " represent " anything besides itself?

When, in ordinary language, we speak of the objective constituent of a perceptual situation as being the "appearance of " a physical object we mean not that it is the appearance which appears but that it is the physical object which appears. As Dr. Broad himself very fairly puts it, "the object (or, at any rate, a literal part of it) seems to be ' given ' bodily "; and the perceptual judgments which we make about it " seem to be ' read off ' from the object itself " (p. 248). But I cannot help thinking that Dr. Broad's account of the " perceptual situation " varies considerably according as he is attempting to describe what as psychologists we actually find it to be and what in order to suit the exigencies of his theory it must be. (*a*) On the one hand, he insists that the perceptual situation is " intuitive " in character, that the object apprehended, the " epistemological object " if you will, is directly and immediately apprehended. He is emphatic in insisting that we do not get at either the nature or existence of the object by a process of inference from the nature of sensa (*e.g.*, p. 151), and he further urges that, at the purely perceptual level, we do not have the special experience called " belief " or " judgment ", but simply act as it would be reasonable to act *if* we believed so and so (p. 153). In short, the intuitive awareness which it is asserted we have of sensa is likewise the kind of awareness which admittedly we seem to have of physical objects. Indeed, this is an under-statement of the case. For it is acknowledged that, as a rule, we do not notice the presence of sensa or their properties at all, unless we specially look for them. The part they play in " our perceiving a physical object " is, it is said, analogous to the part played by printed words on the occasion of our reading a book written in a familiar language. What usually interests us is the meaning of the print, not the print itself, and we do not notice the latter unless there be something peculiar about it (*S.T.*, pp. 246-7)[1]. In other words, the sensa serve as " signs " of physical objects—we " use " them in perception, we perceive " with " them (*e.g.*, p. 298) ; but, so at least one would gather, they are not themselves the objects which we apprehend. Dr. Broad, in fact, is constantly writing as though he meant that in perception we somehow break through the circle of sensa and directly apprehend physical objects. (*b*) On the other hand, however, when we come to closer quarters with the matter, we find that, according to the sensum theory, the things which we do intuitively apprehend consist exclusively of " series of correlated sensa " ; and that, although everyone does take the sensa to depend on conditions outside the series, no one

---

[1] The analogy is evidently imperfect, because the meaning of the print does not stand before us as an object. We should never talk about seeing or hearing the meaning, as we talk about " seeing a table " or " hearing a bell ".

can be logically compelled to do so (*S.T.*, p. 277). When we see, as we say, a penny, what we really see are visual sensa, to which shape and brownness both belong. When we move about and continue, in familiar phraseology, to " look at the same object ", we are aware of a series of sensa, each having shape and colour, all very much alike in these respects, though varying in certain ways which we commonly overlook. When we touch or feel, as we say, the penny, and meanwhile look at it from various points of view, the series of visual sensa is correlated with an invariant tactual sensum, in shape very much, but not exactly, like that of most of the former. The tactual sensa have coldness and hardness ; and solidity is no less genuinely a quality of some visual sensa than colour is. In short, all the qualities which we usually ascribe to the penny when we speak of " perceiving " it turn out to be qualities either of sensa or of images of formerly experienced sensa, and we never really intuitively apprehend anything else.

It may, to use an expression of Bradley's, come from a weakness of the flesh which continues to blind me, but I cannot reconcile the latter account of the matter with the former. If what we are directly apprehending in every perceptual situation be the qualities or properties of sensa, then surely it cannot at the same time be true that, as a rule, we use sensa merely as signs and do not notice their qualities or properties. For there would be nothing else that we could notice. The most that we should be entitled to assert would be that we do not usually recognise that they are qualities or properties *of sensa* ; we should not, for instance, be entitled to assert that we " select a certain part of a sense-field " [1] in order to "perceive with it " (p. 298). For what, under these circumstances, could such an assertion imply? Hardly, I take it, that we " use " some sensa in order to apprehend others, since if our apprehension of sensa be immediate and direct, the intervention of " signs " would

[1] See *infra*, p. 60 *sqq.*

only be a hindrance. But I imagine I am not the only reader of Dr. Broad's works who has experienced perplexity in trying to discover how he would answer the question, *what is it that we perceive*? A perceptual situation comprises, he tells us, " (*a*) a sensed and selected sensum ; (*b*) certain bodily feelings connected with the adjustment and excitement of the relevant sense-organs ; (*c*) certain bodily feelings connected with the adjustment of our muscles, etc., in order to respond to the situation ; (*d*) *possibly* certain images ; and (*e*) *certainly* vague but characteristic feelings, due to the excitement of traces ". The whole of these, it is added, " are bound together into a complex of a unique kind, in consequence of which the whole situation has such and such an external reference " (p. 312). Now, of these (*b*) and (*c*) and (*e*) are presumably subjective constituents of the situation, and the same apparently is true of the " external reference ", which is described as a certain *conviction* we have that the " objective constituent " is part of a physical object. There remain, then, only (*a*) and (*d*) as constituents of the object. And one is left in bewilderment as to why the physical thing should be described as a perceived *object* at all.

4. I have urged that if sensa be taken to be existent entities jointly produced by external physical things and our own bodies, it is, to say the least, misleading and confusing to speak of them as " appearances of " those physical things. And one reason why it seems to me to be so is that any writer who is dealing with problems of knowledge is bound to use the phrase in another and totally different sense. What I mean will become clear from the following considerations.

Dr. Broad is severe upon a criticism of the sensum theory which before now I myself have ventured to press.[1] I have argued, namely, that those who conceive a sensum to be an existent, distinct and separate from the physical thing to which it is said to be uniquely related, and regard it as an object upon which an act of so-called sensing is directed, are

[1] See *supra*, p. 29 *sqq.*

compelled to acknowledge that it may *appear* to be different from what, in fact, it is and that, therefore, the same sort of antithesis breaks out in regard to sensa as, upon another theory, breaks out in regard to physical objects. Dr. Broad seeks to dispose of that objection by insisting that we ought to distinguish between failing to notice what is present in an object and noticing what is not present in an object. He contends that there is no difficulty whatever so far as the former is concerned, that it may well be the case that certain sensa are, for example, much more differentiated than we take them to be, and that two sensa really differ in quality when we take them to be exactly alike. I cannot admit that the objection is thereby met. You cannot usually eliminate features in an object and leave those that remain unchanged. If out of twelve characteristics of a sensum I discern only six, the six by themselves will in all likelihood appear different from what they would appear had they been presented along with the other six. And so, too, in reference to Stumpf's case, if we take two sensa to be exactly alike, when as a matter of fact there is a qualitative difference between them, it is not merely a question of the relation between them; the recognition of likeness or difference rests upon what the compared terms are apprehended as being, and if we judge them to be alike when as a matter of fact they are not, our act of so judging has come about because either one of the terms has appeared different from what it is or both have appeared different from what they are. Or, to take another instance, Dr. Broad himself somewhere refers to the fact that ordinarily people do not take the elliptical shapes presented by a penny seen from various distances to be elliptical. The sensa *are* elliptical, but they *appear* to these people to be round, and often you cannot convince the doubters that they are elliptical. It will not do to reply that the difference is a very small one and easily overlooked. The fact remains that the sensum appears different from what it actually is.

It is not needful, however, to have recourse to instances of this sort. Admittedly in every perceptual situation we do, as a matter of fact, take the " objective constituent " or sensum to be a part of the physical object, while according to the theory it is nothing of the kind. The sensum, then, habitually appears to be something quite other than it actually is. The answer will probably be made that it is one thing to judge that a sensum is a part of an external thing and another thing to immediately apprehend it as such. But this answer can hardly be made by Dr. Broad. For, as already mentioned, he has emphasised in more places than one that, at the purely perceptual level, people do not have the special experiences called " beliefs " or " judgments ", and presumably he would not deny that at the purely perceptual level people do intuitively take a sensum to be a part of an external thing.

5. There is one line of thought in Dr. Broad's account of the sensum theory which is an innovation of his own, and an innovation, it seems to me, of a very significant kind. I refer to his conception of " sense-fields " and " sense-histories ". Sensations are, he urges, distinguished by means of the different sensa which form their objects, and these sensa are well-nigh always outstanding differentiations of larger wholes, or " sense-fields ", such sense-fields being in their turn parts of longer strands, or " sense-histories ". The various special sense-histories—visual, auditory, tactual, etc.—constitute for each individual mind a " general sense-history ", which goes on throughout the whole of the individual's waking life, though there may be gaps in any one of his special sense-histories. And the contention is that there is no reason for postulating a special act of sensing for each separate sensum or for each sense-field. On the contrary, the more likely hypothesis would, it is argued, appear to be that at each moment of our waking lives there is a general act of sensing, and that the successive general acts are linked together so as to form a single general process of sensing, this

constituting the subjective correlate to our general sense-history which is its object. Furthermore, it is advanced as a probable view that the general process of sensing is kept up by the continuant and occurrent general cerebral conditions, which are involved in being " awake " and " conscious ", these being dependent on more general somatic conditions, which supply the general process of sensing with a continual series of internal sensa as objects. Accordingly, the function of the special occurrent conditions (*e.g.*, visual and auditory stimulations) is not to produce acts of sensing but to produce outstanding sensa in our special sense-histories, and thus to furnish the general process of sensing with various objects. In other words, stimulation of the special sense-organs is purely a bodily affair and does not, as such, influence the mind ; it produces changes in the brain and cerebral system, and these changes generate the special sensa (*e.g.*, visual and auditory sense-objects). And the general process of sensing, already permanently provided with a somatic sense-history, is to be thought of as grasping the special kinds of sense-field in its stride, as they are supplied by special occurrent conditions (*S.T.*, p. 516 *sqq.*).

The view, which I hope in trying to be brief I have not mis-represented, has certain points of similarity to Ward's con-ception of a presentational continuum, and is, to say the least, extraordinarily ingenious. And I am inclined to agree with Dr. Broad that the sensum theory, when fully worked out, must take some such form as he has thus delineated. But, at the same time, it seems to me that in attempting in this way to surmount certain obvious difficulties of the theory as it has usually been presented, he is confronted with others which are of a sufficiently formidable kind.

Let us look for a moment at the notion of a " general process of sensing ". So far as I can discover the process in question resolves itself for Dr. Broad into a mass of bodily feeling.[1]

[1] When a visual, tactual or auditory sensum is intuitively apprehended, it stands, he writes, " in a unique kind of relation to something which is not

Now I am not, by any means, concerned to dispute the contention that running through the successive phases of the mental life there is to be found what may not inappropriately be called a mass of corporeal feeling. I have frequently urged that it is, in no small measure, owing to the presence in the inner life of such continuous undercurrent, if one may so describe it, of feeling that the gradual emergence of self-consciousness, in the strict sense of the term, is possible. For feeling is emphatically the subjective, the personal, factor in our experience ; it is, as Hamilton expressed it, " subjectively subjective ". But I discern a curious inconsistency in Dr. Broad's use of the term " feeling ". On the one hand, he speaks (p. 307) of feeling as a " mode of cognition ". And that, I should urge, it never is. We do not apprehend in and through feeling ; what is felt is never regarded by us as an attribute or quality of an object. We may, no doubt, in introspection, contemplate, or attempt to contemplate, feeling as an object ; but that, of course, is a totally different matter. On the other hand, he strenuously insists that the terms " sensation " and " feeling " indicate two quite different kinds of experience, one of which can and the other of which cannot be analysed into act and object. We talk, as he says, of a sensation of red, but never of a feeling of red (*S.T.*, p. 225). Nevertheless, he proceeds to suggest that " the general cerebral and the general somatic conditions co-operate to give a continuous series of unitary bodily feelings, in which no distinction between act of sensing and sensum can be drawn ", that this series of feelings constitutes the somatic sense-history, and that the somatic sense-history is just the " general process of sensing ". Accordingly, " getting sensed " may be taken to mean " coming into such relations with the somatic sense-history as to form with it a

an auditory, tactual or visual sensum ". And this " something " he takes to be " the mass of general bodily feeling of the percipient at the time " (p. 215). And, again, he tells us " the sensum is apprehended by entering into a certain specific relation with a general mass of bodily feeling " (p. 220).

general sense-history ". A sensation of red would be, then, a red sensum so related to a somatic field (consisting of a unitary series of feelings, and forming the subjective factor in sensation) that they constitute together a general sense-field in a certain sense-history (*ib.*, pp. 522-3). In other words, whereas the general sense-history was formerly said (*e.g.*, *ib.*, p. 518) to be the *object* of the general process of sensing, it is now identified with it.

If the sensing of a red patch be analysable into a red sensum standing in a relation of sensible simultaneity with a mass of feeling, one of two things must, I take it, be true. Either, on entering into the relation, the feeling retains its nature as feeling ; and, if it does, there can be no ground for refusing to speak of a " feeling of red ", since, in that case, sensing must, at least, be a kind of feeling. Or, if a " sensing of red " is not a " feeling of red ", the mass of feeling, on entering into relation with the sensum, must lose its character as feeling and become something else. Whichever alternative be selected, the untenability of the position becomes, I venture to submit, sufficiently apparent. (*a*) The sensing of red may be, and I should say undoubtedly is, accompanied with feeling, but the feeling is not identical with the sensing. The latter is an act—an act that involves a facility, in however rudimentary a form, of distinguishing, comparing, relating. If the so-called sensum be, for example, a red triangular patch, awareness of it implies, *inter alia*, awareness of the plurality and connectedness of its parts, and of its difference from other sensa in the sense-field. The feeling, on the other hand, is not an act, but rather a mode of being affected ; and, although under normal circumstances it varies along with variation in the sensation which it accompanies, it may and often does vary while the sensation remains the same. (*b*) No less inconceivable is it that, through entering into relation with a red sensum, a state of bodily feeling could be converted into an act of sensing that sensum. For feeling in itself is blind, and it is impossible to see how the mere presence of a red sensum could in itself influence feeling. There would need first to be *awareness* of the sensum before feeling could be brought into relation with it ; the sensing is the prior condition of feeling becoming associated with the sensum, not the feeling the prior condition of the sensing. And I am at a loss to see how the occurrence of this act of sensing is to be accounted for except by supposing it to be incited by the specific stimulation that is transmitted by the optic nerve to the brain.

So far from it being the function of the special occurrent conditions to produce outstanding sensa in our special sense-histories rather than to occasion acts of sensing, I have more than once tried to show grounds for asserting the opposite, and, of course, what Dr. Broad names the " multiple relation theory " necessarily presupposes the opposite. To argue the point in a paragraph is out of the question, and I must here be content with some cursory considerations. If processes in external physical things and in our bodies jointly produce, as is contended, sensa, it would, on the face of it, seem extremely improbable that the production should take place in, or through means of, the brain. Why, for instance, should it be necessary that, in visual apprehension, the stimulation should have to be conveyed to the occipital cortex? The retina is amply provided with nervous elements ; and, if visual sensa be the joint product of processes in external physical things and living nervous matter, one would naturally expect that the sense-organ itself would be the seat of their production. On the theory we are discussing, it is hard to make out what possible purpose can be served by the elaborate mechanism through which sensory impulses are conveyed to the central nervous system. If, on the other hand, the function of the special occurrent conditions be not to produce sensa but to occasion acts of sensing (or, as I should say, of perceiving), the fact I am referring to becomes, at least, intelligible. For we know, at any rate, that in the human being mental process is closely connected with

changes in the cerebral cortex ; and it is reasonable, therefore, to surmise that mental activity is directly conditioned
by these neural occurrences. Nor is that all. The intimate
junction between the sensory and motor mechanism of the
body points to the same conclusion. In the case of vision, for
example, what seems to happen when the afferent impulse
reaches the visual area of the cortex is not the production of a
sensum but the transmission of the impulse to the efferent
neurones that pass down to join the motor system which
causes the eyeball to rotate in such a way as to enable the
object to be more clearly seen. Once more, in regard to the
suggestion that the " general process of sensing " is kept up
by the continuant and occurrent general cerebral conditions
which are involved in being " awake " and conscious, I think
that if, instead of a " general process of sensing ", Dr. Broad
had spoken of a general or continuous state of feeling, his
suggestion would have had not a little to recommend it.
For it seems far from likely that there exist in the bodily
organism any nerve structures *specially* concerned in the
conditioning of feeling, and there are physiological grounds
for suspecting that a continuous state of feeling is kept
up by processes taking place, apart from specific stimulation, in all nervous tissue, even that of the spinal cord
and the peripheral nerves. But for a " general process
of *sensing* " I can find no physiological warrant. Even
the vague, indefinite, so-called " organic sensations " seem
to be due to special occurrent conditions ; the viscera and
internal organs of the body are amply provided with nerve
fibres.

I confess that when we are bidden to conceive a " general
process of sensing ", the notion of " sensing " seems to me to
have reached the breaking-point. A process of " sensing "
that is capable of apprehending one after another of the
innumerable sensa which make up our so-called general
sense-history, of distinguishing them, of co-ordinating visual,
tactual and auditory sense-fields, of discerning, in fact, all

E

the various sense-qualities with which we become acquainted in their relations and connexions, would surely be evincing all the powers which Ward was in the habit of ascribing to what he called the faculty of "attention". In short, I would urge that psychologically there is a fundamental identity in nature between the simpler activities of mind, those that are misleadingly called "acts of sensing", and the more elaborate activities which we designate "acts of judging".

6. It is worth while perhaps calling attention to the different result reached by Dr. Broad, with respect to the status of the "objective constituent", in his treatment of perception and introspection respectively. He lays great stress upon the strong analogy which he considers may be drawn between the two processes. And yet, in regard to the point which one would have thought was above all fundamental he would constitute apparently a striking contrast. Every genuinely introspective situation, he insists, carries with it the claim that its "objective constituent" is literally a part of the empirical self; and he can find no positive reason for rejecting that claim, such as he does find in the case of the analogous claim which the perceptual situation makes for its objective constituent. It seems to me excessively difficult to suppose that there can be a vital difference of this kind between the two mental processes. The supposition would mean, if pressed, a resuscitation, in modified form no doubt, of the Cartesian standpoint, that the only certain and assured knowledge we possess is that we have of our own mental states and processes, unless, indeed, it could be maintained that no gain so far as knowledge is concerned accrues from the fact that the perceptive act is in immediate relation with its object. I do not imagine that Dr. Broad would wish to defend the latter proposition. But if he does not, an awkward situation confronts him. Fenced off though we are from the external world by a substantial network of sensa, we have yet acquired somehow amazing insight into the nature of that

world and of the physical agencies operative in it. Face to face though we are with our own mental states, we can hardly lay claim to any accurate or reliable acquaintance with them ; such meagre information about them as we have acquired has been painfully and laboriously won, and betrays no mark of immediacy.

III

SENSIBLE APPEARANCES AND MATERIAL THINGS

THE term " sense-datum " found its way into epistemological discussion some years ago, mainly through the initiative of Professor G. E. Moore and Mr. Bertrand Russell. The object of coining the new word was to have a term to denote that the reality of which everyone would admit without implying any specific theory of its nature. " If we want to indicate ", Professor Moore writes in one of his numerous papers on the subject, " what kind of entity is meant by ' sense-data ', in a way which can leave no doubt that there certainly are entities of the sort, I do not know that there is any clearer way of doing so than by saying that they are the sort of entities about which we make such judgments as ' this is a coin ', ' that is a tree ', etc., where we are referring to something which we are at the moment perceiving by sight or touch. Everybody can easily discover for himself the entity about which he is talking, when, under such circumstances, he judges ' that is a tree '. And in calling this entity a ' sense-datum ' we by no means imply either that it is not identical with that part of the surface of the tree which he is seeing, nor yet that the opposite philosophical view, according to which, so far from being identical with this part of the surface of the tree, it is merely a sensation in his own mind, may not be the true one." [1] The significance, then, which Professor Moore wishes to attach to the term is sufficiently apparent. And it is obvious that an expression such as " sensations ", even when it is used to denote not acts of apprehending but features apprehended, is not of the non-committal character

[1] *Proceedings of Aristotelian Society*, supplementary vol. ii, 1919, pp. 181-2.

which he desiderates, but carries with it an implication that the features referred to are, in some way, " in the mind ". Even the term " presentations ", which James Ward was in the habit of employing, is not free from ambiguity, for, although Ward in his later writings persisted that he did not conceive " presentations " to be subjective modifications, yet he still spoke of them as " psychical " or " internal " objects, thus assuming a particular theory as to their nature.

I am, however, far from satisfied that the term " sense-datum " is so perfectly freed from implications as is here claimed. In the first place, it certainly does seem to suggest that what is thus designated is something " given ", rather than something found. But that is not all. Professor Moore affirms that the phrase " sense-datum " is primarily used " simply as a name for entities, the existence of which no one disputes ".[1] He is implying, that is to say, that the entities in question are existents ; and this, again, is just one of the assumptions which at the outset, at all events, one wishes to avoid. The fact is, I think, that, for a concept of this sort, it is impossible to invent a name that will be satisfactory to everybody. The parallel to which Dr. Moore appeals—the term " judgment ", namely, which means primarily something which we all acknowledge to be a fact, whatever our theory of its nature may be—is no true parallel. For, by long usage, the term " judgment " has acquired that primary meaning, whereas in the present instance we have no such long usage to fall back upon. In what I have to say, on this occasion, I shall speak generally of " sensible appearances ", and make no claim that the phrase is free from theoretical implications.

What I mean by the phrase " sensible appearance " I can best make clear by means of an illustration. Three persons, A, B and C, are, we will suppose, sensuously apprehending an object which is ordinarily described as a red rose. A, we will say, is an artist, B is a botanist and C is colour blind. In

[1] *ibid.*, p. 181.

such a case, the red colour of the rose, let us call it R, will seem different to each of these persons—slightly different to A and B, while to C it may seem barely distinguishable from the hue of the leaves. It will seem, we will say, as r_1 to A, as r_2 to B, and as r_x to C. The question, then, with which we are now concerned is as to the nature of r and of its relation to R, which, meanwhile, we are taking to be an actual property of a real existent object in the natural world. The epistemological problem of the nature of perception and of the object that is apprehended in perception arises largely, at any rate, from the circumstance that what we have reasons, good or bad, for describing as the same material thing *appears* differently to different percipients, and even to the same percipient at different times and under differing conditions. Were there no such variations in the way in which what we regard as one and the same material thing appears, did that thing always manifest itself uniformly to percipients, however they might be situated, there would no doubt be, in this connexion, an epistemological problem, but it would assume a form quite other than that which it has assumed for us. In such circumstances, certainly, the theory that the *esse* of sensuous things is *percipi* would hardly have been propounded; it is scarcely conceivable that any serious doubt would then have been felt as to the essentially non-subjective character of sense-qualities.

This consideration itself suggests the kind of inquiry it is at first requisite to pursue. If what we have reason for regarding as one and the same material thing appears differently to different percipients, there is at least a *prima facie* ground for suspecting that the differences in question will be traceable to differences in the process by which there have come to be appearances of the thing at all to the percipients concerned. In other words, the *natural* procedure will not be forthwith to assume that, if the sensible appearances are different, the percipients must be apprehending different objects, but rather to start from the position which in ordinary experience we all take to be true, and which, save for the circumstance to which I have referred, probably philosophers would not deem it necessary to dispute, and endeavour to ascertain from a scrutiny of the perceptive activity whether an adequate explanation may not be furnished of the different appearances presented by one and the same material thing. I emphasise this point on account of a contention, about which I shall have something to say in due course, that has been put forward in much recent discussion.

To determine the character of perceptive activity is, of course, a psychological problem, and here I can only indicate, in the briefest manner, the mode of interpreting that activity which I should be prepared to defend. It seems to me that what it is now usual to call the sensum theory—the theory, namely, that sensory appearances are separate existents, caused in some way by the action of physical entities either upon the body or the mind of the percipient—is open to the objection which has long become a commonplace objection to the older empirical theory which originated with Locke and Hume, that it constitutes so violent an antithesis between the process of sense-apprehension, on the one hand, and that of thinking or judging, on the other, as to preclude the possibility of giving an intelligible psychological account of either of these processes. Here, again, an illustration will be the shortest way of explaining what I mean. When a percipient is aware of two so-called sensa or sense-data, say r_1 and r_2, two shades of red, and not only apprehends each for itself, thus holding them apart, but pronounces them to be like one another or different from one another, he is obviously using the *notions* or *concepts* of likeness or difference, and it is equally obvious that these notions or concepts are not explicable by the mere presence of r_1 and r_2 alone. It is not part of what is taken to be the datum r_1 that it is like r_2 or different from r_2 ; and it is equally not part of the assumed datum r_2 that it is like r_1 or different from r_1. If, now, it be said that the sensa or sense-data r_1 and r_2, having occurred and having been apprehended, give rise to the idea or notion of their likeness or difference, the language thus employed simply conceals the entire absence of explanation in what is said. The assumption is that r_1 may be simply and immediately apprehended, and that r_2 may be likewise simply and immediately apprehended. What, then, is it that takes place when r_1 and r_2 are somehow held together in an act vaguely called an act of comparison, and the new idea of their likeness or difference arises ? The fact is that, in such a case, we should be wholly unable to explain in any way what we mean by the holding of r_1 and r_2 in the mind together, or to see how from that supposed act the new idea of likeness or difference emerges. We should simply be falling back upon the perfectly barren hypothesis that it *is* the nature of the psychical mechanism (using Lotze's phrase) to hold separate sensa or sense-data together in an act of awareness and to produce, under these circumstances, automatically so to speak, ideas of relation. But to suppose that, at any period in the life of mind, ideas of relation spring up in this manner *de novo* when sensa or sense-data, already clearly and distinctly marked off from one another, are somehow compared and brought into connexion, is tantamount to resting content with the assumption of a wholly unintelligible procedure on the part of what we call the mind, We come here, in short, to the *impasse* of being obliged to postulate, as Kant was obliged to postulate, a unique faculty of thinking or judging suddenly emerging full-fledged into being, possessed from the very start with a whole apparatus of categories, and concerning which all we can do is to point to the results to which, *ex hypothesi*, it gives rise. I suppose some would be inclined nowadays to view this as an instance of " emergence " ; but I am persuaded that no psychologist who is really serious with the problem can be content to leave the matter there. He is bound to ask himself how *ideas* of relation gradually come to be formed out of contents of apprehension of a more primitive or rudimentary type. Now, that means that he must radically change the Kantian conception not only of thinking but also of sense-apprehension. If the process of conceptual thinking be, so to speak, of one piece with the process of sense-apprehension; if it be, in other words, a more evolved type of a process that is genetically one and continuous—and that is how psychologists are constrained to regard it—then it is certain that experience does not begin with separate, distinct and definitely marked-off sense-data. Sensuous features or characteristics can only be clearly and sharply distinguished from one another through and by means of those very ideas of relation the origin of which it is the business of psychology to investigate. Or, to put the matter otherwise, if " *ideas* of relation ", psychologically regarded, be, as I conceive they obviously are, outcomes of psychical development, so also are those sensible appearances which are misleadingly called sense-data. The definiteness, the distinctness, the separation, which in mature experience they exhibit, is by no means an original characteristic of them, but a derivative characteristic—a characteristic that is due to the gradual development of the mental process of apprehending. And if this be so, we gain at once an insight into the nature of the mental process in question. For there is, so far as I can see, only one way in which an apprehended content can become more definite, more distinct, and more precise, and that is by being differentiated from other contents and by being contrasted with them. We are thus led to recognise that the act of apprehension is from the very first a process of discriminating, of distinguishing, of comparing—that in its earlier stages, whilst differing, of course, vastly in degree of completeness from those acts which we are in the habit of describing specifically as acts of comparing and relating, or, in other words, as acts of thinking, is yet in nature essentially akin to them. We are led, in short, to recognise that, as we trace back the stages of mental development, we come upon a discriminative activity that evinces itself in ever cruder and more rudimentary phases—a discriminative activity which is prior to that in which what Lotze called " *ideas* of relation " are consciously used, and on the basis of which those " ideas of relation " are subsequently formed and applied.

I would insist, then, upon the necessity in regard to our present theme of being in earnest with the conception of *discrimination* as indicating the essence of any act of apprehension, however primitive and crude that act may be. Just as Kant maintained that the act of synthesising *is* the very act of knowing, so I would maintain that the act of discriminating *is* virtually the act of knowing, or, at all events, the fundamental characteristic of that act *quâ* act. And the importance of this consideration is illustrated, it seems to me, by several recent discussions of the subject. In dealing, for example, with what he calls " the multiple relation theory of appearing ", by which title he intends, I believe, some such theory as that which I have tried to work out, Dr. C. D. Broad represents it as based upon the assumption that there is an ultimate relation of "appearing or seeming" [1]; and, in such case, the difficulty is, of course, to find any ground for supposing that we are, in fact, aware of any such relation. But if by " ultimate " be meant here, as I suspect is meant, not further explicable, then I should refuse to admit that the relation in question is " ultimate ". On the contrary, I should urge that this characteristic of "appearing " is in large measure explicable from the very nature of perceptive activity itself. Always in sense-perception there *must* arise the contrast between what I have called the content apprehended and the content of the actual object upon which, as I take it, the act of apprehension is directed. Any material object whatsoever consists of a vast number of elements and features, and those features of it which are discriminated, and of which there is, therefore, awareness, will be at the best but a fraction of the totality of features which the object itself possesses. The *sum* of

[1] *The Mind and its Place in Nature*, p. 178.

qualities actually discriminated in and through the percept- ive act will clearly, therefore, be different *as a sum* from the *sum* of features characterising the object. Could some god be induced to transform, by a creative fiat, the *sum* of qualities in question into a sum of qualities characterising an existent object, while at the same time annihilating the act of appre- hension on the part of the human mind in and through which alone the sum of qualities, as apprehended content, had its being, then to that god's observation the newly created object would be by no means a mere reduplication of the original object. Were the god further induced to annihilate the original object and to substitute in its place that which he had just called into existence, then, as a con- stituent of the interconnected realm of existence, the latter object would play a part quite different from the former. Advancing knowledge might, in other words, be likened to a pattern gradually coming out. Only the process of " coming out " is never completed ; there is always more to come out ; there is always a vastly greater amount of detail than our limited powers of discriminating are capable of discerning ; there is always a more elaborate network of connexions than we have been able to trace. In all stages of the development of the process of apprehension, the contrast between what actually has been discriminated and the more that remains to be discriminated must of necessity hold. In contradistinc- tion to the richness, the fulness, the completeness of a really existent object, the term " appearance " or " phenomenon " carries with it, therefore, the significance of fragmentariness, of incompleteness, of mutilation—peculiarities that point to the abstraction characteristic of apprehension in all its stages.

" It is always difficult ", Dr. Broad writes, " to understand how anything can seem to have characteristics which are other than and inconsistent with those it really does have." [1] If what I have just been urging be justified, the difficulty would, on the contrary, rather be to understand how, under

[1] *ibid.*, p. 284.

certain circumstances, a thing could fail to seem to have characteristics other than those which it really does have. To take our former illustration. Suppose that the petals of a rose are veritably characterised by a specific shade of red. Is there, in that case, any occasion for surprise in the fact that their actual colour will seem different to two observers who view the rose from different distances, or when one of them observes it in daylight and the other in twilight, or when one sees it through a pair of dark spectacles and the other with the naked eye? Surely the surprising thing would be if the fact were otherwise. Or, again, if normal vision be a means through which the actual colours of things are more or less accurately apprehended, is it, on the face of it, reasonable to expect that there will be equally accurate apprehension of the red petals of the rose on the part of the person who is afflicted with red colour-blindness? Why the red petals should appear to the colour-blind person precisely as they do is no doubt a psychological problem that is by no means easy of solution. Much as we know about the structure of the eye, it is still true that we know extremely little about the manner in which it functions as the organ or instrument of visual apprehension. In what way does it subserve not merely the physical process of stimulation, but as an apparatus through and by means of which a mental act is directed upon an object? One has only to frame a question of this sort in order to realise how far off we are from being in a position to answer it. But if it be part of the work of a pair of normal eyes to function in this respect to some extent after the fashion of a pair of colourless spectacles, it is not perhaps a wild stretch of imagination to surmise that in cases of red colour-blindness the eyes function to some extent after the fashion of a pair of coloured spectacles. However that may be, I can find nothing in the ascertained facts of delusive perceptual situations that tends even slightly to render improbable what I am contending with respect to sensible appearances. On purely psychological grounds, I think we are entitled to assert that the appearance of a physical thing is a way in which that thing is cognised, a way in which knowledge of it is had, that we know a physical thing in and through its appearances, and that in our mature experience, although we may frequently be the victims of delusive appearances, the appearances of a thing in veridical perception are partial views, so to speak, of the thing's actual characteristics.

Considered, then, in abstraction from the physical object, sensible appearances are not, I have contended, existents ; they are not entities that *have* characteristics, they *are* characteristics or complexes of characteristics. Dr. Broad has himself distinguished with sufficient clearness between what he calls " abstracta " and " existents ".[1] In the first place, an existent can, he points out, be referred to in a proposition *only* as a logical subject. But this property some abstracta share with existents. In the second place, however, all existents are either directly and literally in time, or appear to human minds to be directly and literally in time. Abstracta, on the other hand, although some of them are closely connected with existents and thereby become indirectly connected with time, neither are nor appear to be directly and literally in time. And, under the head of abstracta, he includes qualities, relations, numbers and also propositions and classes, if there be such entities. Now, my contention is that sensible appearances, when regarded in and for themselves, are just qualities, or complexes of qualities, and that they are, therefore, abstracta in the sense indicated, that they are real but not existents. A sensible appearance is, *quâ* sensible appearance, outside the region of temporal flux and change. Nothing can alter it, for the simple reason that it is not a concrete existing entity that can be operated upon, acted on or affected, in any way whatsoever. Moreover, as it is not in time so also it is not, strictly speaking, in space. Sensible appearances do not, as such, act and react upon each other ;

[1] *The Mind and its Place in Nature*, p. 18 *sqq.*

they do not obey the law of gravitation, or any other physical law ; they do not exert force, they are not modes of energy. Neither are they mental entities—they are not, that is to say, states of feeling, or of cognising, or of conation.

Nevertheless, according to the theory worked out by Dr. Broad, sensa, although neither physical nor mental, *are* existents—they are, that is to say, particular entities which *have* literally and dyadically the characteristics which the objective constituents of perceptual situations seem on inspection to have. Shapes, colours, temperatures and so on " inhere " in sensa. Admittedly, these sensa are existents of a very peculiar kind. In having spatial and certain other characteristics they resemble physical things as ordinarily conceived ; in their privacy they resemble mental entities ; they are " transitory " and " short-lived " ; they are occur-rents in a special kind of continuant, which is a sort of sub-stance, though not a physical substance. I fail to see what the warrant is supposed to be for the assumption of a realm of existents of this curious nature. And, further, not only is the assumption a flagrant violation of the maxim which Mr. Bertrand Russell considers should inspire all scientific philosophising, *entia non sunt multiplicanda praeter necessi-tatem,* but it seems to me to be beset with difficulties out of all proportion more formidable than any which it may be alleged to remove. I will only refer briefly to certain of these. Dr. Broad himself acknowledges that the status of sensa in a world which consists mainly of physical events and objects is " certainly most peculiar ".[1] But more peculiar still is the supposed mode of generation by which they come to be. Confessedly, the generation of sensa by physical and physio-logical processes must be considerably different from the causation of a change in one physical thing by a change in another,[2] yet why physical existents acting on other physical existents should give rise to existents which are not physical is obviously a mystery which has to be left as such. Nor is it

---

[1] *Scientific Thought,* p. 527.   [2] *ibid.,* p. 539.

the only one. The generated entities retain certain of the characteristics of the entities that produce them—the primary qualities, namely—but exhibit an array of other characteristics—the secondary qualities—which are nowhere else to be met with in nature. So far as the latter are concerned, we are confronted here with the enigma which baffled the older materialism ; and, so far as the former are concerned, there is the additional conundrum thrown in of accounting for the circumstance that these generated entities are like their physical antecedents in some respects while they are wholly unlike them in others. Moreover, it would appear that, in spite of the assertion to the contrary, some of the sensa at least are after all, according to the hypothesis, physical. For admittedly visual and tactual sensa possess the " differentiating attribute " of extension ; and, consequently, by Dr. Broad's own showing, they should be existents of the kind called " material ".[1]

The objection that I am, however, at present mainly concerned to press is that sensa, conceived as existents of the kind indicated, have no title whatever to be described as " appearances of " material things. Professor Moore, it is true, lays it down that " it is no part of the sensum theory to assert that corresponding sense-data, *if* they are sensa, can be properly called ' appearances ' of the physical object to which they correspond, and, therefore, it can be no objection to that theory to urge that they cannot ".[2] The reply is that it certainly does form part of the sensum theory, as Dr. Broad has delineated it, to make that claim. We have seen [3] that acccording to Dr. Broad a sensum *s* may be said to be an " appearance of " a physical object *o*, if *s* has to *o* a certain relation *R* which it has to no other physical object. And this relation *R*—the relation of " being an appearance of "—he would apparently analyse

[1] *The Mind and its Place in Nature*, p. 22.

[2] *Proceedings of Aristotelian Society*, supplementary vol. vi, p. 188.

[3] *Cf. supra*, p. 53 *sqq.*

into a causal relation, although he acknowledges that the causation involved is of " a very odd kind ". Nor is this the only sense in which he speaks of sensa as " appearances of " physical objects. He is constantly implying that physical objects, or the qualities of physical objects, either are or seem to be made *manifest* to us by means of sensa. But how can sensa be "manifestations" of physical things when, *ex hypothesi*, they are altogether different from physical things? So far as the secondary qualities are concerned, instead of manifesting to us the properties of physical things, sensa exhibit properties which, according to the theory, it is "neither necessary nor useful" to suppose are in any way analogous to the properties of physical things. So far as the primary qualities are concerned, while it is argued that the correlated variations in the shapes and sizes of visual sensa are unaccountable unless "quasi-spatial" qualities and relations be ascribed to their permanent conditions, yet admittedly the only shapes and sizes directly apprehended are the shapes and sizes of sensa, and there is nothing in these sensa to force us logically to the conclusion that there must be something beyond them, having the constitutive properties of physical objects.[1] And, even if we were to allow that, on the basis of the theory, the probability of there being physical things with "quasi-spatial" qualities could be sustained, still the shapes and sizes and positions of visual or tactual sensa, as they occur in visual or tactual space, would be in no way manifestations of the shapes, sizes and positions of things that are not in visible or tactual space, and the structure of which must confessedly be totally different from the structure of sensa.

For my part, I am at a loss to understand what precisely Dr. Broad means by the term " perception ". Perception he does not hesitate to describe as " perception of physical objects ".[2] In every " perceptual situation ", he avers, there are present sensa, having properties such as shape, size,

---

[1] *Scientific Thought*, p. 268.   [2] See, *e.g.*, *ibid.*, p. 243.

hardness, colour, loudness, coldness and so on, Certain of
these sensa are " selected " by the mind, and some of the
selected sensa are " used " for perceiving. More, however, is
meant by perceiving a physical object than just sensing these
sensa. The notion of a physical object contains, as an essential factor, the notion of a persistent something which joins
up the various isolated sensa, and this persistent something
is said to " show itself " to the conscious subject partially
and imperfectly through them.[1] Yes ; but the trouble is
that there are, according to the theory, absolutely no ways
by which a physical thing could thus "show itself". It is,
indeed, pointed out that common-sense identifies what it
calls the " real " shape of a perceptual object with its felt
shape, and that it is mainly by " active touch " that we learn
about the " real shapes " of such objects. At the same time,
active touch evinces itself as partly a movement experience
and partly a tactual experience ; so that by its means we do
not get beyond the region of kinaesthetic and tactual sensa.
And, although physicists conceive that the regions in the
movement-continuum are literally occupied by certain objects composed of protons and electrons, after the manner in
which a sensum occupies a sensible place in its own field, yet
more searching analysis reveals, it is contended, that the
movement-continuum is itself part of the general sense-
history correlated with each human body, and that sensa are
not literally in " physical Space-Time ", nor physical events
literally in any sensible Space-Time. How, then, do these
physical events "show" themselves to a percipient ? Furthermore, Dr. Broad insists that shape, size and position cannot be the only characteristics of physical existents, if there
be such things. Nothing he argues, can possibly be *merely*
extended and movable ; *if* spatio-temporal characteristics
be primary, they cannot be the *only* primary characteristics.
" Whatever is extended must have some other characteristic,
which is capable of covering an area or filling a volume as

---

[1] *The Mind and its Place in Nature*, p. 420.

F

colour and temperature do in sensa." [1] Yet this other characteristic, this "extensible characteristic", as he calls it, need not, he urges, be colour or temperature, or any other quality that inheres in sensa ; it may be mass or electric charge. This is as much as to say that it may be a characteristic with which we become acquainted—very vaguely and crudely, no doubt—through the avenue of touch and the so-called kin-aesthetic sensations. The truth is that although the contention that the "objective constituent" of a visual situation is never part of a physical thing may be made to seem plausible, a similar contention in regard to the "objective constituent" of a tactual situation or of resistance to bodily movement cannot be ; and, as a matter of fact, I think Dr. Broad in more places than one is virtually assuming the opposite. But, on the one hand, it is, to say the least, extremely unlikely that the perceptual situation is so fundamentally different in the two cases ; and, on the other hand, there is surely no reason for supposing that visual apprehension is, in any way, less adapted than tactual apprehension is for disclosing to us the character of physical reality.

Lastly, not only does the assumption of sensa as existents land us in extraordinary perplexities in attempting to unfold the nature of perception, but it offers, so far as I can discover, no compensating advantages in other respects. To determine the specific kind of relation that subsists between a quality and that which it characterises is, of course, a metaphysical problem of extreme difficulty ; but, in regard to the matter before us, the problem is not in the smallest measure lightened by the supposition that the existents characterised are of the peculiar kind which the theory I have been criticising represents. In what conceivable way is it easier to think of secondary qualities as "inhering in" sensa than as "inhering in" physical objects? As I have already urged, there is, in truth, nothing in the scientific theory of physical things incompatible with the view that they possess

[1] *The Mind and its Place in Nature*, p. 207.

such qualities as colours and temperatures ; and, if it be objected that " there is not the slightest reason to believe they do " possess them, the rejoinder is, at any rate, near to hand that neither is there the slightest reason to believe they do not. The fact that, when we are perceiving what we take to be (say) a luminous red object, vibrations of a certain period are impinging upon the eye and stimulating the retina is, as Dr. Broad has himself more than once pointed out, no proof at all that the existent entity which is emitting these vibrations is not itself red. For it may quite well be the case that the particles of the physical object, the motions of which give rise to the vibrations that initiate the act of perception, are themselves red ; or, if they are not, that the complex whole, of which they are constituents, is thus characterised. Why not? There may surely be a relationship of a unique kind between a physical thing, the constituents of which are vibrating at a particular rate, and the quality (say) red such that when those conditions are present the quality in question evinces itself ; and, if that be so, the vibrations may be the means of bringing about the act of perception in and through which the red colour is seen, although the thing itself will be thus characterised whether it is perceived or no. When one contemplates the constitution of a physical thing, as it is now conceived by physicists, and tries even vaguely to picture the ultimate elements as units of electric charge, it would seem more probable far that *it* should be characterised by such a quality as red than that such a nondescript kind of entity as a sensum should be. It has, indeed, been objected to the former supposition that, when submitted to scrutiny, it puts too great a strain on credulity. For, it is argued, it would imply that perceived things contain in themselves all the infinitely varying characteristics they exhibit to different percipients. One man, with normal vision, sees an object as red ; his neighbour, who is colour-blind, sees it as gray ; another, who has taken santonin, sees it yellowish ; while a fourth, looking at it through blue glasses, sees it bluish. We should have to assert, so the contention runs, that all these colours characterise the object simultaneously. Now, I grant at once that if that implication were involved, it would be straining credulity vastly too far ; and, in that case, I, for one, should unhesitatingly reject the theory as preposterous. But I shall have failed in my purpose if I have not made manifest that no such implication is involved in the view I have been trying to substantiate.

IV

ON THE NATURE OF IMAGES

Retention or Revival, an ultimate fact for psychology. Impossibility of "presentations" persisting in a region of sub-consciousness.

1. *Imagination continuous with Perception. Nature of Perception. What it is that is revived or reproduced. Influence of Revival in the field of Perception.*
2. *Transition from Perception to Imagination. Ambiguity of the term "image". "Images" in the strict sense. Instances of the presence of a nucleus of perceived fact in "images" that appear as objective.*
3. *Imagery in Dreams. Evidence of the presence of a nucleus of perceived fact as the basis of dream-imagery. The effect of Attention upon an "image".*
4. *The problem as to how subjective factors can affect the character of the content apprehended. What occurs in Einfühlung analogous to what occurs in imaging. Subjective factors do not necessarily vitiate the act of perception.*

THE subject I propose here to handle is notoriously one of exceptional difficulty. Psychologists have sought to ascertain, and have been more or less successful in determining, the circumstances which are favourable to the retention or revival of former experiences; they have investigated the various types of imagination—visual, auditory, verbal, etc.; they have discussed in detail the characteristic differences of what Hume designated "impressions" and "ideas"; and they have brought to light a large number of interesting empirical facts relative to the processes of remembering and imagining. But the problem of the exact nature of so-called ' 'images ", of the precise character of that which in and through an act of imagining is immediately presented to the apprehending mind, has rarely been seriously faced either in the standard treatises on psychology or in special monographs dealing with imagination and memory. And yet it is, I believe, becoming more and more manifest that the crucial questions of the psychology of cognition centre round this problem, and that any conception we can form of the structure of the mental life cannot but be defective so long as it is ignored.

One circumstance which has undoubtedly tended to deter inquiry from the field I have in view ought to be referred to at the outset. As psychologists, we are compelled to accept what is expressed by the terms retention and revival as an ultimate condition of mental life. We have, that is to say, no means of getting behind the facility thus designated, and of exhibiting the grounds of its possibility. Attempts to do this have, it is true, been made ; but the results of such attempts no one can pronounce encouraging. What, for example, is gained by speaking of psychical phenomena as being subject to a law of " mnemic causality ", in contra-distinction from the law of physical causality that holds of physical phenomena? Does it amount to more than using new termimology to describe that which eludes explanation? And the like is true of the phraseology which Bergson is fond of employing. What is really gained by speaking of a conscious state as being " permeated " or " interpenetrated " by others that have preceded it, unless some definite notion of the *modus operandi* of the process thereby indicated be forth-coming? For these phrases are in themselves in no sense explanatory ; they are but pictorial ways of re-stating that which calls for explanation. Nor do I think that in the present connexion much help is afforded by the analogies to which Hering and other physiologists have pointed in the behaviour of nervous tissue and of organic matter generally. It may, no doubt, be safely asserted (*a*) that the original perception which is, as we say, revived, itself involved or depended upon certain changes in the organic conditions, and (*b*) that the revival involves or depends upon changes partially, at all events, similar to those which accompanied the original perception. And there would appear to be ample justification for the further assertion that the whole complex of organic conditions does not remain uninfluenced by such changes but that in truth the network of organic processes comes, by dint of repeated modifications, to be altered in its structure and to respond in a fashion different from what it otherwise would have done to any stimulation similar to that which occurred previously. Accordingly, it is natural enough to look upon " organic habits ", so-called, as a sort of provision already made in the bodily organism itself for the retentiveness and the revival of experience that is characteristic of the mental life. And I am not in the least anxious to question the important part that may be, and in fact must be, played, in this respect, by the bodily mechanism. But, in the first place, the extremely limited extent of our knowledge of these organic conditions precludes any but highly hypothetical conclusions being based upon them. We do not even know what physiological processes are involved in having the original experience which is afterwards revived —much less, therefore, the kind of modification they undergo by repetition. And, in the second place, the completest knowledge of the organic conditions would not in itself enable us to form any conception of what it is that is conditioned by them. It is, in truth, only on the analogy of " habit ", as exemplified in the mental life, that we are enabled to speak of " organic habits " at all ; and, for a matter of that, the analogy utterly breaks down in regard to the one feature which from the psychological point of view is the most significant.

We have, then, to acknowledge that we have no psychological explanation to offer of the fundamental fact of retentiveness or revival. But we *can*, when trying to deal with the matter psychologically, avoid introducing into our descriptive account metaphorical expressions which are readily seen to be not only erroneous but positively mischievous. I will not dwell upon such hopelessly unscientific and misleading figures of speech as " calling up a visual (or other) image ", although they are still frequently employed in a way seeming to imply that the phrase " calling up " is an exact and literal representation of what, as a matter of fact, actually takes

place. I am thinking rather of expressions such as " residua "
and " traces " (the equivalents of Aristotle's term μοναί),
which, if they mean anything, point to a mode of operation
on the part of the mind for the existence of which there is not
the slightest evidence, and which suggest conceptions of the
structure of the mental life wholly irreconcilable with what
we now do know of its nature. It is, as F. H. Bradley once
said, mere mythology to talk of a " copy ", which a presentation has sloughed off, persisting in some sub-conscious
region of the mind, there awaiting in disconsolate exile, until
association announces resurrection and recall ; or, as Professor Ward put it, of images or representations being
accumulated and " somewhere crowded together like shades
on the banks of the Styx ".[1] Even the less objectionable
term " disposition ", used in such a context as that presentations leave behind them dispositions for revival, can only be
allowed to pass provided it be understood to carry with it no
theory of what is actually taking place when a presentation
is no longer, as current phraseology has it, " in consciousness ".

My purpose in the following pages is to set down the out-
lines of a theory, to which by various lines of reflexion I have
been led, of the nature of the content presented in and through
the act of imagining. In conformity with what I have just
been contending, I shall proceed on the assumption that
retentiveness is an essential characteristic of the mental life ;
or, in other words, that the mental life, so far as we are
familiar with it, invariably evinces a certain degree of con-

---

[1] It is surprising that Aristotle's doctrine of φαντασία, or τὸ φανταστικόν,
has lingered on, in the way it has done, down to the present time. Aristotle
conceived that αἰσθήματα, sense-impressions, do not perish when the act
of perception has ceased to be. They leave, he thought, traces (μοναί) of
themselves, and these are somehow stored up " within us ". Through the
exercise of the faculty of φαντασία, and by means of the μοναί, images or
φαντάσματα are brought into clear consciousness. There is much in
Aristotle's psychology that would be of value to the modern investigator ;
but it is unfortunate that this particular doctrine of his should have re-
asserted itself so persistently.

tinuity, that it is not confined to what is directly experienced
at the moment, but that, in some form, what has been continues to be.   How the continuance is effected I shall make
no attempt to determine.   The theory I am about to advance
appears to me to have a considerable body of evidence in its
favour, and to be compatible with the facts that can be
fairly said to be established.   But I am putting it forward
tentatively, and in the hope of eliciting criticism which may
either assist in its further elaboration or suggest a better way
of attacking the problem.   For, in a matter of this kind, even
a wrong theory may be of service, in so far as it directs
attention to an inquiry that might otherwise be indefinitely
postponed.

1

A sufficiently safe proposition from which to start may be
expressed in the form that imagination is continuous with
perception and grows out of it.   Few modern psychologists,
at any rate, would, I conceive, be willing to acquiesce in
what seems to have been J. S. Mill's position that the difference between a " sensation " and an " idea " is an " ultimate
and primordial " difference.   It is worth noting that even
Mill himself apparently accepted the description of an "idea"
as a " consequence " of a " sensation "—a " consequence "
which, although it can be distinguished from the "sensation"
and treated as something different from it, " is yet more like
the sensation than anything else can be ", in fact so like that
it can be called a copy or an image of the sensation.[1]   Apart
from the many awkward questions that might be pressed in
respect to the term " copy ", it is enough to urge, in the
present connexion, that if one thing is said to be a " copy " of
another the implication is that some definite relation of
dependence subsists between the former and the latter.   And,
in truth, the dependence of imagination upon perception is

[1] See James Mill's *Analysis of the Human Mind*, i, p. 52 and J. S. Mill's
Notes, pp. 68-69 and pp. 402-523 (especially pp. 412-413).

rendered obvious by several very ordinary considerations. For one thing, imaginative activity is clearly limited, and strictly limited, by what has already been apprehended through the instrumentality of sense. Be the powers of " productive imagination " never so great, they do not enable us to create for ourselves an absolutely new colour,[1] or an absolutely new sound. Moreover, even so far as the ordering and arranging of the material is concerned, the facility of combination and separation is confined within certain circumscribed boundaries. If two features have been invariably conjoined in perceptive experience, we cannot represent them to ourselves as apart. Thus, while we may imaginatively vary at pleasure the colour of a material object, it is not possible for us to imagine it without any colour at all. " The liveliest imagination is not able to picture a fairy-world which is not so constructed that its constituents can in essence be brought under the categories of physical things. The task of giving an exhaustive scientific description of so chimerical an entity may be difficult ; but the difficulty does not prejudice the principle ; any ' castle in the air ' whatsoever has its architecture." [2] *Prima facie*, therefore, there would appear to be abundant justification for regarding perception as the primary process and for making it the starting-point in any discussion of imagination.

Nevertheless, the reverse method has sometimes been followed (as, for example, by Berkeley), in which case it is, as Professor Alexander has observed, impossible not to be struck with the spectacle of mental activity, so that, well-nigh without misgiving, " images " are taken to be purely mental products ; and thence, coming to perception, the temptation is strong to interpret its data as mental entities likewise. A good illustration of the procedure is to be found in Taine's

---

[1] Hume's hypothetical case of a possible exception to this rule (in the first section of Book I of the *Treatise*) is, as he says, " so singular that 'tis scarce worth our observing, and does not merit that for it alone we should alter our general maxim ".

[2] Münsterberg, *Grundzüge der Psychologie*, p. 341.

treatise *De l'intelligence,* a book that in many respects is still of psychological value. Beginning with what he calls " images " and the laws of their revival, Taine proceeds to view perception as in fact a process of imagining which turns out to be in harmony with external things [1] ; instead of describing a hallucination as a false external perception, we ought, he argues, to describe an external perception as a true hallucination. In short, what in perception we are immediately aware of are, he maintains, just images, or " internal phantoms ", which present the aspect of external objects. The objects we touch, or see, or perceive by any one of the senses are nothing more than semblances precisely similar to those which arise in the mind of a hypnotised person, a dreamer, or an individual subject to illusions. No more need here be said of this doctrine than that it completely fails to account for the extraordinarily assumed fact of " internal phantoms " appearing as external objects at all.

The analysis which I have sought to give of the nature of perceptive activity is based upon a radically opposite principle—the principle, namely, that in perception the knowing mind is directly apprehending given external fact. I have tried to show that perception consists neither in the passive reception of what is given nor yet in merely contemplating the given, but that it is essentially an act of discriminating, of distinguishing, and of comparing the features or characteristics of the given. Such misunderstandings as have arisen respecting the analysis, as I have described it, have, so far as I can judge, been chiefly due to the circumstance that the critics have not realised the fundamental significance one is attaching to the *function of discriminating.* If once the notion of discriminating were taken seriously, and the implications it carries with it recognised, I suspect that many of the difficulties which some writers have felt in following the exposition would disappear. It has, however, to be remem-

---

[1] One can hardly help surmising that Bergson, in some of the arguments of *Matière et Mémoire,* must have been considerably influenced by Taine.

bered that, in the history of mind, discrimination exhibits the most varied stages of development—starting with the crudest possible distinction of that which appears as an obscure somewhat from the vague indefinite background, and extending to the deliberate use of ideas of relation, such as we are familiar with in conceptual thought.

Let me briefly re-state the whole position in a manner somewhat different from that in which I have hitherto stated it. The *occurrence* of any act of perception, the occasioning condition of its *existence* as a state of the mental life, is, I have allowed, undoubtedly traceable to the physiological event of bodily stimulation ; its *character* or *nature*, on the other hand, is not thus to be accounted for, but is explicable only by viewing it from within and as in relation to that upon which it is directed. The distinction between existence and essence or content, between the " that " and the " what " of any concrete fact, is as old as Aristotle ; and, thanks to F. H. Bradley, it has become sufficiently familiar in current philosophical discussion. Now, in the situation we describe as " perception of an object ", two concrete facts are involved—on the one hand, the given object and, on the other hand, the act or process of perceiving it. Each of these concrete facts exhibits, then, the two aspects of existence and content. But, in view of what occurs in this situation—the gradual discrimination, namely, by the conscious subject, of the content of the object—a further distinction is here requisite. It is requisite, that is to say, to distinguish that which I have been in the habit of calling the " content apprehended " both from the content of the object and from the content of the mental act. To bring out the import of this distinction, Professor Ward's well-chosen illustration (employed by him, however, in a different context) of bestowing in the course of a few minutes half a dozen glances at a strange and curious flower will serve. Assuming that the act of apprehension is directed upon the actual flower, as a concrete fact in the external world, we may assert that the cognising subject will gradually discriminate a multiplicity of its features—at first the general outline, next the disposition of petals, stamens, etc., afterwards the attachment of the anthers, position of the ovary, and so forth—he will, in other words, become aware by degrees of a variety of features constituting the content of the flower. And this *awareness* of the features of the flower is not, it will be conceded, something that can be severed from the act of being aware—*i.e.* the act of apprehending. If one describes it as the content of the act of apprehending at a particular stage of its progress, or as that which gives to the act in question its specific character and enables it to be distinguished from other cognising acts of the same conscious subject, one will be doing no violence either to language or to the facts. No one would wish to maintain that this *awareness* is that which in the instance we are considering is cognised, that *it* is the object upon which the act of apprehension is directed. No one would, I should suppose, wish to deny that such awareness is a characteristic of the act of apprehension, when that act has reached a certain measure of completeness. In contrast with this, the " content apprehended " is that which is frequently designated the " appearance " of the object to the percipient. It, likewise, is not the object upon which the act of apprehension is directed. For the object is, *ex hypothesi*, the actual flower, an object which the conscious subject gradually comes to recognise has a variety of characteristics—shape, size, colours, etc. But the sum of the characteristics which the conscious subject will be aware of at any specific moment will be different from the sum of characteristics which he will be aware of at another moment, and either of these will only be a fragment of the much larger sum of characteristics which there are good reasons for believing the flower itself possesses. Clearly, therefore, the sum of *apprehended* features (*i.e.* the content apprehended, or the " appearance " of the object) is *distinguishable* from the larger sum of characteristics constituting the *whole* content of the object. Just as clearly the

former cannot be an existent fact, be it called a " presentation ", or a " sense-datum ", or what not. For it is, if one
may use the term in this connexion, a selection from the
features forming the content of the object, and we have
already premised that the content or nature of any concrete
fact, such as a flower, is not to be confused with its existence,
that its " what " is distinguishable from its " that ". So far,
then, from this selection of features being there, as an existent fact, prior to the act of apprehension, and in some way
calling forth that act, it only comes to be in virtue of the act
of apprehension having been first of all directed upon the
actual object and apart from such act would have had no
" being " of any sort.

One other point is worth emphasising. In the threefold
distinction just insisted upon, the term " content " has been
employed quite consistently and unambiguously. Throughout it has signified a sum of characteristics. The content of
the given thing is the sum of its characteristics or properties ;
the " content apprehended " is, we may say provisionally,
so many of those characteristics as are, for the time being,
cognised ; and the content of the act of perceiving is the sum
of those characteristics of the said act which is described as
awareness of the features just referred to.

When we go on to deal with the facts of revival or retention, the importance of the distinction between " content
apprehended " and " content of the act of apprehending "
becomes at once apparent. For, if the foregoing analysis be
on the right lines, it can alone be the *awareness*—the content,
namely, of a mental act—that is capable of being revived or
" reproduced ". The " content apprehended " cannot itself
persist after the act through and by means of which it has its
being has ceased to exist. It cannot persist in and for itself,
simply because it is not an existent, not what W. E.
Johnson called a substantive proper, not, that is to say, either
a continuant or an occurrent.[1] And it cannot persist in the

---

[1] *Logic*, vol. ii, pp. xi-xii. *Cf.* vol. i, pp. 199-200.

mind, because it has never been " in " the mind, in the strict sense of the term.[1] On the other hand, the contents of our own cognitive acts, the awarenesses, if one may be permitted so to name them, which we live through, or *erleben*—these are the mind's own property, or rather go to constitute its very being, and these we are forced to recognise it has the power of retaining in some form and of reviving. Even they are not, of course, to be conceived as isolated, independent entities. Even they are not brought back again as objects, simply because they never were objects. Nor are the specific acts or states of mind themselves literally " reproduced " or " recalled ", because an act or state of mind is an event or an occurrent, and an event or occurrent can only happen once. But, in accordance with what we have agreed to accept as for psychology an ultimate fact, we can say that it pertains to the very being of a mind that it has the facility, in and through subsequent states, of " reproducing " or " recalling " the awareness which was the content of a previous state and of utilising this retained awareness in the life of the present and of the future.

The next point to insist upon is that no act of perception occurs in our mature mental life without being immensely influenced by the facility just alluded to. In dealing with perception so far I have treated it, and for the sake of simplicity it was allowable so to treat it, as though it took place on each occasion *de novo*. The conclusion reached as regards its essential character will be in no way invalidated by now introducing the factor one had deliberately neglected. The act of perceiving remains from first to last an act of discriminating, and of thus becoming aware of the features of its object. But that process is enormously furthered by the circumstance that it takes place in a mind which by long and repeated practice has come to perform such acts more or less habitually, and by aid of the facility of retention or revival. The well-

[1] The only sense in which it can be said to be " in " the mind is that it is present *to* the mind, or apprehended *by* the mind.

worn illustration which Stout cites from a book of Hutcheson Stirling's will here suit my purpose. When one fine morning a ship unexpectedly appeared on the horizon, *what* it was was evident at a glance to Crusoe. Yet what to Crusoe was a ship was to his man Friday only an amorphous blur, a perplexing, confusing, frightening mass of detail, which would not assume for him the form of a definite, coherent object. There was, that is to say, a tremendous difference between the contents apprehended by these two individuals confronted though they were by one and the same object. The external conditions were similar ; the dissimilarity between what they respectively perceived was largely traceable to their previous mental histories. Crusoe had seen ships scores of times before, and a revival of his former awareness came at once to his aid. What he was actually discriminating at the moment was probably far less than what Friday was discriminating, and yet Friday was at a loss to make out what the mysterious thing out there could possibly be. The instance is a typical one. In ordinary perception, there can be no question, a vast deal of what we suppose ourselves to be immediately discerning is not, as a matter of fact, immediately discerned ; it is discerned through the aid of the revival of previous awareness of similar objects. In other words, the perception of a mature mind is interpenetrated[1] with what accrues to it from a long series of former perceptive acts.

Thus, as the mental life develops, our apprehension of things tends to become less and less immediate and direct. The contents of what we call our knowledge, of what we are said to know about objects, gradually come to assume the form of an inward possession, constituting almost an instrument wherewith we proceed further to differentiate and to grasp the nature of the world to be known. Consequently, in the case of a familiar object—and the great majority of the

[1] Bergson's term may perhaps be used in this context without the risk of misunderstanding.

objects we encounter are familiar—we do not require on each occasion to discriminate afresh its manifold characteristics. The act of perception is certainly directed upon that object, but its familiarity saves us from the necessity of going through the whole process of discriminating anew. It is enough that we discriminate at the moment only a relatively small number of its features ; these immediately suggest the awareness of features previously discriminated ; and the apprehension in question is attained with an ease and rapidity that would otherwise have been impossible. We have here, in fact, an example of that economy of labour which consciousness throughout its procedure exemplifies. In short, our perception tends to become less and less dependent upon what, at the time, is actually given ; we bring to bear upon what is given a wealth of awareness which ensures that no perceptive act is ever, even in its incipient stage, devoid of specific content. Furthermore, it is precisely this wealth of accumulated awareness that constitutes what we are in the habit of describing as our experience ; and in a very real sense it can be said that it is its experience which *makes* a mind. This, I take it, is part, at any rate, of Bosanquet's meaning in insisting that " mind is always a world ". " There is ", he says, and quite truly, " nothing to be called ' the mind ' of which there are empty acts exercised upon objects ".[1] In themselves, acts of discriminating, regarded in abstraction from the wealth of accumulated content, would form so much psychical mechanism, as Lotze styled it ; but when we speak of a mind, it is invariably the totality of its experience to which we are referring, and not merely to the mechanism of its modes of activity.

2

The term " imagination " is no doubt a vague term covering a great variety of processes. But there is, so far as I can see, no valid objection to employing it, in a general way, to

[1] *Three Chapters on the Nature of Mind*, p. 20.

G

include both " reproductive " and " productive " imagination ; and no useful psychological purpose that I can discover is served by confining it, as some writers would do, to
the latter of these, and re-naming the former " imaging ".
For, in the first place, as we shall see, " reproductive "
imagination is not always " imaging " ; and, in the second
place, we certainly require a term to denote that which is
common to both these modes of mental activity. Taking the
term, then, in this wide sense, I shall now try to show reason
for holding that the process of imagining is, in truth, of one
piece, so to speak, with the process of perceiving, as we have
viewed it, the chief difference being that in imagination a
relatively larger proportion of revived factors are involved.

It is easy to make the transition from the one process to
the other by means of instances in regard to which this is
manifestly true. An imaginative child is, let us suppose,
gazing at a mass of fleecy clouds in the play of the sunlight.
Soon the shapes and forms of its various parts will assume
for him the appearance of chariots, and horses, and warriors,
like a scene in ancient legend. The child will, that is to say,
be apprehending the given object through the medium of his
revived experience of pictures, story-books, tales to which he
has listened, and so forth. J. M. Barrie has somewhere tried
to indicate what a map of a child's mind would be like, and
singles out, amongst other things, the recollections of savages
and lonely glens, and gnomes who are mostly tailors, and
caves through which a river runs, and princes with six elder
brothers, and a hut fast going to decay, and one tiny old
lady with a hooked nose. Some such map would account for
what happened on that midnight journey with the beehives
which Tess took with her small brother Abraham, in Thomas
Hardy's novel. The little fellow, as he more fully awoke, so
the novelist relates, " began to talk of the strange shapes
assumed by the various dark objects against the sky ; of this
tree that looked like a raging tiger springing from a lair ; of
that which resembled a giant's head ", etc. And even for

Tess herself " the mute procession past her shoulders of trees and hedges became attached to fantastic scenes outside reality, and the occasional heave of the wind became the sigh of some immense sad soul ". Most people could, I suppose, supply parallel instances from their own experience. There is here, to put it briefly, as there is in perception, a certain nucleus, if we may so express it, of actually discriminated fact, although no doubt less than what is usually discriminated in normal perception. And round this nucleus of actually perceived fact there is, in consequence of the revived awareness suffusing, as it were, the act through which the discrimination takes place, a penumbra, so to speak, of features that seem to share with the nucleus the characteristic of objectivity. That a large number of so-called " images " which appear to stand over against the conscious subject as objects are thus susceptible of explanation is, I take it, scarcely open to question. Even those who maintain that images are " physical facts forming part of the world of physical things " [1] would hardly, I should think, wish to contend that, in the neighbourhood of the trees against the dark background, there were veritably in the external world " images " of tigers and of giants' heads, upon which Abraham's perceptive activity was directed. At all events, it would generally be admitted that here, round the nucleus of actually discriminated fact, features due to the boy's revived awareness of tigers and giants, which he had previously either seen in pictures or heard accounts of, gathered, and led to his interpreting the given objects in the way he did. For such imagery, then, we have an explanation that certainly looks as though it were a correct explanation. I believe, and shall attempt to show, that it is a mode of explanation which may be extended to a variety of other cases where its applicability is less obvious. The gist of the explanation, it will be observed, is not merely that sense-stimulation is involved, but that in imagination, where objective

[1] *Cf.* J. Laird, *A Study in Realism*, p. 67.

imagery is present, there is, as in perception, a real object upon which the act of discriminating is directed, and that this accounts for the objective character which the content apprehended seems to possess, although the number of the features of this object actually discriminated is considerably less than in perception, and the portion of the apprehended content traceable to revived awareness considerably greater, and more arbitrary and haphazard. We must be prepared, no doubt, to recognise that bodily factors, and not only extra-organic things, may, in some situations, function as objects.

One proviso must, however, be insisted on. In speaking, in familiar language, of " images " of imagination, people are wont to group under this term things which are, in truth, radically different. And one fundamental difference that is of great importance in the present connexion is this. Some so-called " images "—certain visual and auditory images more especially—seem to stand over against the apprehending subject, and to be for him objects in space, no less decidedly than the physical things of nature seem to stand over against him and to be for him objects in space. If, for instance, one is reclining on a sofa in a state of fatigue and relinquishing oneself to idle reverie, as it is called, it is a familiar experience that, without any deliberate resolve on his part, visual images (say) of faces, sometimes little resembling those of people he has known, flit before him, and that these appear to be stationed in space not far distant from the visual organ itself. But, on the other hand, when we talk in particular of " memory-images ", it is quite certain that we often do not mean definite objective pictures of this kind. I can remember, for example, what stood on my breakfast-table this morning, and enumerate the different articles there accurately enough, without having any definite picture of the breakfast-table standing over against me at the present moment. Galton's well-known researches carried out in 1875, with respect particularly to visual memory-images, established once for all the fact that there is

extraordinary divergence among individuals in the power of
what he described as visualising. While the great majority
of the men of science to whom he applied protested that so-
called " mental imagery " was unknown to them, he came
across numerous cases where visual images, in the sense indicated, were especially vivid. And he concluded that, on the
whole, such imagery was more frequent in childhood than in
adult life, that it was more frequent in persons engaged in
some kinds of occupation—artists, for example—than in
persons engaged in other kinds of occupation, and that it was
almost entirely absent in the case of those occupied in mental
work involving abstruse generalisation and abstract thought.
Memory is not, then, necessarily dependent upon concrete
objective imagery. There can be memory—and memory of
a very reliable kind—without any representation in the form
of an " image " of what is remembered. Here, no doubt,
verbal or other signs are extensively, if not always, employed ; and these would be, for the most part, objects, in
the sense I am understanding by the term. I do not propose
further to discuss this sort of memory ; it is clearly explicable
on the lines I have indicated.

It seems to me that the term " images " ought to be re-
served for such contents as in memory and imagination do
appear to stand over against the cognising mind as objects,
and upon which the act of apprehension seems (to the
conscious subject in question) to be directed. At all events,
it is with " images " of this description [1] that, in the following
pages, I shall be alone concerned. And the view of them
which I shall endeavour to base upon empirical grounds is, I
repeat, that there is always, in their case, a nucleus, however
scanty and concealed it may be, of something actually
present to the senses upon which the act of discriminating is

[1] That such " images " do occur, and in the case of certain individuals
with great frequency, is, I think, indisputable. Dr. L. Arnaud Reid's
attempt to sustain the proposition that " there are no images but only
imaging of real things " (*Knowledge and Truth*, p. 112 *sqq,*) seems to me to
break down in the face of overwhelming testimony to the contrary.

initially directed, and that around this nucleus a penumbra of imagery gathers, owing to the circumstance that the act of apprehension which is directed upon the real object is saturated, so to speak, with revived or retained awarenesses of the nature already described.

The interesting series of experiments conducted by Professor F. C. Bartlett[1] furnish abundant evidence of the way in which " images " are called forth by actually perceived objects. In the last series, in which the method of ink-blots, variously shaded or coloured, on cards, was adopted, the subjects were instructed to see what they could make of them, after the manner in which they sometimes found shapes for clouds and saw faces in a fire. " It is in relation to that which *might* be many different things ", Professor Bartlett writes, " that images most readily arise, although at the same time the image tends to be of something in particular ". He says of one of his subjects that he " ' projected ' his image on to the blot " ; but it is not quite clear, from his account, how far the different blots actually *assumed* for the other subjects the forms which they *suggested* to them. Presuming, however, that in many cases they did, the results fully accord with what one would have anticipated. The enormous variety of the imagery of different persons occasioned by the same object was an outstanding feature. What to one person was a " camel " was to another person a " tortoise ", to another " a dog worrying a table-cloth ", to another " a baby in a cot with a doll falling out ", to another " a picture of Sohrab and Rustum in a book of Arnold's poems ", and so forth. The way in which the special interests of the persons in question came into play was again strikingly apparent, as also the tendency of a certain type of imagery, once suggested, to persist when one object after another was presented to the same subject. But our problem is not so much to discover the

[1] See *British Journal of Psychology*, viii, p. 222 *sqq.* *Cf.* Professor Bartlett's work on *Remembering* (Cambridge : University Press, 1932), p. 34 *sqq.*

kind of imagery that may be occasioned by specific objects as to discover, if we can, the kinds of objects involved in various types of imagery.

Probably one may speak most confidently in regard to images connected with the lower senses. Images of taste, for example, occur in conjunction with sense-perception—the image of a sour taste may be occasioned by the sight of an unripe apple ; or a hungry man, seated before a savoury dish, may have an image of its flavour—but it would, I conceive, be extraordinarily difficult to make out a plausible case for these images occurring otherwise. So, too, olfactory images may arise when, for example, one is looking at a scentless carnation and represents to oneself the pleasant odour of old cloves, or the mention of castor oil awakens an image of a peculiarly disagreeable smell ; but, again, I think it would be excessively difficult to provide an instance of olfactory images where no obvious object is present. Once more, of tactile images the same may be said. " The most vivid touch-images come ", according to William James, " when we ourselves barely escape local injury, or when we see another injured " ; and he quotes an instance given by Meyer of an educated man who, at the moment of his fright at having accidentally crushed the finger of one of his little children in the door, felt a violent pain in the corresponding finger of his own body, that remained with him for three days.[1] Meyer further relates that he himself could excite images of warmth, cold or pressure upon any part of the skin ; and that they might become so lively as to cause him to pass his hand over the place just as if it were a real impression on the skin.

Kinaesthetic imagery is, it need hardly be said, vastly more common than that just alluded to, but is perhaps the least accessible of all imagery to exact inspection. In this reference, it is to be remembered that perception, as it occurs in the concrete life of mind, is by no means a merely cognitive

[1] *Principles of Psychology*, ii, pp. 65-66.

process but involves a change in the state of feeling and, as resulting from both, a certain form of movement. Consequently, every mode of sense-perception has a tendency, more or less marked, to give rise to kinaesthetic imagery ; and, in the revival of such sensory experience, kinaesthetic imagery will be naturally involved. Another circumstance also calls for notice. In the mature mental life, motor presentations have lost their originally chaotic and haphazard character, and fall into regular groups and series. And, in such groups and series, it is certain that motor images repeatedly take the place of so-called motor sensations. Here, too, it seems to me, it would hardly be possible to produce instances that are incompatible with the view I am taking. Those whose imagery is predominantly of the motor type tend to represent things either in terms of the movements they would themselves be prone to make in the presence of the things in question, or in terms of the words they would use in naming and describing them. The frequency with which familiar objects induce motor imagery is notorious. On glancing at one's pen, for example, there may arise the image of grasping it for the purpose of writing, on touching our bunch of keys the image of the movement necessary for unlocking a safe, and so forth. So, too, nothing is more common than a verbal image aroused by an object the name of which, or of something suggested by it, we wish to recall. The instances given by Stricker,[1] whose imagery was mainly of the motor type, and whose treatment of the subject is of special value, all point in a similar direction. Stricker's imagination of movements of any objects whatsoever appeared to be paralysed when there was no actual experience of movement either in his own eyes or in his own limbs. For the purpose of imaging a soldier marching, for example, he would begin to march himself ; and he even succeeded by practice in inducing his eye-movements to " act vicariously " for his leg-

---

[1] *Studien über die Bewegungsvorstellungen* (1882). *Cf.* his *Studien über die Sprachvorstellungen* (1880).

movements in imaging men walking. He shows, too, how dependent verbal imagination is on actually perceived move-ments in lips, tongue, larynx, etc., and Professor J. B. Watson has recently been enforcing similar considerations from the point of view of " behaviourism ".

It is, then, with respect to auditory and visual images that our theory must be chiefly tested. And here, no doubt, the evidence is more liable to dispute. But I believe the reason largely is that, in regard to auditory and visual imagery, it is extremely difficult to draw the line between images which are objective—images, that is to say, in the strict sense—and those which are not. When, for instance, people are said to possess the gift of " internal hearing ", or when they are said to " see with the mental eye ", it is not, in a great number of instances at any rate, implied that they have definite ob-jective images, but that they are capable of introspection in an eminent degree—in other words, of reflecting upon previous mental states of theirs. On the other hand, when a tune is said to be heard in imagination with as much distinct-ness as in the original perceptual experience, or when Coleridge relates that in the course of a profound sleep " all the images (of Kubla Khan's palace) rose up before him as *things* ", we are concerned, I take it, with presented content of quite another description.

Auditory imagery of the objective type is certainly far less frequent than visual imagery of that type, but it is, for all that, by no means infrequent. Taine reports, for example, of himself that, in thinking over a representation of the *Prophète*, he could repeat silently the pastorale from the over-ture and follow, almost feel, not only the order of the notes, their different height, rests and lengths, not only the musical phrase repeated as an echo, but also the keen piercing tone of the hautboy which played it. He adds that every good musician experiences this sort of thing at will, when he follows the lines of music covered with their black marks. Yes ; " when he follows the lines of music covered with their black marks ". And the question I am pressing is whether there is not always something corresponding to these " black marks " when auditory imagery assumes the form it is thus described as, in these cases, possessing. There are persons who declare that after having listened to a performance of the Passion Music of Bach they can recall at will without difficulty in the silence of their homes exactly what they heard in the concert-room. But they can generally be driven to admit that in such recall they are not conscious of actual melodies in the external world, and that the memory-images, vivid though they may be, do not compensate them for being unable to attend another performance of the same music. I surmise, therefore, that what they are in truth reproducing in such cases are the contents of their perceptive acts whilst in the concert-hall. And the imagery that results may well cluster round some nucleus of perceived fact, *e.g.*, sounds which even in the stillness are present, or the voice of a friend, or some visual datum, and thus acquire the objectivity which it displays.

A variety of circumstances accounts for the fact that the contents apprehended through vision come to have assigned to them by the perceiving subject a *pre-eminently* objective character. For one thing stimulation of the eye is ordinarily accompanied by a relatively small amount of organic affection, and of distinctively marked modes of feeling-tone. In the great majority of cases it is wholly impossible to detect any more of the element of feeling-tone than is involved merely as a consequent of alteration in the momentary state of the bodily organ. And comparative immunity from this prevailingly subjective factor renders visual perception more transparently apprehensive of objective fact than it would otherwise appear to be. Another circumstance making for the same result is that we can discriminate with remarkable precision a visually apprehended content from the movements of the eye itself, so that the visual content stands in decided contrast to the eye-movement, which is only in a secondary

fashion recognised as being an objective process at all.
Moreover, visually perceived contents connect themselves
readily with the objective characteristics determined by
tactual and motor experience, because, of all sense-data, they
afford the best opportunity for apprehension of a number of
features simultaneously. Naturally, then, we should expect
to find visual imagery of a more pronouncedly objective type
than is found in imagery connected with the other senses.
And this is, in fact, what we do find. From the accounts
which good visualisers have furnished of their experiences
instances innumerable might be cited in confirmation of the
theory I am advancing. A few must here suffice. An English
painter, quoted by Taine,[1] explains his mode of work in the
following manner : " When a sitter came, I looked at him
attentively for half an hour, sketching from time to time on
the canvas. I wanted no more. I put away my canvas and
took another sitter. When I wished to resume my first
portrait, I took the man and sat him in the chair, where I
saw him as distinctly as if he had been before me in his own
proper person—I may almost say more vividly. I looked
from time to time at the imaginary figure, then worked with
my pencil, then referred to the countenance, and so on, just
as I should have done had the sitter been there—*when I
looked at the chair I saw the man.*" Abercrombie [2] asserts that
a friend of his had one day been looking intensely at a small
print of the Virgin and Child, and on raising his head beheld
at the further end of the apartment (upon which his attention
must have been directed) a female figure of the size of life
with a child in her arms, the figure corresponding exactly
with that which he had contemplated in the print. Taine [3]
mentions the case of a whole ship's crew being thrown into
consternation by the ghost of the cook, who had died a few
days before. " He was distinctly seen by them all, walking

[1] *On Intelligence*, p. 45.
[2] *Inquiries concerning the Intellectual Powers*, p. 63.
[3] *op. cit.*, p. 60.

on the water with a peculiar gait by which he was distinguished, one of his legs being shorter than the other. The cook, so plainly recognised, was only a piece of old wreck." Another case he quotes is also significant—that of a man, seventy-five years old, of sound mind, who came home one day frightened by a thousand phantoms, which were pursuing him. "Whichever way he looked, *objects were transformed into spectres*, representing sometimes huge spiders which ran at him to drink his blood ; sometimes soldiers with pikes." When a bandage was applied to his eyes the visions ceased, but returned as soon as the bandage was taken off, until the patient kept it on uninterruptedly for a night and part of a day. Then he saw phantoms only at long intervals, and after some days they disappeared entirely. These are extreme examples. But they illustrate the kind of thing I am supposing to take place where it is less easy to detect it. Even in such experiments as those of G. H. Meyer,[1] who by practice succeeded in making it possible for himself to call up visual imagery at will with closed eyes, the presence of an actual object, and a visual one, is not excluded. For, not to mention the entoptic phenomena to which I shall refer later on, the black background is still an object. The phenomena of synaesthesia might also be used in support of the contention, *e.g.*, the interesting cases of " coloured hearing ", described by Dr. C. S. Myers.[2] Audible notes, namely, suggest colours, which for one of Dr. Myers' subjects varied with the pitch of the notes.

In the make-believe of children ample evidence can be shown of the way in which the realisation of imagery takes place in connexion with sense-perception. " The stump of a doll, woefully unlike as it is to what the child's fancy makes it, is yet a sensible fact, and as such gives support and substance to the realising impulse." [3] Sully remarks that the

---

[1] *Untersuchungen über die Physiologie der Nervenfaser*, p. 238 *sqq.*

[2] *British Journal of Psychology*, vol. iv, p. 228 *sqq.* and vol. vii, p. 112 *sqq.*

[3] J. Sully, *Studies of Childhood*, p. 51.

impulse to invent imaginary surroundings, and more especially to create mythical companions, is very common among lonely and imaginative children. I will take as an instance a small boy of my acquaintance who, when he was between the age of three and four years, invented for himself two imaginary playfellows, whom he christened respectively Binny and Nurny. Until he reached the age of six or seven years, he was constantly to be found amusing himself with them and conversing with them. He would speak to them through the window, while he was being dressed in the morning (*e.g.*, " Is that you, Binny? Stay a second ; I shall be down in a moment "), or he would exclaim, as his mother was about to take her seat at the breakfast-table, " Oh, *please*, not that chair ! Don't you *see* that Nurny is sitting on it? ", thus obliging her to seek another. Unquestionably these imaginary little creatures were for him distinct objects ; but invariably they were present as an intimate connexion with real things—either seated on chairs, or walking about in the garden, or standing by the counter in a shop, and so on. Actual sense-perception, that is to say, was necessary in order that the make-believe should be realised or come to pass.

3

Some striking confirmation of our theory can be obtained from a consideration of the imagery of the dream-life. Certainly not all dream-imagery can be said to be of the objective type. It is perfectly possible to go through the most vivid dream-experience without being able to discover in what one can remember of it on awaking any objective imagery, at any rate of the visual or auditory kind. But we are here concerned with dream-imagery that is of the objective type. And let it be noted at the outset, as one of the most characteristic features of the night-dream or dream proper, that there is unhesitating acceptance on the part of the dreamer of the contents of his dream-images as real. The conditions under which these dream-images occur are such as to deprive the individual of the possibility of exercising that criticism of what is presented to him which he habitually does exercise in the normal waking life ; and, in the absence of all means of distinguishing the real from the imaginary, he takes every apprehended content to be the content of a real entity. *For the dreamer*, that is to say, the whole realm of the imaginary is literally wiped out—a fact which, so far as I know, has never yet had justice done to it in the rapidly increasing literature of " dream psychology ".

It has long been recognised that at least a very large number of dreams originate in consequence of actual perception on the part of the individual, and several well-known writers have gone to the extent of saying that probably all dreams originate in this way.[1] Those who take this view are by no means necessarily committed to the assumption that " the primary cause of a dream is some stimulus ",[2] any more than those who accept the ordinary doctrine that the primary cause of an act of perception is some stimulus are necessarily committed to the assumption that that stimulus is the primary cause of the content perceived. What the position does imply is, I take it, that the content, of which the individual is (in and through the mental act occasioned by the stimulus) vaguely and confusedly aware, suggests, or starts the suggestion of, those features that play the predominant part in the dream. The evidence which goes to show that this is so could scarcely be stronger than it is.

[1] " It is customary ", writes Wundt, " to regard the majority of dream-phantasms as pure hallucinations. This view is hard to sustain. Probably most, perhaps even all, dream-presentations are in reality illusions, inasmuch as they are engendered by the slight sensory impressions, which are never extinguished in sleep " (*Grundzüge*, 4te. Aufl., Band ii, p. 536). W. Weygandt (*Entstehung der Träume*) takes a similar view. Tissié (*Les Rêves*) declares that " dreams of a purely psychic origin do not exist " ; and Havelock Ellis (*The World of Dreams*, pp. 71-72) holds that " most, perhaps indeed all, dreams that are sufficiently vivid to be clearly remembered on awakening have received an initial stimulus from some external, or at all events peripheral, source ". So, too, Bergson (*L'Energie Spirituelle*, p. 99) asserts that " it is out of real sensation that we fabricate the dream ".

[2] T. H. Pear, *Remembering and Forgetting*, p. 74.

It is hardly necessary to refer to those dreams, frequent enough, that are initiated through " organic sensations " connected with the internal organs of the body. In consequence of the obliteration of the features that divert attention from them in the waking life, these " organic sensations " attain during sleep a prominence in consciousness. Tissié tried to show that disorders of digestion, breathing and circulation can be correlated with definite kinds of dreams ; and there are well-attested instances of premonitions in dream-experience of serious maladies, such as heart disease and typhoid fever,[1] owing to the circumstance that in the dream-experience the incipient symptoms are enabled to assert themselves more pronouncedly than in waking experience. So, too, the pressure of the bed-clothes, an uncomfortable position of any part of the body, obstruction of the supply of air, etc., have often been observed to be excitants of dream-imagery. A slight internal pain may be represented as the bite of a savage dog, a small difficulty in breathing may assume the form of a terrifying incubus such as afflicts us in nightmares, an involuntary extension of the foot may appear as a fall down some vast abyss. The familiar dream-experience of flying or floating through space takes its rise not improbably from a vague consciousness of the rhythm of movement in respiration.

Much of the visual imagery in dreams, especially of the earlier part of the night, is doubtless engendered by the entoptic phenomena, to which Johannes Müller was one of the first to call attention. Müller tells us that he rarely failed to see, before falling asleep, " with closed eyes and in the darkness of the field of vision " a great variety of highly illumined and coloured objects. From his youth he had noticed them, and had learnt how to distinguish them and their rapidly changing forms and movements from the peculiar images of

---

[1] *Cf.* Forbes Winslow, *Obscure Diseases*, p. 611 *sqq.*, and Hammond, *Treatise on Insanity*, p. 234 *sqq.* Even Aristotle (*De Div. per Somnum*, 463a) notes that scientific physicians pay attention to the dreams of patients in diagnosing their symptoms not yet sufficiently evident in the waking state.

dream-life. They rarely took the shape of recognised realities, but usually appeared as fantastic figures of men, animals and what not, such as he had never seen before. " I often follow these appearances ", he says, " for a half-hour, until they finally pass over into the dream-images of sleep ". Helmholtz, too, insisted on the importance of the phenomena in question. In his opinion every eye probably contains *muscae volitantes*, so-called ; and of these fibres, granules, etc., floating in the vitrous humor, the shadows appear in the field of vision as little dark moving spots. And G. T. Ladd, who devised a method of experimenting with himself in order to determine the influence of what he describes as the *Eigenlicht* of the retina upon visual dreams, gives numerous instances of the actual transformation which he had observed of these " thin, pale and almost senseless schemata " into the kind of things seen in dreams.[1] For example, several times on waking from a dream in which he had distinctly seen lines of printed letters forming words and sentences which he had been engaged in reading by sight, he clearly detected the minute light and dark spots, that had arranged themselves in parallel lines across the visual field, to which the illusion was due. There can hardly be any question that such " phosphenes " or " ocular spectra " do supply the objective nucleus of visual imagery in certain dreams. And I know not why they should not likewise to some extent be operative even in the waking life. Indeed, one can in a state of reverie, by fixing attention upon these little objects in the field of vision, watch the way in which imagery clusters round them.

That numbers of external objects and events elicit the attention of a sleeper and set going trains of dream-imagery is matter of common observation. What would be to a person awake an insignificant noise, such as the sound of a bell

---

[1] *Mind*, N.S., vol. i, 1892, p. 299 *sqq.* The method consisted in keeping the eye closed on awaking, retaining the visual images of the dream for a brief interval, and observing them dissolve into the " phosphenes " perceived by the waking consciousness.

or the fall of a tile, may to that same person asleep become a noise like thunder, and he may forthwith picture himself as being at the mercy of the elements and as witnessing a whole chapter of catastrophes. The creaking of furniture, the rain beating against the window, the howling of the wind—these are some of the sounds that are heard and that may be interpreted by a sleeper in all sorts of fantastic ways. Burdach and a companion pass a night during which there is a violent storm at an hotel, and they both dream that they are wandering in the darkness among high precipices. Havelock Ellis[1] relates a dream in which he was listening to a performance of Haydn's *Creation*, the orchestral part of the performance appearing to consist chiefly of a very realistic representation of the song of birds, though he did not identify the note of any bird in particular. Then followed solos by male singers, whom he saw, especially one who attracted his attention by singing at the close in a voice scarcely audible. On awakening, he discovered that the source of the dream was the song of a canary in an adjoining room. This instance is the more noteworthy because he had never heard Haydn's *Creation*, except in fragments, and it could only have been its reputation as regards the realistic representation of natural sounds that had been instrumental in occasioning the dream. So, too, external objects visually perceived constantly form the starting-point of dream-phantasy. Two cases quoted by Bergson[2] from Tissié's account will serve as illustrations. One person dreams that the theatre of Alexandria is on fire, that the whole place is lit up by the flame. Then he is transported to the fountain in the public square, and a line of fire is running along the chains which connect the great posts placed round the basin. After that, he is back in Paris at the Exhibition; it too is on fire, and he is taking part in the scene. On awaking, he finds that his eyes were catching the beam of light thrown by the lantern of the hospital nurse going her round. Another person dreams that he is in the

[1] *op. cit.*, p. 82.　　　　[2] *op. cit.*, pp. 93-94.

H

navy, in which he had formerly served. Soon there is a battle going on and he beholds fire belching from the cannon. Again the dream is provoked by a beam of light from the lantern of a hospital nurse. A very common form of visual perception giving rise to dreams is that of bright moonlight, and of the early sun's rays. An amusing instance is quoted by Radestock[1] of Krauss, who once, when twenty-six years of age, caught himself, on waking, stretching out his arms towards what his dream-fancy had pictured as his mistress, but which turned out to be the full moon. And Radestock thinks it is not improbable that many of the dreams of celestial glory which persons of a mystical religious temperament are said to experience are occasioned by the rays of the sun or moon.

I submit, then, that we may fairly take the ways in which dreams are fabricated as a clue to what happens in the formation of "images" strictly so-called in normal waking experience. In each of the instances just cited what happens is clearly analogous to what we noted as happening in the case of a child gazing at a mass of fleecy clouds, or in that of the boy Abraham on the occasion of the night-journey with his sister. And I would invite the reader to compare the instances I have given of dream-imagery in this section with the instances given in the previous section of imagery in the waking life. In point of fact, neither dream-experiences nor the working of imagination in the waking life can be understood except by reference to what takes place in normal perception. In normal perception, the sense-content directly apprehended serves as the pivot around which we group a mass of revived factors and concepts, interpreting the whole in objective terms. The standard of interpretation is our normal experience. The data presented will be misinterpreted if either they are themselves apprehended with insufficient precision or if the circumstances attending the apprehension of them are in any way unusual. If the quantity of the con-

---

[1] *Schlaf und Traum*, p. 110.

tent presented be too small, if its elements be confused, if the time available for the discrimination of those elements be excessively brief, it must be a matter more or less of haphazard or chance what specific interpretation be put upon the data in question. And considerations such as these make manifest, I think, (a) how impossible it is to draw any fixed line between what we call imagination and what we call perception, and (b) the probability that in imagination as in perception there is actually given sense-material, for the most part vaguely and confusedly apprehended, and often, no doubt, intra-organic in nature, which serves as the pivot around which the suggested "imagery" is grouped and hence interpreted in objective fashion.

One characteristic difference there *is* between perception and imagination, but it tends to strengthen rather than to militate against the view I am taking. In sense-perception, the exercise of attention increases the clearness and distinctness of the content apprehended. And such increase of clearness and distinctness is due to the increasing number of the features of the object that are differentiated by the perceiving subject and which are by him compared with, and related to, one another. But in regard to imagination a like rule does not appear to hold. On the contrary, direction of attention upon, or the effort to attend to, the imaginary object seems rather, in a large number of cases at any rate, to dissipate it, to have the effect either of causing it to disappear or of transforming it into something else.[1] It may, indeed, be urged that if this be so, the disappearance of the " image " ought, on our theory, to result in the real object exhibiting itself, and occupying the place previously occupied by the " image ". The reply is that, in numerous instances, this is exactly what does happen. If the child who discerns chariots and horses and warriors, when gazing at a mass of

---

[1] It is difficult at times to perform the experiment effectively, because what we take to be an effort of attention may be simply an effort to hold the image in consciousness.

fleecy clouds, can be induced to attend more specifically to
the actual shapes and structure of the clouds he will probably
see them very much after the manner of his less imaginative
parent, and the fantastic objects will vanish. And, similarly, in the case of the visual images that occur in reverie the
exercise of attention results in the discovery of the actual
objects. The reason why in other cases it does not is fairly
obvious. In a large number of cases, the encroachment of
penumbra upon nucleus will have been so great, and the
latter will have been so confusedly and fragmentarily apprehended, that it is not surprising it should afterwards elude
detection.

4

If our inquiry has been conducted so far along the right
lines, we are confronted, it is true, at the end with a problem
of fundamental importance. We have been admitting,
namely, that in and through the act of imagination subjective
factors influence to an extraordinary degree the appearance
presented by that which is really objective. What are actually
revived or recalled are never, we have insisted, so-called
" presentations ', but contents of previous acts of perception
—in other words, the awarenesses in which those acts have
culminated. And the awareness of a characteristic, or sum of
characteristics, is never, we have contended, itself an object ;
it never stands over against the individual subject as that
upon which his act of apprehension is directed. How, then,
does it come about that in the process of imagination these
admittedly subjective factors do affect the " content apprehended " in a most pronounced manner, and give rise to
constituents in it that seem to the imagining subject to be
unmistakably objective?

The problem is undoubtedly one that goes to the very root
of the psychology of cognition, and it has, I think, to be confessed that we are not at present in a position to solve it.
But, in seeking for a solution, some light may come from the

consideration of certain phenomena, particularly in the sphere of aesthetics, which in late years have led to a considerable amount of discussion. Ruskin once spoke of a tendency of human imagination which, as he expressed it, " rejoicing in its own excessive life, puts gestures into clouds, and joy into waves, and voices into rocks " ; and the term *Einfühlung*—empathy (" feeling into," parallel with the term sympathy, " feeling with "), as Professor Ward would render it—is but a technical name for that tendency. In its simplest form, *Einfühlung* consists in reading into impersonal and inorganic objects conscious feelings, emotions and desires which are really in ourselves. To borrow some hackneyed illustrations, the pinnacles of a Gothic tower may seem to us to be striving upwards, as we ourselves should strive against a load threatening to crush us ; or we may attribute peacefulness to a gently murmuring brook, anger to the boisterous waves in a storm, seriousness to the movement of a melody in music. Poetry abounds, of course, with examples. Take, for instance, Wordsworth's well-known lines about the daffodils on the shore of Ullswater,

> The waves beside them danced ; but they
> Outdid the sparkling waves in glee ;
> A poet could not but be gay,
> In such a jocund company.

In all such cases the act of perception is markedly toned with subjective feeling, and the object perceived appears to be different from what it would appear to be were it apprehended in and through acts of perception not thus toned. The experience " felt into " the object is at once an experience of the apprehending subject and seems to be a characteristic of the content apprehended by that subject ; that which is peculiarly psychical is thus seemingly combined with the physical and other characteristics of the object to form a whole, after the manner in which these latter are combined with each other into wholes. Not only so. These psychical features are not merely " thought into " the object conceptually ; they are, so to speak, *seen* in the object. " The conscious subject ", as Witasek[1] puts it, " represents intuitively (*anschaulich*) the psychical features expressed in the object by re-living them and inwardly perceiving them ".

The relevance of all this to our present theme will be at once apparent. The feelings and other psychical factors involved in the process of *Einfühlung* are, in the terminology I have been using, contents, or partial contents, of mental acts ; yet, inasmuch as the aesthetic object is contemplated in and through the mental acts of which they are contents, it wears the aspect of itself possessing them among its other properties. No doubt, among its other properties there must be some that are the inducing conditions of the affective characters which belong to the apprehending subject being thus ascribed to the object. But the essential point is that here those factors of the inner life which Hamilton designated " subjectively subjective " are capable of influencing in a very prominent way the content apprehended. If this be true, then, of states of feeling, there need scarcely be hesitation in allowing a similar statement to be true of what we have called revived awarenesses. For these, although they are likewise contents of mental acts and are not, as such, objects, do, for the most part, refer, if I may meanwhile use the conventional phrase, to what is objective, and there is in so far the more reason why they should influence the content apprehended than states of feeling which have no such objective reference.

I am not for a moment suggesting that the comparison I have been making affords us any means of solving the problem which, as I have said, confronts us at the end of our inquiry. For in none of the extensive literature on the subject can I find any approach to a satisfactory explanation of the process of *Einfühlung* itself. All such phrases as " externalisation ", " transference ", " projection ", " projicience " and the like seem to me to be in this context purely figurative

[1] *Grundzüge der allgemeinen Aesthetik*, p. 132.

and metaphorical, and to help us not at all in understanding what it is that really takes place. But the circumstance that we have, at present, no satisfactory explanation to offer of the facts of *Einfühlung* ought not to prejudice us in recognising the facts themselves. And what I *am* suggesting is that the explanation, whatever it be, of these facts would in all likelihood enable us to solve the problem to which I have been referring.

It may be worth while to add a few words upon one other point. The objection may be pressed that, in developing a theory of the nature of images, we have been forced to admit an influence of subjective factors that would fatally vitiate any act of *perception*. If, for example, in the illustration borrowed from *Tess*, the strange shapes of the trees, etc., were so readily transformed into phantasms, is it not possible that the subjective play of revived experiences may equally transform for us every object of perception? It is, I think, a fair rejoinder that there is nothing, so far as is known, in the mode of operation of retention or revival that must necessarily lead to such vitiation. In any complex cognitive act, and an act of perception is obviously complex, we are, of course, exposed to manifold possibilities of error ; and that we are perpetually liable to illusion in perception is notorious enough. The first vague and confused apprehension of an object must needs be defective ; it is only in and through the refinement of the process which comes from repeated exercise that the chances of misinterpretation are by degrees reduced. And this general consideration applies in regard to the objection just mentioned. Undoubtedly, acquired experience may and often does lead us astray with respect to what we suppose ourselves to be immediately cognising. But advance in discriminative capacity, the consequent refinement and perfecting of that function, operates with respect to the revived factors precisely as it operates with respect to what is immediately cognised. We come gradually to a more and more accurate and circumscribed use of the revived factors ; we learn gradually to turn them to relevant and exact account, we acquire a dexterity of rapidly selecting those that are appropriate and of utilising them in the right way. And then, so far from falsifying perception, revived experience adds enormously to its efficiency. It at once sets the perceptive activity free from having to go through a lot of work it would otherwise have to perform, and it supplies elements that further the process of discrimination itself. It is true that when the presented nucleus is diminished beyond a certain limit and there is a preponderatingly large penumbra due to retained experiences, the play of fancy may run riot. Yet, even so, the play of fancy does not, in our waking life, as a rule deceive us ; we do not usually take it to be other than a play of fancy. As William James reminded us, the means at our disposal for distinguishing between real and imaginary fire, or real and imaginary water, are, in our normal experience, sufficiently efficacious ; imaginary fire does not burn, and imaginary water does not extinquish flames. So that "around the core of reality the world of laxly connected fancies and merely rhapsodical objects floats like a bank of clouds ".

V

CONCEPTUAL THOUGHT AND REAL EXISTENCE

1. *The Reflective Character of Conceptual Thinking.*
2. *Analytic and Synthetic Nature of the Process of Judging.*
3. *The Objective Reference involved in Conceptual Thinking.*
4. *The threefold Distinction of Act, Content and Objective Reality.*
5. *Existence and Subsistence.*
6. *Bergson's View of Conceptual Thinking.*
7. *Bradley's Theory of the Nature of Judgment.*
8. *Subjectivity of the knowing process* not *a vitiating influence in respect to Knowledge.*

By the older writers on psychology a sharp and decided antithesis was instituted between sense-apprehension, imagination and memory, on the one hand, and conceptual thought and reasoning, on the other hand. These were looked upon as distinct and separate mental functions. And even at the present time that view sometimes lingers on. The earlier writers (Locke, for example) were in the habit of contrasting the two processes by help of the opposition between general or universal and individual or particular. Perceiving and imagining seemed, namely, to imply reference to a determinate fact or individual object, while conceptual thought or thinking seemed to imply reference to features which are by no means restricted to any one specific thing. Thus, for instance, the contrast between the mental processes of perceiving a colour and thinking of one would have been illustrated by pointing to the single, isolated nature of the coloured object perceived and the common, widely spread nature of the colour itself, as conceived. But, as a result of our examination of the facts of perception and imagination, we can at once assert that, whatever kind of contrast subsists between that which is perceived and that which is conceived, there can be no absolute severance between the two mental processes in question. The activity of thinking does not stand aloof from the process of perceiving as something entirely new superadded. As we have repeatedly seen, perception is very far indeed from being a simple attitude of mind, such as might be described by speaking of it as the direct or immediate apprehension of an individual fact. On the contrary, we have found it always to be an active process of differentiating and distinguishing the characteristics of the object upon which it is directed. It is, therefore, perfectly legitimate to insist that thinking or judging is involved in cognitive activity throughout, that even a rudimentary act of cognition is already in essence an act of judging. From a psychological point of view there is, however, a certain disadvantage in extending thus widely the scope of the terms " thinking " and " judging ". If we recognise that the elementary functions of discriminating and comparing are implicated in cognitive activity from the outset, we may reserve the terms " thinking " and " judging " for those higher developments which involve not only the functions referred to but also the results attained by them in the sphere of sense-perception. For, unquestionably, the terms " thinking " and " judging ", as customarily employed, denote extremely complex reflective acts, which are distinguishable from acts of perceiving and imagining, although it by no means follows that the kind of activity involved in the former differs in essence from that involved in the latter. Taking, then, the term " conceptual thinking " in this specific sense, I propose, at the outset, to call attention to some of the more prominent features that seem to mark off conceptual thinking from other modes of cognition.

1. I note, in the first place, an extremely familiar feature of thinking, so understood, as compared with perceiving—that which, for want of a better word, one may call its inwardness or reflective character. By this I mean that the individual thinking subject appears to himself to stand in a

less direct, in a less immediate, relation with the external
world of existent fact than he appears to himself to stand
when perceiving a particular object. In both cases the apprehending subject is, or may be, aware of his own activity as
either thinking or perceiving ; in both cases there is a certain
content apprehended as the indispensable correlative of his
activity ; and in both cases there accompanies this content
what meanwhile I will call " reference " to the real order of
existing things apprehended in and through the act either of
thinking or perceiving. But in the act of thinking the
conscious subject seems to himself to be at a farther
remove from the world of objective fact than he is in the
act of perceiving. In consequence, thinking comes to be
looked upon as *pre-eminently* an inner activity ; and I
suppose it is largely on account of this circumstance that
in recent times the charge indicated by the ridiculous name
of " intellectualism " has been levelled against reflective
thought.

There follows at once from this a further peculiarity which
logicians have long fixed upon as appertaining to conceptual
thinking. Thought, as they have viewed it, is *mediate*
knowledge—that is to say, the real things thought about are
not directly apprehended but are represented by some marks
or properties assumed to belong to them. Thus, the perception by a conscious subject of a particular man would be
called immediate knowledge, whereas what is indicated by
the general notion or concept " man " would be described as
mediate knowledge. Further, when one duly inspects this
first distinguishing feature of conceptual thinking, it forthwith becomes evident that no concept, in the sense just
specified, could make its appearance in the history of mind
until the difference had been recognised between the real
order of fact apprehended in perception and what we may
call the ideal constructions of imagination and the ideal
reproductions of memory. Now, psychologically regarded,
recognition of this distinction between what is ordinarily,

although misleadingly,[1] called the real and the ideal is
virtually equivalent to the recognition on the part of a
conscious subject of the self as having a mode of existence of
its own, other than and distinct from the order of facts apprehended in perception.

"The advance of thought, in my view", wrote John
Grote, "is the simultaneous development of the distinct
conception of ourselves, or our personality, and the distinct
conception of objects of thought as independent of us ; and
each conception brings out the other. By an object of
thought, as distinctly conceived, we mean something standing off from, though connected with, our thinking, and we
cannot mean this without a *co-conception* of ourselves, from
which the other is relieved ; nor is there any means of setting
ourselves before ourselves, as something to be thought of,
without distinguishing ourselves from something else."[2] As
to the intimate connexion between the development of self-
consciousness and the development of the process of conceptual thinking, there can be no question ; a thinking mind
and a mind conscious of itself are, as Adamson put it, two
ways of naming the same thing.[3] In short, the activity of
conceptual thinking comes to be looked upon as pre-eminently
a voluntary process, a process whereby the mind lays hold
of and interprets in its own fashion what is offered in experience.

2. I note, in the second place, certain peculiarities of the
generality usually ascribed to thoughts or concepts. Roughly,
generalising may be said to be the process of selecting a
mark or feature, or combination of marks or features, and
liberating it from other marks or features with which it has
been presented in perceptive experience. Generalisation, in

---

[1] Misleadingly, because, strictly speaking, the ideal is also real. The
distinction is, in truth, that between the order of real *existent* fact and the
order of the real *subsistent* contents of imagination and memory. *Cf. infra*,
p. 138 *sqq.*

[2] *Exploratio Philosophica*, part ii, pp. 146-147.

[3] *Development of Modern Philosophy*, vol. ii, p. 290.

other words, is reached through means of abstraction ; and by means of abstraction a perceived or imagined content is freed from a variety of accidental or temporary concomitants and dwelt upon for itself apart from these. Generalisation is certainly not exhausted in the act of abstracting. Meanwhile, we can, however, confine ourselves to the latter. This process of abstraction depends, of course, for its exercise upon the supply of apprehended material ; it is, in no sense, an isolated activity which may be exercised in a purely arbitrary manner. It rests upon, and is, indeed, involved in, the comparison of, the discrimination of, relations among the contents offered in perception and imagination. An inner life which had before it a mere stream of given contents, of presentations and so-called images, as, for example, Hume conceived to be the case, could never advance to the stage of isolating any aspect, quality or relation from the whole in which it had originally made its appearance. For, as we have previously seen, whatever else may be given, it is clear that the difference (say) of any one content from another cannot be given in either of those contents taken singly[1] ; and, without some recognition of difference the initial step in the liberation just referred to could never be taken. In our ordinary experience no content can be recognised as in any way different from another without thereby becoming to a certain extent generalised—loosened, that is to say, from some of the numerous details along with which it had been originally apprehended ; and every item, thus detached from the perceived content, and released from the limitations imposed upon it in that context, acquires by this very circumstance a new significance.

The mental process to which I have been referring may be rightly described as involving both analysis and synthesis. Some fact is separated out from the mass of detail offered in sense-perception and is then connected with other facts, perhaps widely separate from the given fact in space and time.

[1] *Cf. supra*, pp. 71-72.

The act of judging is analytic in character because it breaks up or sunders or differentiates what is previously apprehended as a more or less confused whole ; it is synthetic in character because it unites these sundered features in another order, and by doing so both enriches what is called the subject of the judgment and specialises the generality of what is called its predicate. So that our knowledge, which advances by a series of judgments, thus exhibits a twofold mode of progress—on the one hand, an increased number of distinctions come to be recognised, and, on the other hand, by means of these distinctions, that about which we are judging is brought for us into connexion with the vast environment to which it belongs. Or, to put the matter in another way, it is only in and through the operation of judging that we arrive at that discernment of individual objects, with which we are prone to believe experience begins. In truth, experience begins with what in strictness cannot be described as either individual or general. It is only by breaking up the composite mass of what is originally offered in experience that the apprehending mind gradually arrives at a recognition of individual objects, on the one hand, and of generalities, on the other. Every new discrimination affords therefore, it may be said, the basis of a judgment of which the subject-term denotes the individual entity and the predicate-term that which is general ; and, through the synthesis thus effected, we come to regard the individual object as possessing qualities and standing in relations.

It may be well to bring out more explicitly what exactly it is that the operation of synthesising really amounts to. Take any elementary judgment of perception, such as that " this desk is solid ". In asserting that judgment, I must obviously already have reached the stage of discrimination at which I am aware of that which is expressed by the subject-term as a particular, individual object. And I am saying that among its properties or qualities is that property or quality to which we give the name of solidity. But, clearly, the quality " solidity " is a quality which " this desk " shares, or has in common, with a great multiplicity of various other objects; I could not predicate it of " this desk " unless I had previously become familiar with it as a quality of other objects. In assigning it, therefore, to " this desk ", I am, at the same time, connecting " this desk " with a number of other things likewise possessing the quality of solidity. So again, if I assert that " this desk is smooth ", I am also attributing a quality to it which it possesses along with many other things. And thus I might go on, gradually exhausting more or less the qualities of " this desk ". Every one of these qualities would turn out to be a quality which " this desk " possesses in common with numerous other things and, in ascribing to it any one of these quali- ties, I shall be *ipso facto* connecting it with those other things ; whilst, in ascribing to it a multiplicity of such qualities, I shall be virtually viewing it as belonging to a net- work of qualities and relations of a very far-reaching kind. This, then, is what is meant by speaking of an act of judging as an act of synthesising ; and obviously such function is an extremely important function so far as knowledge is con- cerned. It enables us to conceive of the vast multiplicity of objects in nature as forming together a more or less systematic whole.

By means of the activity of synthesising we obtain, so to speak, an arrangement of the world's components in a logical order as contrasted with what, in one sense, may be called the contingent, accidental order in which they come before us in perception. Relevant features are grouped together, irrelevant features are discarded or left out of account ; and, in this manner, the apprehending mind is enabled to gain knowledge of larger and larger portions of its vast environment, and to contemplate huge stretches of time and space, whereas in sense-perception it is confined to that relatively infinitesimal section of the environment which is in the immediate vicinity of the bodily organism.

Whilst, then, in one way conceptual contents are undoubtedly more abstract than contents perceived, in another way it may legitimately be said that the latter are more abstract than the former, because in sense-perception the multiplicity of relations in which the particular object perceived stands to other objects is only partially apparent. In sense-perception, that is to say, abstraction is largely and unconsciously made of the setting in which the particular object has its being, and apart from which its true character can only be imperfectly grasped. So that it might be said that what thought loses in minuteness of detail is counterbalanced by what it gains in width of extent.

We reach, then, concepts, or conceived contents, by a process that is at once analytic and synthetic. But the analytic function of thought would be misconstrued were it taken to be a *mere* dropping out of certain features from the complex whole of what is given in perception. Like every cognitive act, an act of conceptual thinking is, let me once more repeat, an act of discriminating, comparing and relating. The concepts which result from such comparison are based upon the resemblances discerned or discriminated in the empirical order of fact. These points of resemblance are, so to speak, mentally brought together in consequence of the comparison ; and, in order thus to compare, there must necessarily be to some extent what I have been metaphorically describing as a " breaking up " of the given material. Nevertheless, this " breaking up " is not a *mere* act of abstraction. No doubt, if we want resemblances, especially if we want exact resemblances, we must ignore differences ; and *to that extent* abstraction, in the sense of merely leaving out, *is* a means of attaining what we call a general notion or concept. It is, however, not so much " leaving out " as " singling out " that is really requisite for the purposes of reflective comparison. That this is so becomes apparent when we consider that the features which we compare, and from which comparison our general notion or concept is formed, are not at all likely to be found lying side by side. As a rule they will, at least, be parted in time and space, and they will almost certainly come before us embedded in a mass of detail from which they have got to be extracted. So that to serve for comparison these features must evidently be made to stand out in relief, as it were, more or less distinctly—in other words, they must be " singled out ", and in mature reflexion they will be deliberately singled out. They must be known for what they are.

The process of discerning resemblances is, accordingly, much more a positive than a merely negative process. The recognition of distinct common features is the main thing. The particular instances and their setting may or may not be left out. If they are, it is simply a matter of intellectual economy, not at all an absolute necessity so far as the concept itself is concerned. Not only so. If the common content be taken merely as a content, it will lose the character of generality ; it will become, then, just another individual entity, and we shall be guilty of hypostatising an abstraction. We may legitimately enough drop out of sight this or that particular instance ; but, if we ignore the consideration that the common quality is, after all, a characteristic or quality of particular instances, we shall almost inevitably fall into the blunder of conferring upon the content conceived a mode of existence which from its very nature it cannot possess. It will, then, be set over against the particular objects as another particular object, and some superior kind of reality will be assigned to it as compared with that of the former. This is what Hobhouse once christened " the fallacy of the supersensual "—a fallacy which, as he said, is always in essence the same, though its forms may be various. Professing to be superior to what it despises as " sensationalism ", this fallacy rests on a view of reality which is quite as crude, sometimes, indeed, cruder, than the " sensationalist " view. Its reality must be something which it can metaphorically touch and see ; it must have an object distinct, crystallised out, and unchangeable. " It insists upon what is intellectually solid quite as much as sensationalism insists upon what is physically solid." [1]

I may add that it is in connexion with generalisation that we can see most clearly the all-important function discharged in our thinking by language and the use of signs. It would be well-nigh impossible to preserve the generalised contents attained by conceptual thinking without the establishment of associations between them and some concrete empirical facts, such as words, which serve to retain these generalised contents at our command. A name or symbol never suggests all the detail of the perceived object ; it suggests what, rightly or wrongly, we have taken to be its essential nature, and what we tend to regard as remaining the same amid a variety of unessential concomitants.

3. Abstraction, we have been contending, is only one phase of the process of generalising. " The concept ", as Nettleship put it, " is not *made* general by being abstracted ; its generality *means* its capacity of being abstracted ". A concept or general notion is certainly very much more than a merely attenuated or impoverished particular, very much more than a " wandering adjective " divorced from the content of a mental image. Were it no more, what Bradley described as thought's chief characteristic—its invariable reference to an *objective* [2] connexion in the real world—would be inexplicable. Let us look, for a moment, at this characteristic. Thinking seems to stand, as it were, aloof from the mechanical order in which our presentations and representations happen to come and go ; and to refer to that which, in Lotze's phraseology, has its being and meaning in itself, and which continues to be what it is and to mean what it means whether we are conscious of it or no. In other

[1] *Mind*, N.S., vol. vi, 1897, p. 149.

[2] " Objective ", as here used, is not, of course, to be taken as meaning simply what can be presented as an object. It is here used as the correlative of " subjective ".

words, in conceptual thinking, despite the fact of what I have called its inwardness or reflective nature, we find invariably a reference either to the objective order of real existent entities or, at any rate, to a real order that is other than the merely subjective occurrences in the inner life. A connexion thought about is taken by the conscious subject to be an objective connexion—that is to say, a connexion in the nature of things, whatsoever those things may be. What I mean will become apparent if we consider the difference between a judgment and a train of associated ideas. Take, for example, a fairly simple judgment, such as " snow is white ". When I judge that " snow is white " there may, of course, be present to my mind a conjunction of presentations or re-presentations through means of which I am aware of the object, white snow. But, in addition to any such conjunction of presentations or re-presentations, there is further involved in the judgment " snow is white " the thought of a real connexion of a quite peculiar kind, such as is indicated, however imperfectly, by the very form of the judgment. I mean that " snow " and " whiteness " do not merely come together in my experience, but that they actually are connected in point of fact.

In any judgment, then, there is involved reference to a connexion of an objectively valid kind—that is to say, of a kind altogether distinct from the mere conjunction of such presentations or re-presentations as may be involved in forming the judgment. Now, we may translate the term " objective validity " by the equivalent term " necessity " ; and we may say that it is characteristic of conceptual thinking that the contents thought about are conceived as necessarily connected. By " necessarily connected " is not, indeed, to be understood necessarily valid. It is not to be supposed that the act of conceptual thinking is infallible in its procedure. The " necessity " is still necessity as conceived by us ; and, so far as that goes, it is involved no less in an erroneous judgment than in a correct one. Whether we are in error or not we view the facts referred to in our judgment as having connexion of an objective or of a necessary character.

Whence, now, comes this peculiar trait in our thinking? It is needless to emphasise here its supreme importance in knowledge. Clearly it is of vital concern that we should thus distinguish in our thinking between what is merely subjective, what merely pertains to our own modes of experiencing, and what in contradistinction thereto is objective and necessary. But it is important here to emphasise that this same distinction we have already had before us, in a cruder and less pronounced form doubtless, in dealing with perception. For in the process of perceiving there is involved exactly that operation of thought which here in more explicit fashion comes before us in the case of judging. Even in the more rudimentary modes of perceiving we invariably attach to the object perceived general characteristics which at once give it a significance of an objective kind—remove it, that is to say, from what is a mere episode in the conscious subject's transient experience. Once more, therefore, we are driven to the conclusion that perceiving and thinking are not disparate faculties of mind, but that they involve common functions—functions the results of which are relatively implicit in perceiving and relatively explicit in thinking. Accordingly, to repeat what I have already said, it is not a sudden introduction of a new factor that we have to contemplate in the act of judging; what we find there is rather the explicit unfolding of what was implicitly involved in the more elementary processes of mind, those processes whereby apprehension of the difference between self and not-self, inner experience and outer world of reality, gradually took its rise. Without the elementary functions of discriminating, comparing and synthesising, no recognition of that distinction could have been effected. With these functions and with recognition of that distinction, there becomes possible and, through increase of experience, there is gradually made actual the higher developments to which the name thinking is commonly restricted.

If, then, it be granted that, in the history of mind, we start with vague, indefinite and crudely differentiated contents, that what comes first in experience can be described neither as general, if by that we mean the generality ascribed to concepts or notions, nor yet as individual, if by that we mean the individuality ascribed to the concrete objects of our mature perception,[1] it would seem to follow that progress in knowledge ought to be conceived as taking place along two lines of advance, which need not by any means be diverging from one another, but may well be tending towards a common goal. A careful scrutiny of the activity of knowing would yield abundant evidence of the soundness of this position. No apprehending mind ever rests content with a bare abstract generality. Each generality acquired enables the relatively indefinite experience from amid which it has been gathered to be viewed as a group of more determinate individual facts. And each individual fact, thereby rendered more or less determinate, is apprehended as sharing in features belonging also to other individual facts, which latter facts are in their turn increasingly individualised and differentiated from one another. The child mind that has extracted from some fact of perceptive experience, say a chair, the elementary idea of hardness never keeps this quality floating in the air, as a " wandering adjective ", but forthwith proceeds to find it in as many other facts as possible. By a series of rudimentary judgments, the vague objects from which the child mind starts are seen to have general characteristics, and the larger the number of such characteristics recognised, the less vague, the more individual, do the objects of its experience become. And, conversely, the larger the number of objects to which a general characteristic is ascribed, and the greater the amount of difference they are otherwise seen to possess, so much the more definite and

[1] *Cf. supra*, p. 126.

distinct does the general characteristic become. The child's
first apprehension of a general notion is certainly no less
vague than its first apprehension of a particular object ;
only by slow degrees does the essential meaning thereof
gradually begin to appear. And what is true in this respect
of knowledge in its earlier stages in true likewise, *mutatis
mutandis*, of knowledge in all its stages. Every great
scientific generalisation carries with it a more and more
definite individualising of the particulars in which it finds
exemplification. If the story were true, although apparently
it is not, that Newton abstracted from the particular phenomenon of a falling apple the law of universal gravitation, this
falling apple must have immediately become transformed
for him into a much more pronounced and distinctive individuality than a falling apple had ever been before. By
discerning in it an identity with all other moving bodies he
would at the same time have been determining with greater
precision its points of difference from them. Moreover, even
that highly specialised mode of reflective thinking which
makes the inner life itself a subject of its contemplation can
only be carried out in so far as that inner life is conceived as
related to, and in intimate connexion with, the world of
extended things in space.

4. Before proceeding further, I wish to point out that the
threefold distinction on which stress was laid when dealing
with perception holds equally in regard to conceptual thinking. It is essential, namely, to distinguish the act of cognising a universal both from the universal itself and from the
way in which that universal, in and through the act in
question, is cognised. A mental state of conceiving or
thinking is, undoubtedly, a concrete event or occurrence ;
and as such it is neither a concept nor a universal. It is
characterised, of course, as every other concrete fact is
characterised, by a plurality of properties which it has in
common with other mental states, whether of conceiving, or
of perceiving, or even of willing ; but in itself it is as defi-

nitely *particular* as any fact in nature can possibly be. Again, a concept is a way in which a universal is conceived, a mode in which it is grasped by thought, or, in other words, a content apprehended (corresponding to the so-called " presentation " [1] or " appearance " in sense-perception) ; and, obviously, is not to be confounded with the act through and by means of which it has been attained. A concept, as Bradley put it, does not happen, neither can it possess a place in the series of events. And lastly, although it is usual to identify concepts and the universals to which they refer, and although for ordinary purposes no serious misunderstanding is thereby occasioned, yet it needs but little reflexion to realise that the identification is in strictness illegitimate and may readily lead to downright error. A concept is a product of thought—of thought exercised doubtless upon a world of objects which are found to exhibit certain identities of character. Its manner of formation can be more or less psychologically traced and its actual nature determined. As we have seen, it is reached by a process that is at once analytic and synthetic ; a process, on the one hand, of singling out what is imbedded in a matrix of reality, and, on the other hand, of bringing together what is presented in numerical difference. The universal to which it refers is a quality characterising a number of particulars, often widely removed from one another in space and time—a " pervasive character of things," as Professor Alexander expresses it.

5. In thus distinguishing a concept from the universal to which it refers we are entangling ourselves in a controversy which has been waged from scholastic times as to the being of universals. Many philosophers have maintained, and some would still maintain, either that universals are purely mental constructs, formed by a process of abstraction from the contemplation of individual entities—that is to say, are

---

[1] Professor Ward, who used the term " presentation " in a very wide sense, did not hesitate to class concepts under the head of " presentations ".

concepts—or else that they are mere names attained through the instrumentality of language. Locke, for instance, adopted the former position, that traditionally known as conceptualism. " Universality ", he insisted, " belongs not to things themselves, which are all of them particular in existence " ; general ideas are solely the workmanship of the mind, they are not the workmanship of nature. Berkeley and Hume went further and denied that there are even general notions or concepts of qualities or characteristics—in the sense, at any rate, in which the term notion or concept is usually understood. " An idea ", declared Berkeley, and by " an idea " he meant a perceived or imagined object, " an idea which, considered in itself, is particular, becomes general by being made to represent or stand for all other particular ideas of the same sort." In other words, there is no need to assume that there are such universals as " whiteness " or " triangularity " ; we require simply to accept the fact that there are certain particular objects which are white, certain particular objects which are triangles, and then to affirm that anything else is white, or anything else is a triangle, which bears the right sort of resemblance to these chosen particulars.

Perhaps the most direct way of showing that this position is untenable will be to lay stress on the consideration that there may be other kinds of universals than those which we describe as qualities or characteristics. The relation, namely, of resemblance or similarity, which is, of course, but one of many modes of relation, would appear itself to be a universal. Seeing that admittedly there are numerous things which are white, even though the " white " in each case is alleged to be a different " white ", yet a resemblance or similarity must subsist between respective pairs of white things ; and this relation of resemblance or similarity must, at least, be general or universal. It will not do to argue that there is a different resemblance or similarity for each of the pairs, because then one would be forced to admit that these different resemblances resemble each other ; and thus, in the end, there would be no avoiding the conclusion that resemblance or similarity itself is a universal. Had Berkeley been in this way driven to acknowledge that the relation of resemblance is a universal, he would scarcely have thought it worth his while to have resisted the contention that " whiteness " and " triangularity " are likewise universals.

He might, however, still have contended, as, indeed, with reference to relations he did later contend,[1] that these so-called universals are simply notions or concepts, and that they have no mode of being apart from the mind which conceives or thinks them. But consider what that would mean. Take such a judgment as that " Oxford is south-west of Cambridge ". This judgment asserts a relation between two portions of the earth's surface ; and it is surely enigmatical to lay it down that there can be no such relation as this except in our thought. On becoming aware of the fact that Oxford is south-west of Cambridge we become aware of something which has to do with Oxford and Cambridge. The truth of that judgment is not at all dependent upon our coming to be aware of it ; on the contrary, our coming to be aware of it is dependent upon its being a truth prior to any such act of awareness on our part. Even if in the course of some future war-madness all human beings who speak about south and west were wiped out, it would still be a fact that the part of the earth's surface where the city of Oxford stood would be south-west of that part where Cambridge stood. We may, therefore, I venture to urge, safely conclude that the fact in question is not a mere construction of our thought. Now, this fact involves, as one of its constituents, the relation " south-west of " ; and, if the whole fact is not a mere construction of our ways of thinking, it follows that its constituent, the relation " south-west of ", which is a uni-

---

[1] Berkeley only recognised " notions ", as distinguished from " ideas ", in the second edition of the *Principles*, published in 1734, twenty-four years after the appearance of the first edition.

versal, is likewise no mere construct of ours but is, on the contrary, a condition of things which we find or discover *in rerum natura*.

The conclusion we have just reached does not by any means imply that a universal such as the relation " south-west of " is an *existing* entity, on a par, in this respect, with the existing streets and buildings composing the towns of Oxford and Cambridge. In modern times it has been pre-eminently the great Austrian philosopher Alexius Meinong who has emphasised the fact that the whole of what exists, including what has existed and will exist, is, after all, infinitesimal when compared with the whole of the entities that are or may be known. That this consideration has been so easily lost sight of is due, so Meinong averred, to that " prejudice in favour of the actual (*wirklich*) " which has driven us to the extravagance of supposing that the non-existent is something too trivial with which to concern our-selves. To put the matter briefly, we need to recognise that the term " being " or " reality " is a vastly wider term than the term " existence ". There are various groups of entities which have being, or, to use Meinong's phraseology, which subsist (*bestehen*), and many of them are of tremendous moment for what exists, yet in and for themselves these entities can, in no sense, be said to exist. Similarity and dissimilarity are, for instance, entities of this description ; they may and do subsist between existent entities but they are not themselves bits of existing entities. So, too, numbers do not exist alongside of the counted things, when the latter are existents ; and entities that do not exist may be counted. Pure mathematics has, indeed, solely to do with ideal or subsistent entities ; and our " prejudice in favour of the actual " leads us here to the extraordinary, although not, of course, explicitly recognised, dilemma : either that to which our knowing refers exists in the actual world or it exists, at least, in our thought. And the word " ideal ", in defiance of its history, has come to stand for the latter.

What does not exist outside of us must, at any rate, exist within us—this we take involuntarily for granted, and it seldom occurs to us to reflect how futile and meaningless the subterfuge is. " Everyone except a philosopher ", Mr. Bertrand Russell once wrote, " can see the difference between a post and my idea of a post, but few see the difference between the number 2 and my idea of the number 2. Yet the distinction is as necessary in the one case as in the other. The argument that 2 is mental requires that 2 should be essentially an existent. But in that case it would be particular and it would be impossible for 2 to be in two minds, or in one mind at two times. Thus 2 must be in any case an entity, which will have being even if it is in no mind." [1]

We cannot define either of the terms " existence " or " subsistence " in the ordinary sense of the phrase definition, any more than we can define such ultimate terms as " red " or " blue ". We can only point to the sort of entities included under each ; we can only seek to describe as unambiguously as possible what these terms mean for us. Take then, first, the term " existence ". An existent entity is always, in the first place, a particular, concrete entity ; something which *has* qualities or characteristics and is not a mere sum of characteristics or qualities, however difficult we may find it to explain what " having " in this context precisely means. Or, in Bradley's phraseology, it is always a " that " qualified by a " what ". It is true that we cannot perceive the " that " in abstraction from the " what " ; we perceive, as I have said, only its qualities or characteristics, the " what ". Yet this is, in itself, no reason, of course, for doubting its presence. In the second place, an existent entity is always in time ; it is always undergoing change. And, in the third place, I am inclined to say that an existent entity is always a centre of activity. And, if this last mode of description be valid, we can, in some measure at least, understand why it is we do not perceive that which *has* qualities, but only the qualities. In the

[1] *The Principles of Mathematics*, 1903, p. 451.

case, for instance, of a material thing, that which *has* the qualities would be the complex of atoms and molecules, the activity of which occasions the act of perceiving by which we become aware of its qualities but which is not itself revealed. Consider, next, what we have designated subsistent entities. Perhaps it is true that these entities cannot be unambiguously described except by saying that they are real but non-existent.[1] And that means that we can lay down certain negative statements concerning them. In the first place, a subsistent entity is not a particular concrete fact; it is destitute, so to speak, of that factor which Bradley called the " that ". In the second place, it is not temporal in character ; although white *things* may change into black things, whiteness maintains its status as whiteness. Time, that is to say, does not affect it. And, in the third place, a subsistent entity is not a centre of activity—whiteness, for example, exerts no compulsion on the things which it characterises ; they are simply characterised by it. Of such subsistent entities we may enumerate the following : (*a*) qualities or characteristics, (*b*) relations, (*c*) numbers, (*d*) truths and (*e*) moral and aesthetic values.

The " plain man " would, I suppose, brush aside what I have been contending by bluntly asserting that nothing can be without existing. But, unless he can show that there is no status in reality other than the status which such entities as stones and storms, trees and horses, persons and toothaches possess, his objection counts for nothing. As someone has wisely said, " a lively sense of reality is doubtless a salutary thing, but it has to be proved and not merely felt that a Plato's sense of reality is inferior to the ploughboy's ". Far more serious is the argument which certain philosophers have advanced, that if we allow there are such entities as subsistent truths, we shall have to allow likewise that there are such entities as subsistent falsehoods, and this is in itself well-nigh incredible. While " there would be some dignity ", it has

[1] *Cf.* C. D. Broad, *The Mind and its Place in Nature*, p. 19.

been said, " attaching to a subsistent truth or an eternal
verity, no such dignity could be felt to attach to subsistent
falsehoods or eternal lies ". Formidable, however, though on
the surface this objection may appear to be, it does not seem
to me to be really so. Neither Meinong nor Husserl have felt
constrained to admit the being of subsistent falsehoods.
And I conceive it may quite well be the case that, while
there are subsistent truths, there could be no falsehoods if
there were no minds to make mistakes. Just as we may fall
into error in regard to existing things, so may we fall into
error in regard to subsisting truths. A straight stick partially immersed in water looks bent ; but we do not, on that
account, consider it needful to suppose that the stick
actually is bent. And so, in like manner, if it appears to an
uneducated person that " twice nine are sixteen ", we need
by no means assume that there is veritably subsisting the
proposition " twice nine are sixteen ". That erroneous
belief may surely be simply due to the uneducated person's
misapprehension of the true subsisting proposition that
" twice nine are eighteen ". I fail to see, therefore, that the
view of subsistent truths is, in any way, undermined by an
argument of the kind just noted.

But it is needful to consider more in detail those subsistent
entities which are very closely connected with existent facts
in the actual world. A very large number of those universals
which we have described as qualities characterise particular
things or events, and numerous relations relate now one set
of things or events and now others. It does not, however,
follow from what we have been contending that our concepts
or notions will be exact pictures or representations of such
subsistent universals, or yet of the ways in which they are
connected with existents. Granted that a concept or notion
is a way in which a universal is known or cognised, it can
nevertheless, in no sense, be said to be a duplicate or replica
of that universal. We have seen that in perception the cognitive activity of the conscious subject is directed upon a real

physical object, and that the so-called " presentation ", or
content apprehended as we have named it, is not a *tertium
quid* between the cognising mind and the object, but is rather
a way in which the object appears to the cognising mind.
And obviously such an " appearance " can never be a copy
or likeness of the real external thing, if only because it can, at
the best, disclose no more than some of the numerous features
and constituents of that external thing.   Much more decidedly does a like consideration hold in reference to thought-
contents or concepts.   In what possible manner could the
concept or notion of gravitation, for example, be a copy or
picture either of gravitation itself or of the way in which it
characterises bodies in space?   Clearly it can be no other than
a way in which gravitation is grasped by a thinking mind.

In a valuable chapter of his *Logic*, Lotze argues truly
enough that the constitution of the logical notion does not
strictly correspond to anything which takes place in things
or external objects themselves.   Thus, for example, in the
notion, or, at all events, in some of its more prominent
forms, the relation which we describe as that of general to
particular is implied ; yet this relation, as thus conceived,
cannot have any precise counterpart in the realm of nature.
" There is no moment in the life of a plant in which it is
merely plant in general or conifer in general, awaiting some
subsequent influences answering to the subsequent logical
determinations in our thought, to settle the question what
particular tree it is to grow up into."   So, too, as concerns
the subordination of notions or concepts to one another in
classification, there is nothing exactly answering to it in the
actual structure and development of things themselves.
" This horse was not to begin with animal in general, then
vertebrate in general, later on mammal, and only at the last
stage of all a horse ; nor can we by any means at any moment of its life separate off as an independent set of qualities
the more fully defined group of properties which make it a
horse, from the more general and less determinate which

would make it a vertebrate, or from those most indeterminate of all which would merely constitute it an animal as
such." [1]

All this, so far as it goes, must, of course, be unreservedly
acknowledged ; and if notions or concepts be supposed to be,
as so-called " presentations " in the case of perception have
been supposed to be, existent entities upon which the thinking process is directed, instead of ways in which a reflective
mind interprets the nature and relations of the real universe,
then, in the light of these considerations, conceptual thinking
will evince itself as vitiated by a cardinal defect. For concepts are formed by means of generalising ; and although,
as we have seen, generalising is by no means merely a process
of abstraction, it is that to a considerable extent. Consequently, on the supposition just mentioned, we shall seem to
get what F. H. Bradley designated " floating adjectives ", cut
off, as it were, from the stream of perceived fact—loose, disconnected, discrete entities, that is to say, interposed between us and the real world, which would altogether mislead
us as to its true nature.

6. This is virtually the burden of M. Bergson's indictment
of conceptual thought. Nature, he maintains, is a perpetual
becoming ; its central and fundamental feature is fluidity,
life, creativeness. But conceptual thought, fashioned by
evolution for the exigencies of human practice, must needs
work with stable elements and invariable conditions ; and so
singles out from the flowing current of reality those factors
which, taken in abstraction, bear the aspect of sameness or
identity. Preoccupied beyond all else with the necessities
of action, reflective thought is limited to taking, at intervals,
views that are instantaneous, and by that very fact is debarred from apprehending the true evolution, the radical
becoming, of the real world. The thinking intellect takes a
number of snapshot views at the passing procession of
events, makes these the contents of its picture, and, then,

[1] *Logic*, § 342.

entrenching itself in a network of concepts obtained in this artificial manner, is for ever vainly attempting to entangle and retain in its stationary web the moving reality that is meanwhile hastening on. These concepts may, indeed, glide into one another like a succession of pictures in a cinema show and thus give a semblance of continuity and life, but it is a semblance only. In point of fact, it is urged, the cinematographical character of reflective thinking renders it impotent to seize and adequately to represent the continuous stream of real process. If we would gain access to the real as it veritably is in its togetherness, and restore the continuity which conceptual thought has murdered in dissecting, we must return to that innate mode of knowing which in its unconscious phase as instinct is sympathetic action, and which becomes in its conscious phase as intuition sympathetic insight, a mode of immediately discerning what is present to it. And these two, intuition and conceptual thinking, require to be sharply distinguished the one from the other.

Two obvious considerations in regard to the contention I have thus summarised suggest themselves at once. In the first place, if the character of thought or reason be such as is here depicted, if it is constantly falsifying the reality which it purports to reveal, leading us to suppose that what is moving and living is inert and lifeless, then surely it is a peculiarly *unpractical* instrument to serve the ends of practical utility, and the *élan de vie* must be perpetrating upon us a strange and inexplicable trick in evolving it as our means of actively carrying on the business of existence. And, in the second place, if the truth of life is revealed by intuition, while intellectual thinking is prevented by a natural inability to grasp the truth of life, it is, to say the least, a curious circumstance that, as a matter of fact, all we really know of life and evolution has been discovered by the latter, in spite of its natural inability. The notion of cosmical evolution, or, indeed, of any of the forms of continuity which are recognised by science, is manifestly not yielded by immediate or intuitive apprehension. There is no immediate awareness of the continuity of the acorn with the oak, or of the amoeba with the mammalia, or of the mammalia with the human species. To the untutored mind, dependent mainly on crude sense-perception and incapable of understanding the conceptual categories of biology or of history, the continuity of the lower animals with man has never been particularly apparent. In truth, the theory of evolution, in common with every other large scientific generalisation, such as the law of gravitation or of the conservation of energy, is a principle of continuity applicable to an extensive area of the real world, which immediate or intuitive awareness is wholly unable to cover.

But furthermore, although it is certainly the case that conceptual thinking is essentially a process of distinguishing and differentiating, and is on that account compelled to follow the discursive path where predicates are treated more or less abstractly, yet, as we have seen, the synthesis involved in the process of judging is as necessary an aspect of it as discursive analysis. To think or to judge is to connect and to unify no less than to discriminate and hold apart ; in fact, to differentiate and to relate are two sides of one and the same process. It is, indeed, impossible to relate without recognising different factors to be related ; if continuity is to be discerned there must be recognition of the several items between which the continuity subsists. Again, it is to be noted that so-called immediate apprehension, or intuition, is in its own way likewise discursive, so that discursiveness does not originate with conceptual thinking. In the sensibly continuous masses of so-called immediate intuition, such as the perception of continuous space, the continuity in question is only relatively undifferentiated. Even in the awareness of a simple movement in space there must be involved the awareness of so much discreteness as is implied in speaking of the " starting point ", " direction " and " goal ". What reflective thinking really does is to unfold more fully and

K

explicitly the continuity in discreteness, or the identity in difference, to use a Hegelian mode of expression, which is implicitly involved in unreflective experience. And, as the work of reflective thinking proceeds, the original continuities become transformed for us not into purely discrete elements, as M. Bergson supposes, but into other types of continuity, such, for example, as the continuity of equivalent amounts of energy, the continuity of biological evolution, of purposive activity, and so forth. The difference, then, between immediate or intuitive experience and that same experience when worked over and illuminated by thought is not that the continuities of the former have been replaced by the rags and tatters of thought's analysis, but rather that the crude and more or less contingent continuities of sense have been supplanted by those more comprehensive and far-reaching principles of continuity which scientific investigation has brought to light.

In arguing that no effort of conceptual thinking could ever render intelligible to us the significance of change, M. Bergson is, indeed, following in his own way what has been a traditional doctrine in speculative philosophy. Repeatedly it has been maintained that there is a radical and fundamental difference between thought-contents and what is revealed to us in and through perceptual experience. Briefly expressed the antithesis amounts to this. Thought-contents are, it is urged, unaffected by change ; each remains eternally identical with itself, timeless and unalterable. And the relations of these contents are not merely permanent ; they are altogether independent of time. They are the very types for us of the unchanging and the timeless. Of the possibility as of the fact of change no conceptual thinking could, therefore, inform us. It is only immediate sense-perception, only in M. Bergson's view instinct or intuition, which accepts the " given " as its datum, that can in any way bring before us the fact of change. Now, I submit, in the first place, that a contention of this sort rests upon the assumption of a separation which we have already seen ample reason for discarding as illegitimate. Doubtless, if we start by confining conceptual thinking to the range of those inner activities which operate on already given apprehended contents, then what is thus asserted of it would be true. So contemplated, the activity of conceptual thinking would have before it not concrete existent facts, but the contents of so-called " presentations " or " re-presentations ". What, however, are we then to make of a perception or intuitive function which has in it no element of discriminating activity? What are we then to make of an experience which is " opposed to " conceptual thinking, and which must, therefore, be assumed to be altogether disparate in nature. It is true that M. Bergson contends that there is no complete severance between " instinct " or " intuition " and " intelligence " ; that as complementary they accompany one another ; " there is ", he avers, " no instinct that is not surrounded with a fringe of intelligence ". Yet these phrases are purely metaphorical ; and it is difficult, if not impossible, to see how the two processes can " interpenetrate " each other, if the difference be a " difference not of degree, but of kind ". In point of fact, when perception and conceptual thought are thus contrasted the comparison has been wrongly made. On the one hand, it is certainly the case that perceptive activity is dependent on sensory stimulation ; and it is equally the case that what is apprehended through such activity is a present fact—that is to say, part of the total content apprehended is a determination of present time. But, then, the *act* of conceptual thinking is likewise dependent on temporal conditions ; it too takes place, namely, at one time and not at another ; and there is no reason why there should not be a temporal determination in the content which is apprehended in and through such thinking activity. On the other hand, if the content apprehended be regarded in abstraction, then there is no fundamental difference in respect to the element of time in the two cases. A thought-content, taken thus in itself, is certainly independent of time ; but a content apprehended in perception, when taken in itself, is no less timeless than a content of conceptual thinking.[1]

To assert, then, that conceptual thinking does not bring before us, could not bring before us, the notion of change appears to me as valueless as to assert that conceptual thinking does not bring before us, could not inform us of, any specific sense-quality we might choose to select. No one ought for a moment to suppose that conceptual thinking is capable of being thus severed from the rest of our experience, or that in any other than the narrow acceptation convenient for psychological purposes conceptual thinking is to be separated from perceptive activity. In the second place, however, I would meet M. Bergson's contention in a more direct way. Admittedly, every truth, as distinguished from existing fact, is changeless ; a truth, in other words, transcends time, temporal relations do not affect it. But if we had before us nothing but a stream of continuous change, it *would be* impossible that we should ever become aware of, or know anything about, time or change at all. There is, as James Ward once expressed it, all the difference in the world between a succession of presentations and the presentation of succession. Were the psychical life a mere flow of unbroken happenings, a " continuous progress of the past which gnaws into the future and which swells as it advances ", it could never attain to a consciousness of itself as such. It is, then, precisely because thought-contents or concepts are changeless that they afford us the means of obtaining a knowledge of change ; it is, so to speak, by translating the temporal into terms of the timeless that cognition of the temporal is possible. A thinking mind is, therefore, in a very real sense a denizen of two worlds. As existing, it is in the stream of succession ; as knowing, it transcends that stream and contemplates even it *sub specie aeternitatis*.

7. I suppose it may be alleged that a more radical view of

---

[1] *Cf. supra*, p. 77.

the shortcoming of conceptual thinking as an instrument for interpreting the realm of existent reality is that advanced by F. H. Bradley. He too emphasised the discursive or abstract character of the process in question. An act of thinking or judging consists, so Bradley maintained, in predicating, as he was wont to express it, an ideal content of a given subject-term. But the idea which is predicated is never the same as the fact of which it is predicated, so that, in judging, the existent fact and the meaning are necessarily divorced. Thought has, then, to recognise this division of existent fact from its meaning, or of the " that " from the " what " ; and it cannot join these two features so as to get rid of mere ideas or notions and arrive at actual reality. The content which it supplies to reality has, when applied, no genuine existence—it is an " adjective " cut loose from its " that " ; it is a characteristic which, as we are aware of it, is ideal and not a characteristic of existent fact.[1] Nor can it be ever rejoined to existent fact in such a way as to constitute a portion of the real world. Consequently, conceptual thinking inevitably exhibits a distortion or dissection and never the full richness of what is real. Accordingly, Bradley concluded that since thought is not identical with the existent reality it purports to know, it cannot be adequate to the task of disclosing the nature of that reality, although he admitted that could it become identical with such existent reality, then it would be thought no longer. Or, to put the point somewhat differently, since the process of thinking is not the whole of the reality to which it refers, it must be unable to grasp that reality, and its inability is due to the circumstance that its very procedure consists in tearing asunder that which in reality is not thus torn asunder.

With respect to this theory of the nature of judgment, worked out by Bradley in elaborate detail, I must be content here to offer the following observations. In the first place, if we start, as Bradley did, with a mental state,

[1] Cf. *Appearance and Reality*, chapter xv.

assumed to be experienced in some unique way, in some way, that is to say, absolutely different from the way in which the facts of the objective world are or can be apprehended by us, and if that unique experience furnishes the only hold we can secure on existent reality, then it becomes a question whether the thinking activity does not labour under a more serious disability than even Bradley took to be the case. For see how we stand. Our mental life consists of psychical states or events, each possessed of two aspects, existence and content, the content being the complex of qualities and relations constituting the character of the existent in question. These psychical states are our data ; their occurrence *is* our experiencing ; in their case reality (or such degree of reality as belongs to them) and experience are one and the same. So far there is no thought and no logical judgment. But certain of these psychical states, so-called " sensations ", are, *quâ* existents, signs of an immediate relation to, a direct encounter with, a reality beyond themselves. In sense-presentation we are in actual contact with this objective reality, but such contact in itself only assures us *that* the objective reality is and not *what* it is. By means of the judgment we qualify, interpret, impart meaning to the signified real. And we are enabled to do so because the psychical state, which *quâ* existent is in contact with the presented reality, is *quâ* content a mental image, part of which can be used ideally and referred to that which is beyond itself. The subject of the judgment is the signified real, the predicate a portion of the content of the mental image, abstracted from the rest, fixed by the mind as a universal and attached to the signified real. It is, then, clear why the unification involved in an act of judgment never can present us with a concrete reality, such as that which has been mutilated in order that the act of judging should take place. The subject of the judgment cannot own its predicate in the same way as the mental image owned its contents, and that for two reasons. On the one hand, it is a different existent from the mental image, and there is no reason whatsoever for supposing that its content must coincide with the content of the mental image. And, on the other hand, it is hard to understand how a fragment of content torn from its particular setting in one context has thereby been fitted, by being deprived of its clothing,[1] for transportation into another context, " to live on strange soils, under other skies, and through changing seasons ". As thus cut loose from its own existent, this fragment is an " adjective ", a " meaning " ; and is referred to an existent reality which is other than the mental image. On what grounds are we, however, entitled thus to use an adjective abstracted from a psychical state to qualify an existent beyond it? If we are to take the immediate experience of a psychical event as our criterion of reality, then to dismember this reality which is immediately experienced and to use one of the *disjecta membra* to qualify a supposed reality which is not immediately experienced seems to contradict in violent fashion the assumed criterion. Accordingly, the conclusion would appear to be inevitable that the procedure of conceptual thinking on this view of it is altogether misdirected and is leading us farther and farther away from the objective reality it purports to decipher. In the second place, I would unreservedly reject the contention that conceptual thought must in the long run suffer shipwreck because it can never be immediately identical with that which it essays to know. On the contrary, it seems to me obvious that thinking or knowing must in this sense be distinct from and other than the objective existents which confront it—in the sense, namely, that it is an act or process of the individual mind itself. There could be no knowledge of any sort without that antithesis between knowing and the known ; even complete or perfect knowledge would not transcend it, for it is implied in very notion of knowledge as such. To demand of knowledge that it shall be one with the object known is tantamount to demanding that knowledge

[1] *Cf.* Bradley : *Principles of Logic*, pp. 9–10.

shall both be and not be knowledge. Yet, " does it not seem absurd to say that by interposition of mind, by which alone knowledge is possible, knowledge is at the same time impossible? What alone renders something possible, alone renders it impossible! I know, but because I know, I do not not know! I see, but because I see, I do not not see ! Is it a fact, then, that because both—subject and object—are present in cognition the one must be destroyed by the other, and not that cognition may be made true, but that it may be made false? In a word, is it not worth while to consider the whole antithesis—an object is known because there is a subject to know it ; an object is not known because there is a subject to know it." [1]

8. The consideration here suggested is one that may be approached from many sides ; we have been approaching it along the road of psychological inquiry. And if our analysis of conceptual thinking has been rightly conducted, we have obtained a result of no small importance with respect to the antithesis just propounded. For we are now in a position to assert that the subjectivity which is of necessity implied in all knowledge, inasmuch as knowledge is dependent on the activity of a knowing mind, has not in itself a vitiating influence upon the knowledge it is the means of obtaining. The activity of knowing throws no colour of its own upon that representation of the world of fact which through it is possible, simply because it has no colour of its own to throw. In essence, it is throughout a process of discriminating, comparing and relating ; and there is nothing in such a process that need of necessity distort or falsify the contents which thus come into recognition. As an activity of this kind, it cannot itself get in the way of that which it discriminates, compares and relates ; it gives no *form*, in the Kantian sense, no portion of its own being to the contents that in and through it make their appearance.

[1] J. H. Stirling, Annotations to Schwegler's *History of Philosophy*, pp. 391-392.

Against this conclusion there is, indeed, one objection that might be pressed which it may be well briefly to consider. We have seen, namely, how the contents of acquired knowledge come gradually to be looked upon as the property of the self, which, in mature experience, it is generally assumed we are able to make an object of our contemplation.[1] The self comes thus to be regarded as possessing a body of knowledge, as having at its disposal and in its keeping, so to speak, a whole storehouse of notions and categories wherewith to arrange and interpret the details of experience. In receding from sense-perception to ideas of imagination and concepts of discursive thinking we seem to be withdrawing from the real world of fact into an inner world of our own construction, and the question may accordingly be raised whether the formation of the latter does not in turn distract and pervert our view of the former. In other words, is not the direct and immediate apprehension of an unreflective mind more likely faithfully to discriminate the features of existent reality than the apprehension of a mind that brings to the task a host of ideas and thoughts which may conceivably be irrelevant and misleading? The prominent characteristic of existent fact, it may be pointed out, is its concreteness, while the prominent characteristic of our ideas and concepts is their universality. In the order of existent fact, it may be urged, the parts seem to be connected through the relatively external relations of co-existence and sequences, while, in the order of thought, ideas and concepts are connected through the relations of logical dependence. Does it not, then, follow after all that our thought proceeds according to a fashion of its own and that it imposes on the materials furnished to it forms that are peculiar to itself? It would, I admit, be difficult to resist this argument on the assumption that thought is a " fundamentally distinct mental function ", which operates upon presentations given to it by means of another " fundamentally distinct mental function ". If,

[1] *Cf. supra*, p. 96.

however, that assumption be, as we have maintained, unwarranted, if the process of conceptual thinking be, in truth,
a development from the more primitive process of sense-
apprehension and continuous with it in nature, then we are
entitled to answer the question just formulated decidedly in
the negative. We are entitled to point out that universality
is not a feature abruptly introduced into apprehended contents when we begin to contemplate them reflectively, that,
on the contrary, it is really involved even in the crude presentations of the rudimentary consciousness, and that, so
soon as a perceived object is regarded as having a permanent
existence of its own, and as being common to a multiplicity
of percipient minds, the qualities discriminated in it are
tacitly recognised as universal. Instead, therefore, of being
simply a form of our individual thinking, universality is a
feature which we discover in all the materials with which our
modes of apprehension are concerned. And so, too, with
respect to the relations of logical dependence. They are in
no sense accidents due to the particular mechanism of conceptual thinking on the part of finite subjects. It is perfectly
true that those relations which we represent by means of
judgments and syllogisms are not to be regarded as precise
copies or counterparts of relations that hold in the world of
existent reality. But, in the first place, we never, in our
thinking, assume any such literal correspondence ; thought
never claims for the relations of logical dependence that they
are other than generalised representations of those modes of
systematic connectedness which we gradually come to discern in reality *as a whole*. And, in the second place, our
activity of conceptual thinking is not some miraculous
function suddenly transported into a world alien to it ; it has
itself originated in and developed as part of that world ; its
growth has been throughout conditioned and determined by
the very material upon which in turn it comes to be exercised,
and which we have no ground whatsoever for supposing has
been engaged in the strange freak of so shaping the discrimin-

ative process as to convert it into a mechanism for distorting and defiling that which went to fashion it. Once more, then, the categories of thought evince themselves as no mere capricious inventions of human intellects ; they are, on the contrary, contents which in the whole of reality discerning minds have discovered, and which those minds bring to bear in interpreting that portion of the whole of reality which we describe as the realm of existent fact. In that process there is, of course, ample room for misunderstanding and error ; but there is no ground for regarding it as inherently incapable of attaining to a knowledge of the environment in the midst of which we are stationed.

VI

F. H. BRADLEY'S TREATMENT OF NATURE

1. *What Bradley meant by " Nature ".*
2. *The Dictum that " to be real is to be indissolubly one with sentience ".*
3. *Physical Nature and Finite Organisms.*
4. *Bradley's Theory of Experience.*
5. *His View of Appearance and Reality.*
6. *Absolute and Relative Truth.*

IT has been said of Hegel that " nature was for him always a kind of step-child ". It would not be fair to apply that saying to Bradley. But, as in the case of most philosophers who have been largely influenced by Hegel, it is noticeable how small a portion of Bradley's work was devoted to a consideration of the physical universe, or to an attempt to estimate the bearing of the results of modern scientific investigation upon his metaphysical theory. His attitude towards natural science was, however, very different from Hegel's. He strongly repudiated any claim on the part of philosophy to criticise its conclusions, so long as it kept within its own domain. A scientist must be credited with understanding his own business, and must be left at liberty to follow his own methods ; and should he persist in rejecting every kind of explanation other than the mechanical, that was his affair and not the affair of the metaphysician. Indeed, the question of the operation of ends in nature was a question which metaphysics should leave untouched. While the business of metaphysics is to deal with ultimate truth, phenomenalism is the one rational attitude in all the natural sciences, including psychology—restriction of attention, that is to say, to events, with their laws of coexistence and sequence. It is only when phenomenalism loses its head, and steps forward as a theory of first principles, that its pretensions become ridiculous.

1. Bradley held, however, that a philosophy of nature, as well as, and in contradistinction to, a science of nature, is possible. Its function would be to give, from time to time, system to the results of science ; and, accepting from the sciences the various kinds of natural phenomena, to set these in an order of rank or merit, according to the degree of reality possessed by each, from the point of view of that perfection or individuality the idea of which is fundamental in metaphysics. But he pleaded his own inability to undertake a task of this sort ; and he confined himself to inquiring generally how far nature, as interpreted by natural science, can be said to be " real " in a metaphysical sense. By " nature " in this context he means, he tells us, " the bare physical world ", the " remainder " that can claim existence when everything psychical has been abstracted.

It very soon becomes apparent that in Bradley's view there is no such " remainder ". He first emphasised the fact that nature to the common man is not the nature of the physicist, and that outside his science, the physicist habitually looks upon the world as what he must believe it cannot be. In the opening chapter of *Appearance and Reality*, by a series of arguments of the kind Berkeley employed, the impossibility had already been shown of separating primary from secondary qualities. The mere skeleton of nature which is the object of the physicist is only " made real ", Bradley here insisted, by the blood and flesh of secondary qualities. Indeed, the boundary of nature cannot be drawn even at them ; tertiary qualities, to use Bosanquet's phrase, can only be excluded by considerations that are purely arbitrary.

2. The question as to the status of sense-qualities in the natural world has assumed an altogether different aspect in late years from that which it assumed at the time when *Appearance and Reality*[1] was written ; and it is unfortunate

---

[1] I am using hereafter the symbol A to denote this work, and T to denote the later work, *Essays on Truth and Reality*.

that Bradley was never induced to deal with the problem in the light of more recent discussion. Had he done so, he would have found many to agree with him in rejecting a " bifurcation of nature " who would yet withhold assent from the Berkeleian thesis that " outside of finite experience there is neither a natural world nor any other world at all " (*A*. 279). And he could scarcely have felt so confident as he then did that a realistic doctrine of sense-qualities would, from a metaphysical point of view, " turn out not worth notice ".

Despite the persistence with which he recurs to the subject, it is by no means easy to determine precisely what Bradley wished to have understood by his proposition that " to be real is to be indissolubly one thing with sentience " (*A*. 146). There can, I think, be discerned in what he has written in its support three different lines of reflexion.

(*a*) Often he certainly seems to imply that all the so-called " things " of nature are psychical in character. " There is ", he declared, " no being or fact outside of that which is commonly called psychical existence. Feeling, thought and volition (any groups under which we class psychical phenomena) are all the material of existence. And there is no other material actual or even possible " (*A*. 146). And again : " We can discover nothing that is not either feeling or thought or will or emotion or something of the same kind. We can find nothing but this, and to have an idea of anything else is plainly impossible " (*A*. 522). What seems to be asserted by statements such as these is that any object which we feel, or think, or will, itself consists of feeling or thought or will, or of some complex of them. And by way of establishing this position, he challenges us to " find any piece of existence, anything that anyone could possibly call a fact, or could in any sense assert to have being, and then judge if it does not consist in sentient experience " (*A*. 145).

It is clear, I think, that any plausibility this argument may be supposed to possess arises solely from the ambiguity of the term " experience ". If by the term " experience " be meant a mental process of experiencing, then there is no difficulty in responding to the challenge. For to allege that " things " consist of sentient experience in this sense is merely to assert what seems to be directly contrary to fact, without producing a shred of evidence in support of the assertion. If, on the other hand, be meant by the term in question the whole complex situation, " awareness of a fact or an existent ", then doubtless we cannot produce that of which we are not, to some extent, aware, but nothing is thereby settled as to the nature of the said fact or existent. Whatever its nature, that would still be true. There is certainly no sense in which we can " continue to speak of it when all perception and feeling have been removed ", but that would still be the case even though it be as different from perception and feeling as a material entity is usually taken to be.

(b) Following another line of reflexion, Bradley proceeded from an " original whole " of feeling, the immediate unity of a finite psychical centre, a " this-mine ", experienced altogether as a co-existing mass, out of which, by a process of " disruption ", everything that comes to appear as objective (and, for a matter of that, everything that comes to appear as subjective) emanates, and on which, as a persisting background, each of these " loosened " contents plays its part, finally returning into it again. Nature is, on this view, but " one part of the feeling whole "—a part which has, by our abstracting thought, been severed from the rest, and, enlarged by theoretical contrivance, been set up as the self-existing. As such it is mere " content " torn from its " that ", not now indeed consisting of either feeling or thinking or willing, for these are *existents*, but of a complex of adjectives separated from their substantives and erroneously taken to constitute an independent reality.

But what proof is offered for supposing that a " whole of feeling " either does or can contain the things which it is thus assumed to contain? I can discover none. Extension, weight, solidity and the secondary qualities are all, accord-

ing to Bradley, included in the " whole of feeling "—" the
idea of the extended has extension, the idea of the heavy has
weight, the idea of the odorous has smell ", for, although
ideas are not what they mean, they can mean nothing but
that which they are (*Mind*, N.S., iv. p. 21). " Unless ", he
wrote, " an idea has, and to that extent is, a quality, there is
no way of understanding how it goes about to show it ". Yet,
surely, there is no incongruity in acknowledging what seems
to be a manifest fact that a quality or characteristic can be
shown or exhibited by means of that which does not possess
it (*e.g.*, a beam of an electric lamp may go about to show
qualities or characteristics which are certainly not qualities
or characteristics of the beam itself). Not only so. Bradley
took for granted that qualities such as extension, weight,
colours, sounds, etc., can be felt or lived through (*erlebt*), just
as a state or condition of the mind itself, a feeling or an act of
attention, is felt or lived through. It was, however, precisely
this assumption that, for the purposes of his theory, he
needed to justify. He would have admitted that when, in the
development of conscious experience, the recognition of the
distinction between subject and object has been reached, and
a sense-quality such as green is cognised as a characteristic of
an object, this characteristic is not as such " felt " or
" *erlebt* " ; but his contention is that prior to its being " got
out into the form of an object " (*T.* 176) the green was immediately experienced, and that subsequently to its being
thus " got out " it still implies a " felt background ". Now,
with respect to the latter point, it is no doubt true that the
act of perceiving, together with its content, in this case the
awareness of green, as constituting part of the actual structure
of the psychical centre, is " lived through ", or, in Bradley's
terminology, " felt " ; but that in itself affords no presumption that the same is true of the content perceived, the green
colour, either at the moment when it is being cognised or
prior to such cognition. In other words, if perception consists in a mental act being directed upon and discriminating

the features of an object, there is no ground whatsoever for supposing that, in the history of the mental life, it was preceded by an altogether different mode of " experience ", in which there was no distinction between the perceiving and the perceived—" an immediate feeling, a knowing and being in one " (*T*. 159). It may readily be granted that the distinction between subject and object would not then have been recognised by the conscious subject, and that the content perceived would have been crude and obscure in the highest degree. Yet from neither of these considerations, nor from both, is there the slightest reason for concluding either that there was, as a matter of fact, no object present, or that the contents which come later to be recognised as standing over against the conscious subject are in truth constituents of that subject's own being.

(*c*) There is yet another line of reflexion followed by Bradley, which differs, I think, somewhat from the one just noticed—that, namely, which comes to light in his treatment of judgment. Judgment, according to his well-known definition, is " the act which refers an ideal content (recognised as such) to a reality beyond the act " (*Logic*, p. 10). In judgment, I predicate an idea of a reality, but neither the reality nor the idea is an existent " in my head ". The reality may be an existent but, in any case, it is not " in my head " ; the idea, in this context, is neither an existent nor is it " in my head ", but a mere " what ", a mere feature of content, divorced from its psychical existent, and used to qualify the " that " of the subject of the judgment.

But here again, although he tried to remove a number of incidental difficulties, Bradley never really indicated what his reply would be to objections of a more radical kind. For one thing, the theory is violently opposed to what appear to be obvious facts. When I assert that " this rose is red ", no scrutiny, however careful, will reveal a process of first discerning redness as a quality of a mental state of mine, of then detaching it from that state, and finally of transferring it to

L

something entirely different. The redness seems to be as little a content, or part of a content, of my mental state as the rose is ; and, so far from thrusting upon the latter a characteristic of my mental state, I appear to be detecting the redness as a property of the object. Judgment may, of course, be an operation quite different from what it appears to be ; but he who takes its nature to be such as Bradley describes has surely the problem staring him in the face of explaining how it comes to " go about " disclosing itself as a process not of adding adjectives to reality but of discerning them as already belonging to reality. Furthermore, the theory presupposes that the subject of the judgment is, in so far, what it purports to be—namely, a reality other than and distinct from the " psychical centre " by which it is apprehended. Yet it is impossible on the theory (i) to see how the *subject* of the judgment ever succeeds in coming to recognition at all, and (ii) to understand why *it* should be taken to be what it appears to be—a reality independent of the finite " whole of feeling "—while its attributes cannot in like manner be taken to be what they appear to be.

3. As regards physical nature, Bradley's position is, then, that it is not, as such, real, but an appearance within Reality, a partial and imperfect way in which the Absolute is manifested. Not from physical nature, either as scientifically interpreted or as presented in ordinary experience, can we gain any adequate conception of the absolute Reality. Such positive conception of it as we can frame is best attained by reverting to those finite " wholes of feeling " with which we are familiar. A whole of this sort, containing diversity and yet not parted by relations, is, it has to be admitted, most fragmentary and unstable ; we hardly experience it as more than that which we are in the act of losing ; but it serves to suggest the notion of a total experience, beyond relations though full of diversity, a unity transcending and yet containing every manifold appearance, a whole in which phenomenal distinctions are " merged ", and possessing the direct

nature of " feeling ", yet at a higher level and without losing any of the richness of relational experience. Physical nature is a mere element in this one totality—an element with a very small measure of reality and truth (*A*. 495), which is preserved in the Absolute only by a large amount of transformation and transmutation.

So much for the moment being granted, it might be the case that the necessary transformation would be partially, at any rate, effected if we could regard all nature as in truth subservient to distinct unities of feeling. But can we? Or, is there such a thing as inorganic nature? The question is not, in Bradley's opinion, one that admits of an answer. Abstractly regarded, there is no reason why in the Absolute there should not be qualities unconnected as a body with some finite soul, although there is no special reason for thinking that there are such qualities. And from the side of concrete facts, it has to be confessed that we know extremely little about what can or cannot play the part of an organism. We assume the existence of other organisms mainly on the basis of a certain degree of resemblance to our own. But, because we have found out the character of some organisms, we cannot conclude that we have exhausted the character of all. For aught we can tell, therefore, every fragment of visible nature might serve as a constituent of an organism unlike our bodies. Our inability to answer the question is, however, of small moment ; whatever the answer, finite organisms are clearly phenomenal only and must be transcended in the Absolute, while the inorganic, if it exists, will need greater transformation still.

More important is the question whether a physical fact which is not *for* some finite sentient being is possible, and, if so, whether there are grounds for taking it as real. Bradley's position is briefly this. He held that it cannot be said to be impossible that there are elements experienced in the Absolute which yet are not experienced within any subordinate focus, because these would still be subordinate to and integral aspects of the whole—a whole that is a single experience. But, although not impossible, there is, he urged, no good reason for believing it to be the truth. For (a) the number of finite centres and their diversity is very great, and may fairly be supposed to extend beyond our knowledge. Organisms unlike our own may very well exist, so that it is quite conceivable that all nature is always in relation to finite sentience, and that even such an object as my brain, invisible to me, may be obvious to some faculty of sense. And (b) while recognising that a line of argument such as the foregoing tends to become extravagant, we should remember that beyond the things perceived by sense there is the realm of thought, and that nature may comprise not only the region that is both presented and thought of but also that which is only thought of. " Nature may extend beyond the region actually perceived by the finite, but certainly not beyond the limits of finite thought " (A. 277). That means, however, that what for us is intelligible only must be more for the Absolute. Somehow, what we merely think must, in the Absolute, be perceived ; and the nature which we know conceptually will in the Absolute, where all content is re-blended with existence, gain once more the form of being immediately felt or sensed, i.e., an intuitional (anschauliche) form.

4. Criticism of the doctrine I have outlined can here be confined to two points. And I am mindful of the advice which Bradley himself has given us that criticism in order to be effective ought to show that the starting-point of the view criticised is untenable, and the principle of development from that starting-point, together with its result, unsound.

(a) Of the two alternatives which he had before him, Bradley evidently inclined to the position that no element of physical nature " falls outside the experience of finite centres ". But what exactly did he wish to have understood by the phrase " falling within the experience of a finite centre " ? In lieu of that phrase, he was in the habit of employing a large number of equivalent expressions. He spoke of physical qualities as " passing through ", as " developed on or filtered through ", as " included in ", as " contained in ", as " entering into ", as " one part of " finite centres of feeling ; yet it is far from easy to determine how much or how little these expressions are intended to imply. So much, however, is certain : he did mean to assert that, in order to be real, physical qualities must be experienced, and that, so far as finite experience is concerned, that only can be experienced which is a " state " or " occurrence " in the mind which experiences it. " Everything that in any sense, however ideal, is present in my experience may ", he averred, " loosely be called my psychical state " (*Mind*, N.S., iv. p. 3). And again, " other bodies and souls and God himself are (so far as I know them) all states of my mind, and in this sense make parts of my particular being " (*A*. 300). Here, then, I take it, we have the starting-point of Bradley's theory of experience, and its untenability is shown, I would contend, by the *impasse* to which it leads. It is truly to land us in the most hopeless predicament before the problem of knowledge to insist that since our experience consists of psychical elements, states of mind, whatsoever is known or experienced by us must likewise be a state of our mind, a part of our particular being. For a finite centre, *as an existent,* is necessarily shut up, like everything else in the world, to its own components or constituents, and what transcends it, *i.e.*, any existent other than it, cannot be *in* it ; although the ordinary naïve notion would seem to be that the mind, as it were, goes out of itself and literally lays hold of things, or throws its net over them. Feelings, processes of knowing and willing—these are the components of the individual mental life, and they have an existence of their own—a mode of existence that is both numerically and generically distinct from that of " things " or of other mental lives. By *means of* certain of these processes—those called cognitive—the finite centre in which they occur is, or appears to be, made aware of the

being and nature of existents other than himself. Yet
neither has this finite centre any magical facility of drawing
these into himself, nor have they any such facility of " passing through " him. In point of fact, it is this separation, this
distinctness of existence, that furnishes the *raison d'être* of
knowledge and gives to it its scope and function. Knowing
bears in its very heart, so to speak, a reference to that which
is other than itself ; it is, on the face of it, impossible that
there should be knowledge without this separation between
knowing and that which is known. It is an antithesis, in
other words, involved in the very notion of knowledge itself.
Now, *in a sense*, Bradley not only acknowledged but insisted upon this antithesis. He points out, for instance, that
the " true existence " of my horse or of my own body is not
that which is present *in* my mind, but rather that which is
present *to* it (*A*. 301). Yet he immediately proceeds to
nullify the whole force of that observation by following it up
with the assertion that " their existence is a content which
works apart from, and is irreconcilable with, its own psychical being ; it is a ' what ' discrepant with and transcending its ' that ' ' ". Taken literally, the statement that the
existence of my horse is a content which has " broken loose "
from my psychical being is nonsensical ; my horse never
existed as part of my psychical being and could not, therefore, have " broken loose " from it! But it is, in truth, no
less nonsensical to speak of the content I am aware of, in such
a case, as having " broken loose " from my psychical being,
i.e., from my act of awareness. The only ground offered for
so enigmatical a supposition is that my horse " must, for me
at least, be nothing but ' experience ', for what I do not
' experience ', to me must be nothing ". And, to that, the
simple answer is that if by " experience " be meant the direct
awareness I have of my own psychical being and its states,
then, although my state of being aware of my horse forms
part of such " experience ", the object I am aware of does
not. I cognise the latter, I experience the former. If, on the

other hand, the term be used in a very wide and comprehensive sense, it is no doubt true that " what I do not experience must be to me nothing " ; but, in that case, the statement in no way implies that there is for me " no discoverable
fact outside of my psychical condition ".

The psychological view at which he had arrived of the
genesis of cognition from a primitive basis of immediate experience probably influenced to no inconsiderable extent
Bradley's thought upon the matter to which I have been
referring. In one of his early papers he described, in a curious
passage, what he conceived to have been the course of development. " Everything in experience is felt and is given first as
a ' this-now '. Then the content of experience separates
itself into groups, a ' me ' and a world of ' not-mes ', ideal
objects to which all is referred as adjectival. And the same
felt content is used at once to qualify both the self and the
not-self. There is first the feeling-green, then the sensation
of something-green, and of my so perceiving it. But, if these
two groups and their adjective and their relation were not
felt, they would not be experienced at all " (*Mind*, N.S., iv. p.
19). That is to say, it is assumed that, prior to the stage at
which such a judgment as that " this leaf is green " could be
made, the quality green " passes through " the finite centre
in the form of a feeling, although it " has no rest till it has
wandered to a home elsewhere " (*A*. 234). Yet nowhere, so
far as I can discover, did Bradley offer any proof of the existence of a huge number of qualitatively distinct " feelings "
of this character, nor do I think that the slightest warrant for
supposing them to exist is to be obtained from psychological
investigation.

(b) Although himself of opinion that the qualities we call
sensible all require to be " filtered through " finite centres,
Bradley, as we have seen, allowed it to be possible that some
sensible qualities exist and are perceived without such mediation. How the " merging " and " re-absorption " of such
qualities in the Absolute is effected we are, it is true, wholly

unable to say, and still less, it should be added, how, under such circumstances, perception of them is possible ; but, it is pointed out, to be inexplicable is one thing and to be incompatible is another. The question I would now raise is, however, whether sentience as characterising the Absolute is not incompatible with sentience in the form in which it has been described as characterising finite centres. It seems to me clearly to be so. For it has all along been assumed that finite feeling centres are only to be met with in connexion with bodily organisms. " Feelings and ideas ", it is declared, " neither act nor exist independent of body " (*A*. 335). An organism, a more or less permanent arrangement of qualities and relations, subserves, it is maintained, each distinct unity of feeling (or, perhaps, in certain cases, several distinct unities of feeling) ; and is connected, immediately and specially, with pleasure and pain, and, again, with sensations and volitions, as nothing else can be. And a theory is propounded of the relation of mind and body according to which every state of mind goes along with a state of body, and what we have is, in fact, always an event with two sides or aspects, the psychical and the physical, inseparably conjoined. It is true that soul acting or existing in separation from body is a thing which is possible ; but the idea is discarded as that of a merely idle possibility, since there is not the smallest reason for supposing a soul of that sort to exist. What, accordingly, are we to make of the notion of the Absolute as a " whole of sentience "? Not only is it maintained that the Absolute does not consist of finite centres, that these as such are there " transmuted " and have lost their individual character, but it is conceded that there may be a margin of physical qualities that find their way to absorption without the mediation of finite sentience, and insisted that what by us is thought of only must be for the Absolute sensible reality. Is, then, the Absolute to be conceived as having an organism in any way comparable to the organisms of finite centres? Bradley would certainly have dismissed such a suggestion as sheer nonsense. But if it be so, one is surely entitled to ask, why describe the Absolute as sentient experience at all? We were bidden at the start to find any piece of existence, anything that could possibly be called a fact, which did not consist in sentience ; and now in the end it turns out that nothing for the Absolute can consist in sentience, in that sense of the term in which we were called upon to produce a fact which did not consist of sentience. One thing, at any rate, is obvious. The consideration that " though unperceived by finite souls all Nature would enter into one experience with the content of these souls " affords no reason for regarding the " one experience " as sentient. For a finite soul's experience is sentient in so far, and only in so far, as its way of contact with reality is through a " limited aperture ", through the felt " this " ; and we are expressly told (*A*. 253) that we are not justified in insisting on the window-frame's rigidity, that it has, as such, no existence in reality, but only in our impotence. So that it would seem as though even the experience of a finite centre when absorbed and merged in the Absolute would lose its sentient character. In any case, it requires to be observed that an " intuitive experience " need not necessarily be a " sentient experience ".

5. A similar conclusion is forced upon us from another set of considerations. Bradley had, in truth, burnt all his boats before he came to treat of the degree of reality that can be assigned to physical nature. Lapse of time and the passage of events, succession and change, separation of one element from another and inter-relation between them— these, as he fully recognised, are the most general and unmistakable characters exhibited by that physical nature with which we, as finite centres, are familiar. But, in the well-known chapters of the first book of *Appearance and Reality*, these features were shown one and all to be illusory appearances ; each evinced itself as riddled by discrepancies and contradictions and was accordingly condemned as unreal. In regard to time and temporal occurrences, Bradley was par-

ticularly emphatic. " At a touch ", he averred, " time falls apart and proclaims itself illusory ". It is " the false appearance of a timeless reality ", and " it proclaims its unreality by its inconsistent attempt to be an adjective of the timeless ". It must be " thoroughly transmuted ", " counterbalanced and, as such, lost within an all-inclusive harmony ". Succession must be banished " as something without rights and as mere appearance ". Change is a fact, but a fact which is as such irreconcilable with the Absolute ; and, if we could not in any way perceive how this fact can be unreal, we should be placed in a fatal dilemma.

What, however, becomes of the dictum that " a physical world, to be real, must clearly be sensible " (*A*. 277), when taken in conjunction with these contentions? I do not mean merely that spatial and temporal properties are essential characteristics of everything in nature that we sensuously apprehend, and that without them a sensible physical world would seem to be a contradiction in terms. This difficulty is doubtless sufficiently formidable to raise the issue, whether if the sense world in order to find a place in Reality must be so "transmuted" and "re-composed" as to have these features eliminated and removed, that does not imply that sentience has itself been so " transformed " and " suppressed' as to render the statement that the being of Reality consists in sentient experience paradoxical. But the difficulty I would press goes, perhaps, more nearly to the root of the matter. Bradley admitted, namely, that " assuredly everything psychical is an event " (*A*. 52) ; he admitted that my thinking, feeling and willing are all events which happen (*A*. 259) ; he admitted that a finite centre of feeling is subject to perpetual change (*e.g.*, *T*. 163), and that psychical existence consists of a series of mental states causally connected (*A*. 333 *sqq.*). In short, a finite centre is confessedly an appearance, and the feeling or sentience of which it consists, its experience namely, is likewise appearance, and therefore unreal. And yet he maintained that " being and reality are one thing with sentience"; that "they can neither be opposed to, nor, even in the end, distinguished from it" (*A*. 146). How can Reality be indissolubly one thing with that which has evinced itself as, in all its essential features, unreal, false and illusory? It is true we are asked to conceive of a totality of sentient experience where feeling and thought and will are harmonious and at one. It is even urged that finite centres of feeling, each possessing a nature of its own, may surely come together and be fused in the Absolute ; and that, so far from such a resolution being impossible, it seems most natural and easy (*A*. 227). Yet how such coming together and fusion can be supposed to obliterate and destroy their character as consisting of temporal events one is at a loss to understand ; and perhaps still more how, if it does, what remains can still be said to be feeling and sentience, thought and volition.

There are manifest, in fact, throughout Bradley's treatment two conflicting views of the relation of appearance to reality, although he never seemed to realise that they are conflicting, and thus he had the advantage of being able to appeal now to the one and now to the other. On the one hand, he is constantly to be found insisting on the "illusory", "self-contradictory", "essentially inconsistent", "irrational" and "unreal" character of appearances. And when this view of them is uppermost, he uses language which implies that in the Absolute they become "suppressed", "lost" and "destroyed", "swallowed up" and "dissolved", so "transcended" and "blended" and "transformed" that they "vanish" as such and "disappear". "We have", he wrote, "an all-pervasive transfusion with a re-blending of all material. And we can hardly say that the Absolute consists of finite things, when the things, as such, are there transmuted and have lost their individual natures" (*A*. 529). In this reference, the doctrine of "degrees of reality" furnishes no help. The whole phenomenal world, in all its grades, would seem to be engulfed in one common "bankruptcy" and "ruin". Physical nature, as we have seen, is declared to be " a mere con-struction for science " and to possess " a very partial reality ". But finite centres are in no better case. As against the sug-gestion that in the Absolute they may be considered to per-sist as such and to be merely ordered and arranged, it is urged that " not like this is the final destiny and last truth of things " (A. 529). The " process of correction " which finite centres must undergo may, it is contended, " entirely dissi-pate their nature ". On the other hand, Bradley was no less persistent in his contention that " Reality itself is nothing at all apart from appearances ", that they are " its revelations ", that " each contributes and is essential to the unity of the whole ", and that " in the Absolute no appearance can be lost ". " We do not know ", he asserted, " how all these partial unities come together in the Absolute, but we may be sure that the content of not one is obliterated " (A. 204). All the various aspects of experience, it is argued, imply one another and point to a unity which comprehends and perfects them. Somehow even the diversity of the material world enters, in all its fulness, into the life of the Universe and is included therein. In fine, Bradley argued as though appear-ances, notwithstanding the drastic transmutation and disso-lution to which they must submit when they come together in the Absolute, might still, as constituents of limited portions of the whole, preserve their distinctive character ; and, within those limited portions, play no less real a part than they would play did they preserve their distinctive character in the Whole as such.

6. Bradley's philosophy may be said to turn upon the notion of a radical difference—a difference amounting to a violent contrast—between the things of ordinary experience (using this term now in its wider significance) and the superior kind of being which he ascribes to the Absolute. The things of ordinary experience had, in his view, the mark of inferiority, the stamp of deficient reality, in that they are mutable, entangled in a network of relations, and

immersed in the stream of time. That which is ultimately real, that which enjoys fulness of being, has the counter-marks of timelessness and unchangeability. And he conceived that the knowledge we obtain of each of these two realms of being displays a corresponding mode of difference. Of the relative and the transitory there can by the very nature of the case be no strict and adequate knowledge. Physical science, the province of which falls within the sphere of phenomena, does not aim at absolute truth ; its concepts are not intended to set out the true character of Reality. The ideas with which it works—those of matter, motion, force and the like—are but working ideas, useful for the purpose of finding out the ways in which temporal phenomena are connected and happen, but inconsistent and worthless if they are supposed to accomplish more. All thinking that moves, as scientific thinking does, by the machinery of terms and relations can be no other than a " makeshift, a device, a mere practical compromise, most necessary but in the end most indefensible ". On the other hand, our comprehension of the Absolute may be miserably partial and incomplete, but it is certain and real knowledge so far as it goes. Here, at least, we can apply with confidence the principle that " what *may* be, if it also *must* be, assuredly *is* ".

A view of this sort, not, indeed, new in philosophical inquiry, implying as it does a complete and irremovable difference between the Absolute and the Relative, cannot be regarded as either satisfactory in itself or sufficiently satisfying to induce acceptance except on irrefragable grounds. To represent metaphysical thinking as different in *kind* from the thinking that is exemplified in the special sciences does violence to the demand we seem entitled to make on thought, that its mode of attaining truth shall exhibit unity of principle and of method. And, if that demand be justified, metaphysics would appear to be distinguished from the special sciences not by reason of difference in the nature of its subject-matter nor yet by the employment of an altogether different set of concepts, but rather by the greater generality, the more fundamental nature, of its problems and of the solutions it offers. In each of the special sciences the chief aim is to reach grounds or reasons which will explain a multitude of specific facts ; and it is not, I think, wide of the mark to assert that the attempt to work further *in the same direction*, the attempt to explain the concepts which the sciences employ, leads to metaphysics. But the work of science would be rendered theoretically barren and nugatory, and the use that metaphysics could make of its results would be negligible, if in any case the " truths " which science claims to have established are to be pronounced " make-shifts " and merely useful " devices ", and if the facts it claims to have discovered require to be thoroughly " transmuted " and " fused " and " blended " in order to be regarded as " real ".

One other word in conclusion. Throughout this essay I have been engaged in criticising adversely, though not, I hope, unfairly, one portion of Bradley's philosophy—a portion, it is true, which is fundamentally related to his system as a whole. And I am bound to confess that in regard to his system as a whole much of the criticism I have been urging seems to me to be fatal. But, however that may be, Bradley's work, both his constructive and his critical work, will, I am convinced, survive as a great effort of human speculation.

VII

THE DYNAMIC ASPECT OF NATURE

1. *Force, in the popular acceptation of the term, not a subjective phenomenon ;*
2. *Nor exclusively based upon physiological conditions.*
3. *Force and Energy in the physical world.   Matter and Force inseparable.*
4. *Modern Atomic Theories and the Concept of Energy.*
5. *General Theory of Relativity and the Forces of Nature.*

1

FIFTY years ago a somewhat lively controversy was being waged as to the exact significance of the term " force " in physical science. Some physicists, notably in this country Tait, of Edinburgh, maintained that there was no such objective reality as " force ", that the term " force " was merely a convenient name for expressing a certain rate of change, the rate of change of momentum, understanding by " momentum " the product of the mass moving into the velocity with which it moves. " Force " ought no more to be regarded as an actual fact than the bank rate of interest (be it two, three or four per cent.) ought to be looked upon as a sum of money, or than the birth-rate of a country ought to be looked upon as the actual group of children born in a year.[1]

That the protest which this contention embodied had a certain measure of justification may be at once conceded. The way in which the term " force " had come to be employed in physical science was no less a scandal than the way in which the term " faculty ", against which Locke inveighed, had come to be employed in psychology. " Accelerating force ", " centrifugal force ", " polarising force ", " vital force ", and a host of others, were freely spoken of as though

[1] *Nature*, vol. xiv, p. 459 *sqq.*, and *Recent Advances in Physical Science*, p. 338 *sqq.*

they were substantive powers, performing functions in the world similar to those performed by the spirits and deities of primitive cultures. Too frequently it had become the fashion to fall back upon these occult agencies for explanation of natural events when other explanation failed—a mode of procedure which reached, perhaps, its culmination in Herbert Spencer's *First Principles*, where " force " appears as " the ultimate of ultimates "—a sort of almighty potentate, directing from without the affairs of the universe.

Nevertheless, I doubt whether it has ever been possible for the physicist to adhere consistently to the use of the term " force " as signifying " the rate of change of momentum " or " the rate of doing work per unit of length ". Tait himself did not succeed in doing so. While insisting with peculiar vehemence upon the definition just quoted, he is constantly to be found making use of the term in the very sense which he had deprecated. Following Newton, he attributed to " force " any change whether in the direction or in the rate of motion of a body. He asserted that " the longer a given force acts the greater will be the change of momentum which it produces ", and in reference to " a certain force acting through a certain distance ", he spoke of the possibility of calculating how much work it will do. That is to say, within the compass of a few pages " force " is declared, on the one hand, to be the agent which does work or changes the rate of motion[1]; and, on the other hand, to be the rate at which some other agent does the work or changes the rate of motion. It is little short of nonsense to plead in excuse that in the former case the term " force " is merely a convenient symbol employed to shorten what would otherwise be a cumbrous mode of ex-

---

[1] *Cf.* Thomson and Tait's *Natural Philosophy*, vol. i, § 183. " *Force* is any cause which tends to alter a body's natural state of rest or of uniform motion in a straight line." Force, it is said, " is wholly expended in the *Action* it produces ", and " may be of divers kinds, as pressure, or gravity, or friction, or any of the attractive or repulsive actions of electricity, magnetism, etc." And again (§ 185), " the *measure of a force* is the quantity of motion it produces in unit of time."

pression. As an affair of terminology it matters not at all whether the term be used in the one sense or in the other. What does matter is that if the latter usage be adopted it shall not be assumed that the reality of that which had been denoted by the former has been *thereby* disposed of. No gain to accuracy, the *sine quâ non*, as Tait affirmed, of all science, can accrue by confusing that which is measured with a way of measuring it.

In point of fact Dr. Broad is, I think, clearly right in denying that anyone " ever does *mean*, or ever has *meant*, by ' force ' rate of change of momentum ".[1] No doubt the perceptive experience from which the scientific concept of " force " was originally derived can be safely said to be the familiar experience of the initiation of movement by us as living beings. The primitive representation of such a situation is crudely anthropomorphic ; the agency is taken to be the agency of the conscious subject. By degrees, however, what may fairly enough be called the mechanical side of the transaction comes to be distinguished from the subjective aspect. The latter comes to be regarded as that in which intention or purpose is prevailingly manifested, while the former comes to be closely connected with bodily effort, the change produced being vaguely thought of as the overcoming of resistance by muscular energy.

On the strength of considerations such as these Professor Tait contended, as so many others have done, that the experience of strain or tension is purely a subjective phenomenon, that we have no warrant for supposing that strain or tension is a real property of physical nature. To vision the universe appears to be filled with light and colour, although reason, as he thought, convinces us that what we understand by brightness, etc., does not exist outside our minds, that the sensation of colour is subjective, the only difference possible between different so-called rays of light outside the eye being simply in the extent, form and rapidity of the vibrations of

[1] *Scientific Thought*, p. 162.

M

the luminiferous medium. In like manner, so he would have us conclude, when the muscular sense induces us to believe that the body is exerting power, as in pushing and pulling, or when we resist the impetus of a gust of wind, we ought to guard ourselves from the anthropomorphism of attributing the strain or tension which we feel to the external world. When the earth attracts, as we say, a stone, it cannot be conscious of exerting effort, nor can the stone be conscious of being pulled.

So far as secondary qualities are concerned I have tried to show that the doctrine which this distinguished scientist accepted as indisputable will not bear the test of critical scrutiny. I have tried to show, further, that a perfectly intelligible and coherent account of the process of perception can be given when colours, sounds, etc., are regarded as characteristics of natural objects, and that strong reasons can, in fact, be furnished for holding that they are characteristics of natural objects. If they are, then obviously the analogy which Professor Tait sought to constitute makes for a conclusion very different from that which he, in common with numerous other writers, would have us draw. He committed, it seems to me, the fallacy of assuming that because vibratory motions give rise to, or condition, our acts of perceiving colours and sounds, these vibratory motions must be the equivalents in the external world of the colours or sounds which we perceive. But that, as we have seen, does not follow—not, at least, until the possibility has been ruled out that both vibratory motions and sense-qualities may be comprised in a natural object, the former conditioning the occurrence of the act of perception, the latter forming part of the content perceived. And what I am desirous first of all of maintaining on the present occasion is that, because we become aware of strain or tension through muscular sensibility, it likewise does not follow that the strain or tension of which we are aware must be subjective in character.

Let me dwell for a moment upon the analogy to which I

have been alluding. As it is requisite to distinguish the *act of perceiving* a colour from the *colour perceived*, so it is requisite to distinguish the *act of perceiving* a strain from the *strain perceived*, or, as Dr. Broad expresses it, our *feeling of strain* from the *strain which we feel*. Manifestly it is absurd to identify " force " with the *feeling* of strain, for in no sense in which we use the term " force " can the feeling of strain be said to be a " force ". But we are no more debarred on that account from maintaining that the strains which we perceive or feel are " forces ", or indications of " forces ", than we are debarred from asserting that the content which we perceive when gazing at a certain object is blue because the act of perceiving it is not blue. Here I cannot do better than borrow Dr. Broad's illustration. Unless, after the manner of Plato or Fechner, we suppose the heavenly bodies to have minds or souls, it is clearly ridiculous to imagine that the sun is conscious of a strain when it pulls the earth. It is ridiculous, as Dr. Broad says, not because the sun could not be exposed to a strain, but because, presuming it to have no mind, it could not be conscious of anything, and not, therefore, conscious of a strain. Consequently, there is no incongruity in describing " forces " as the sort of entities which we become aware of in and through our perception or feeling of strain or effort, nor in asserting that physical bodies, such as the sun, are influenced by and exert " force " in this sense. In other words, there is no more reason for identifying tension or strain with the consciousness of it than for identifying colours or sounds with the consciousness of those colours or sounds. Not only so. Dr. Broad presses, I think successfully, the further point that on the view one is opposing it would be no less unreasonable to say that a physical body, such as the earth, is round or rotates, than to say that it is subject to the strains or stresses which are what we ordinarily mean by " forces ". For the concepts which we form of roundness or of rotation are, after all, grounded upon the particular instances of these universals which we apprehend through means of sight and touch. Without sense-experience of round objects the meaning of the term roundness would be as completely hidden from us as the meaning of the term blueness is hidden from a man born blind. " The person who uses the argument about the sun not feeling strains, as an objection to the view that the feeling of strain is the sensational experience which gives a meaning to the concept of force, may ", writes Dr. Broad, " be invited to consider the following parallel argument : ' How can the concept of roundness be based on our sense-perceptions of sight and touch when the earth, which can neither see nor feel, is admitted to be round?' " And, as he says, " the answer, of course, is that the earth *has* the sort of properties which we have become acquainted with by seeing and feeling, and that it does not need to see or feel in order to have those properties ". Just, then, as the earth has the properties of being round and of rotating without being conscious that it has them, so it may be subject to forces of which it is not conscious, and these forces may be the sort of entities of which we become aware in and through our perceptions or feelings of strain.[1] It is, in short, a gross blunder to confuse " force " with the awareness of force.

I should be prepared, indeed, to carry the argument further, and to dispute altogether the legitimacy of conceiving the mind or the " self " as being either subject to strain, in the sense in which that term is used of material things, or as putting forth energy. The doctrine that in what is called the " will " there is to be found the prototype of what is ordinarily meant by " force ", and that even in mature experience the " will " is the one and only " force " with which we are immediately acquainted, has long been current in certain modes of philosophising. " In willing ", we are often told, " we feel that we are active ; we are aware of exerting energy, and we know it directly ". The so-called " sense of effort " is accordingly pointed to as the essential factor in volition, and

[1] *op. cit.*, p. 163.

this is supposed to yield the information that the " ego " is
pre-eminently the seat of force, which operates upon what is
contained in the realm of the " non-ego " and initiates
changes therein. Nothing, it has been said, sooner brings
home to one the poise and counterpoise between self and
nature than the attempt to shut a door against a furious
wind.[1] If, however, the " self " be regarded as in this sense
an efficient agent there still remains the task of showing how,
in that case, the conscious subject comes to be aware of itself
as this agent. And not only has that task not been fulfilled,
but I think we may safely predict it never will be. It has,
for instance, been contended that, while it is in the act of
willing that the self has existence, yet the self is cognised as a
self only in so far as there is a felt opposition of the muscles
to its activity. In the experience of voluntary movement, so
it appears to be thought, there is supplied a pure inner perception both of the body and of the mental agent that operates through means of the body ; and, somehow, in the duality of will-force and muscular resistance, out of which self-
consciousness is supposed to spring, the ego is revealed to
itself as the originator of the act through which it becomes
known.[2] But can a shred of evidence be furnished of our
having any consciousness, even the vaguest, of a situation
such as is here depicted? Can we, indeed, form so much as
an intelligible conception of the activity of the self being
opposed by the resistance or the organic inertia of the
muscles? In spite, however, of an assumption so extraordinary, it has to be admitted[3] that the contraction of the
muscles is due to the stimulus of the efferent nerves, and then
it is alleged that the volitional force acts upon the latter,
although the awareness of such force only arises through the
kinaesthetic sensations attendant upon the muscular contraction. So that, according to this account, it turns out,

[1] Martineau, *A Study of Religion*, vol. i, p. 199.
[2] *Œuvres inédites de Maine de Biran*, tome i, p. 204 *sqq.*
[3] *ibid.*, p. 212.

after all, that the " sense of effort " is no revelation of will-
force, but that the supposed revelation is, as Bradley
would have said, " an intellectual construction " which may
quite well evince itself as " a thorough misinterpretation "
of the facts.[1] Or, to take a less crude mode of dealing with
the matter, it has been contended that in all voluntary
activity there is, in Professor Baldwin's phraseology, " an
earlier fiat than the will to move, and that is the fiat of
attention to the particular idea of movement " ; that, in
truth, even in muscular exertion, the real " effort " is to be
found in " attending " to the idea. Without seeking to un-
earth the mysteries covered by the term " fiat ", I will content myself with urging two considerations : (a) Apart from
the circumstance that the " feeling of effort " is not always
present in voluntary attention, careful observation has
brought to light the fact that in cases where it is present
attention usually starts before the " feeling of effort " makes
its appearance, and that when the process of attending
attains its highest degree of efficiency the " feeling of effort "
dies away. One would conclude, therefore, that so far from
being a condition of attention it is rather a concomitant,
more or less variable, of the process, and that it by no means
belongs to its essence. (b) It is evident, I think, that the
content we are aware of in the experience described as the
" feeling of effort " is composite in character. It involves

---

[1] In the present instance it is easy to show that it is a misinterpretation of
the facts. De Biran argued that we come to distinguish voluntary action
from instinctive or involuntary movements on account of the unique
character of the kinaesthetic sensations attendant upon the former. In the
case of involuntary movements, the kinaesthetic sensations have a passive
character which reflects the mode of their origin ; in the case of voluntary
movements, on the other hand, the kinaesthetic sensations take on a character of " reduplication " whereby we are enabled to be conscious of (a) the
inertia of the muscles, and (b) the volitional force which causes their contraction. But (i) there is, in fact, no such difference between kinaesthetic
sensations in the two cases : (ii) confessedly contraction of the muscles
comes about through nervous impulse, and if there be resistance on their part
it must be to these impulses ; and (iii) muscular movement is certainly taken
by the conscious subject, in the great majority of cases, not to be opposed
to what seems to him to be his volitional activity but to be part of it.

certainly the awareness of a subjective motive and the idea of
an objective change to be produced. The direct experience
which we may legitimately assume as lying at its basis is no
doubt that which through kinaesthetic sensations we obtain
of what is happening in contracted muscles, stretched liga-
ments and so on.[1] When these constituents are removed,
we may well inquire, with Bradley, what is left of the consciousness of effort put forth? In short, I cannot see that the
content of which in these experiences we are aware gives us
any direct information of the condition of ourselves in such
awareness, for we have no more reason for thinking that the
consciousness of strain or effort is itself a condition of the
strain or effort than we have for thinking that the consciousness of blue is a condition of blue being there in front of us.[2]

Let me not be misunderstood. Nothing could be farther
from my purpose than to imply that willing is not an active
process. Every state of mind, be it of the cognitive or of the
conative type, is, I should agree, essentially a state of activity. None the less, it seems to me a manifest error to as-
similate mental activity to that kind of activity which we
ordinarily ascribe to material things, to suppose that " feeling
and cognition operate as psychical forces which are analogous to physical forces, except that the latter involve spatial
relations ".[3] For, on the one hand, the mental life, the psychical continuant (in W. E. Johnson's phraseology), is obviously not made up, as a material body is, of discrete particles in
various conditions of agitation. A rough illustration may be
permissible. When a horse pulls a cart, we speak of the horse

---

[1] *Cf.* W. James, *Collected Essays and Reviews*, p. 151 *sqq.*, and *Principles of
Psychology*, chapter xxvi. Also Bergson, *Essai sur les données*, p. 16 *sqq.*

[2] *Cf.* my paper on " The Nature of Willing " (*Proceedings of Aristotelian
Society*, N.S., vol. xiii, pp. 57-58), where I have sought to show that, from
what we are able to lay down concerning the development of self-consciousness, it is readily explicable how the effort or strain of which we are conscious
has come, in our mature experience, to wear for us the appearance of self-
activity.

[3] W. E. Johnson, *Logic*, part iii, p. 104. Cf. *Proceedings of Aristotelian
Society*, N.S., vol. x, 1910, p. 269 *sqq.*

as active, as exerting force, meaning that the initiation of the cart's movement is due to the horse's pull. But we cannot point to separable entities in the stream of mental process, one of which may thus be said to act and the other to be acted upon. Psychical causality, assuming we are justified in using that expression, is, at any rate, causality of a kind very different from that of physical causality. And, on the other hand, the relation of the mental act to its object in no way involves that the object is exposed to any exertion of force or energy on the part of the mind. The object is neither attracted nor repelled, nor, so far as is discoverable, in any way affected, by an act of apprehension being directed upon it. In volition, it is true, the mental act culminates, or may do, in the conversion of a *faciendum* into a *factum*, but the actual conversion is effected by the bodily and other physical mechanism. In short, there is no evidence either of one mental state acting upon another mental state or of the mind acting upon matter in a manner at all analogous to that in which one physical entity acts, or appears to act, upon another physical entity.

2

Thus far our argument has been directed to making good the position that " force " or " energy ", as ordinarily understood, is invariably something of which we are conscious, and is wrongly taken to be something either inherent in or characterising the mental life itself. But, even if this position be sound, it does not, of course, necessarily follow that what we are in such experiences conscious of is a veritable constituent, as it appears to be, of physical reality. For our apprehension is liable in various ways to error ; and, although we may have excluded the possibility that the error, if in this case there is one, is due to the importation of a subjective feature into the content of what we take to be the physical world, we have not excluded the possibility of our having, from other reasons, misinterpreted what is presented to us.

I shall attempt presently to point to positive grounds for
thinking that we are not in this connexion misinterpreting
the facts ; but, before proceeding, it will be well to say something in reference to an objection that may at this stage be
pressed.

" Granted that ' force ' or ' energy ' is a content cognised
and not a condition of psychical existence as such, yet it may
still be true," so it might be urged, " that ' force ' or ' energy ',
as thus cognised, is a purely bodily phenomenon, and that
except where physiological processes are in operation is not
present in nature." Now, it has, no doubt, at once to be admitted that, in the experience of tension or strain, what
through kinaesthetic sensations we are *immediately* conscious
of is usually a series of happenings or occurrences in the
muscles, tendons and other tissues of the body. But these
are, of course, material structures, parts of a complex material system, which is in its turn a part of the immense
material system with which physical science is concerned.
Those physiologists who, like Professor J. S. Haldane, insist
that the living organism is not merely a physical and chemical mechanism would not question the truth of the proposition that the contraction and relaxation of muscular tissue
is due to the strains and stresses in the constituent fibres of
which it is composed. Even though relaxation and contraction as they occur in living tissue are subject to guidance and
control of a special kind, yet the mechanism by means of
which such relaxation or contraction is effected differs, it
would be conceded, in no essential way from the mechanism
of inorganic substances. Compress a liquid or a compressible
solid, and you are conscious of *its* exerting a force of expan-
sion which decreases as the compression is allowed to decrease. Stretch between your two hands an elastic band,
and you are conscious of *its* exerting a force of contraction
which likewise decreases as the extension is allowed to decrease. I can find no more ground for supposing that these
strains and stresses are intra-organic phenomena and not pro-

perties of the things they appear to be properties of than for supposing that the movements of the things in question are not their own movements but movements of ours in respect to them. It is true that strains and stresses cannot be apprehended through the organ of sight, while movement can be. Yet, what of that? While no one need be concerned to dispute the tremendous part played by vision in the building up of our knowledge, it would be attributing to it an altogether extravagant pre-eminence over the other senses to regard it as having a monopoly in revealing the characteristics of the external world. Were our experience limited to visual experience, even though supplemented by hearing and organic sensation, the objective scene might present for us a panorama of successive appearances (though I do not think it would) ; but, without the experience of pressure and resistance, we should assuredly obtain no conception of either matter or causality. I agree with Bradley that the experience of resistance is a secondary product, and that it is absurd to find in resistance the one manifestation of reality [1]; but the fact that it is not the sole manifestation of reality does not prevent it from contributing its share to that manifestation. And it is, I take it, certain that visual apprehension would be a vastly less efficient mode of cognising than it actually is had it not been developed on the basis of the experience acquired through motor and muscular sensibility.

The supposition that what we are cognisant of as " force " or " energy " is confined to organic phenomena would, it seems to me, necessitate a theory of vitalism, cruder and more untenable than any hitherto suggested. The advocates of a " vital force " or " vital principle " have not hesitated to make use of physical and chemical explanations of physiological processes so far as they could ; they have invariably taken for granted, namely, that the " forces " and " modes of energy ", differentiated by the physicist, are actually

[1] *Appearance and Reality*, second edition, pp. 116 and 225.

operative in organic structures and account for a great number of the processes which these structures exhibit. Their contention has been that over and above these there is an autonomy of the living organism which is not physically explicable. And, consequently, they have assumed the presence in the living organism of a non-physical influence which co-ordinates, regulates and guides the chemical and physical processes. Professor Haldane's criticism of this view [1] will be sufficiently familiar and I am not now concerned to discuss it. But its difficulties, already formidable, would surely be enhanced, and its unphysiological character be made at once apparent, if it were understood to imply that what we are conscious of as stress and strain is, in truth, rightly attributable to " vital force " alone and wrongly extended by us to processes in the inorganic world.

3

There is, of course, no direct way of proving that strain and stress as we are conscious of them are actual factors of physical nature any more than there is a direct way of proving that colours and sounds are. We can but proceed indirectly, first by showing, if we can, that other and alternative modes of explaining their presence in experience are unsatisfactory and then by attempting to show that those physical theories which either assume or are compatible with the objective reality of these factors are on the whole more coherent and true to fact than those which are incompatible therewith.

That the conception of force is not ultimately a very important one in mechanics, and that the main advantage of retaining it there is for the purpose of making general statements, is no doubt true [2] and is not in the least surprising.

[1] See, for example, *Mechanism, Life and Personality*, p. 24 *sqq.*

[2] C. D. Broad, *Scientific Thought*, p. 167. " You may regard the laws of motion as being expressed by equations, with force on one side and rate of change of momentum on the other. You may regard the special laws of nature as being expressed by equations, with forces on one side and the special configurations, electric charges, magnetic properties, etc., of the

The fundamental law of mechanics, which states how masses move under the influence of given forces, is, as Professor Weyl expresses it, simply a blank schema, which acquires a concrete content only when the concept of force appearing in it is filled in by physics. " The unfortunate attempts which have been made to develop mechanics into an independent science have not ", he says, " been able to help themselves out except by converting the fundamental law into the merely verbal statement that force *signifies* mass × acceleration ".[1] On the other hand, in any particular sphere of physical phenomena, such as that of electrostatics, the investigator is, he urges, confronted with the fact of force, and sees how it is determined from the phase-quantities, charge and field, according to a definite law. Assuming that what we directly observe is the motion of matter, it is, he insists, only this entire network of theoretical considerations that is susceptible of experimental proof.

Modern physics takes its rise, I suppose it may be said, from Faraday's striking and characteristic conception of " lines of force ". Profoundly influenced by the atomic theory of Boscovich, Faraday's mind was imbued with the idea that the space surrounding a body was filled with what he named the " force " which that body could communicate to other bodies ; and he clearly enunciated the view, upon which in recent years Professor Whitehead has so strongly insisted, that an atom is not confined to the infinitesimal portion of space where its material is supposed to be, but that it extends wherever its action extends. In his great paper " On Static Induction " [2] he concentrated attention on the dielectric, the non-conducting medium surrounding electric circuits, and localised the phenomena that occurred mainly

bodies that you are dealing with, on the other. Thus you might just as well express the facts by a single set of equations, directly connecting the configurations, charges, etc., with the change of momentum, and drop the mention of force altogether."

[1] *Raum, Zeit, Materie*, 4te Aufl., p. 60.

[2] *Experimental Researches*, vol. i, p. 360 *sqq.*

in it, not in the conductors as it had been customary to do.
He pictured the space surrounding electric and magnetic
bodies as filled with " lines of force ", resembling those revealed by iron filings in the presence of a magnet, each " line
of force " being conceived as a closed curve that at some part
of its length passed through the particular magnet or electro-
magnet in question.   And a " line of force " could be regarded
as forming the axis of what he named a " tube of force ",
which was so constituted that the product of its cross-section
into the magnetic force was constant along its entire length.
There cannot be the least doubt that to Faraday, at any rate,
these lines and tubes of force involved that stress and strain
were objectively real, and as such fundamental aspects of
nature.   His truly epoch-making discovery of the action of
magnetism upon light-rays enabled him, as he put it, to
" illuminate " the lines of magnetic force.

Then came later, and through the labours of many investigators, the development of the doctrine of energy, anticipated in some measure by Faraday's reiterated belief that
" the various forms under which the forces of matter are
made manifest have one common origin ".   It was partly due
to the circumstance that the steam-engine was coming into
general use, and to recognition of its value as being propor-
tional to the work it could do—in other words, the distance
through which it could move a body against a definite
amount of resistance—that, in England at any rate, the
term " energy " came to be substituted for the term " force "
in many of the senses that Faraday had employed the latter
term.   Energy was defined as " the power of doing work, in
whatever that power may consist ", and work as a transference of energy from one system to another.   So soon as
potential energy (which, by the way, Helmholtz had named
Spannkraft) had been distinguished from kinetic energy (first
definitely by Rankine in 1853), the principle of the conservation of energy could be formulated—a principle which Clerk
Maxwell declared to be " the one generalised statement

which is found to be consistent with fact, not in one physical science only, but in all ". While, then, Faraday conceived of electric and magnetic forces as pervading the space surrounding electric or magnetic bodies, Clerk Maxwell likewise conceived of energy, that by which the bodies in question could do work, as pervading this space or, in some way, stored up in it. Probably he reasoned in some such wise as this. A body, we say, is acted upon by a force, and in consequence moves so as to acquire energy. But there is as little ground for thinking that this energy is given to it immediately, without reference to the intervening space, as there is for thinking that the force acts at a distance. If, therefore, the energy must enter from the surrounding space, the energy may quite well be in the space ; and, it may be assumed, would have been there even though there had been no body to be acted upon. That a body *is* acted upon indicates, in other words, that either moving through or stored up in the space of its vicinity there is energy, ready to be imparted to it. Thus, Maxwell was led to inquire as to the amount of energy there was in the space surrounding electric and magnetic systems, and as to its distribution ; furthermore, he was enabled to determine the relation between the quantity of energy and the force that was being exerted. Not only so. He showed how it was possible to reduce all electric and magnetic phenomena to stresses and motions of a material medium—the former being energy of the potential type, existing in the form of some sort of strain in the medium ; the latter being of the kinetic type, energy of translation. In order, however, that either kind of energy should move from one body to another, or from particle to particle of the same body, it was requisite that both kinds should be present. Only when the strain of the medium had, so to speak, been relaxed could the energy be set in motion. And on investigating the rate at which the energy thus set in motion would travel in a particular case—that, namely, in which the electrical disturbances were of an alternating character—he discovered that it coincided with the rate at which light-waves travel, and was thus led to formulate the modern electro-magnetic theory of light.

Physicists, as Bradley would have said, know their own business, and when they insist upon the necessity, for their purpose, of distinguishing force and energy, it would be ridiculous for the philosopher to raise any question. Obviously if force is to be defined as the change of momentum of a body considered as depending upon its position relative to other bodies it is something very different from that which is expressed by $\frac{1}{2}mv^2$ (i.e., $mv \times v$, not $m \times v^2$). Force, in this sense, is, for example, not conserved ; on the contrary it is perpetually appearing and disappearing. Indeed, even when force is taken to be " that which alters the motion of a body ", it is still true that it is not identical with what the physicist means by energy. Two bodies tend to move towards each other, and this tendency is spoken of as the force of attraction. If the restraining influence be modified and the tendency becomes realised, the bodies in moving towards each other acquire energy. The energy acquired is not the force alone ; but the force is an ingredient of it.

The motive which weighs with physicists in now endeavouring to avoid the notion of force as that which produces change of motion is not far to seek. So soon as the equivalence of energy in its different forms and the fact of its conservation had been established the temptation was strong to confuse energy with force, in the sense just mentioned, and to conceive of force as a separate existent and matter as another separate existent, each possessing the characteristic of indestructibility. But the doctrine of energy, rightly understood, had undermined a conception of that sort. In his classical essay of 1847 Helmholtz protested against the notion of force as something *per se* that acts on matter, and acts across space, or as something lying hidden in material bodies and ready on occasion to leap out of them. " Pure matter would ", he said, " be for the rest of nature a thing of indifference, because it would never determine any change either in other matter or in our organs of sense. Pure force would be something that ought to exist and yet again ought not to exist, for the existent we call matter." In nature, he argued, neither the one nor the other of these " pure " entities is to be found ; we meet there with matter and force only in inseparable connexion.[1] It is, however, one thing to repudiate the notion of force as an entity *per se* and quite another thing to deny that force has objective reality. We are, as Helmholtz said, acquainted with matter only through its activities, but the fact that the activities are its activities does not lessen in the least their claim to be considered real.

If a distinction is to be drawn between space and that which occupies it, and no physical theory of energy has yet contrived to advance a step except on the basis of that distinction, Helmholtz's insistence upon both the duality and the inseparability of matter and force would seem to be incontrovertible. Any occupancy of space, be it even that of a single electron, involves, on the one hand, cohesion of the parts within the space occupied, and, on the other hand, exclusion of parts external to the space occupied. We cannot, that is to say, form any concept of an occupancy of space apart from the idea of mass. But cohesion between the parts of a specific occupant of space implies a mode of force—that which Newton described as *vis insita* and *vis inertiae*. Again, exclusion of parts belonging to other portions of space implies a condition of stress— what Newton described as *vis impressa*. So far Kant's thesis in the *Metaphysische Anfangsgründe der Naturwissenschaft* is justified, namely, that matter, in order to occupy space, must be endowed with the two forces of attraction and re- pulsion. When, however, Kant goes on to contend that as each part of space is infinitely divisible, so also is each part of matter occupying space infinitely divisible, his argument is, I think, inconsistent with the former position. For, if the

---

[1] *Ueber die Erhaltung der Kraft* (Ostwald's *Klassiker*), p. 4.

conditions of space-occupancy be those just indicated, it follows that we must come ultimately to a particle, such as at present an electron is taken to be, which is indivisible. The parts into which any portion of space may be divided are themselves spaces ; but the parts into which a unit occupant of space could be divided would not themselves be occupants of space, because, *ex hypothesi*, space is only occupied by their cohesion. There cannot, that is to say, be a force of attraction except between two parts at least ; so that, if the force of attraction be requisite for the material occupation of space, these two parts cannot, taken severally, be material— the minimum of matter involves their togetherness. In short, the concept of force existing, as it were, *in vacuo* is a pseudo-concept and cannot really be formed. And the concept of merely passive matter, although it may be formed, is, in truth, equally self-contradictory. The very coherence or consistence of matter, that which we apprehend as resistance, compels us to think of it as active and to guard against confusing its inertia with inertness.

4

This conclusion is borne out in a sufficiently striking manner by the revelations as to the nature of atomic structure which have been pouring in upon us during recent years. The old Democritean atom has been relegated to the keeping of the historian more unreservedly than even Helmholtz and his contemporaries could have anticipated ; and the chemical atoms of Dalton have now been shown to be not atoms in the strict sense at all but complex and loose structures, each consisting of a nucleus, wherein nearly the whole mass is concentrated, and of the much lighter electrons (or, in the case of hydrogen, of one electron) circling round it. As everyone knows, the nucleus is positively charged and the electrons are negatively charged, and thus electrical attraction plays the part in this minute system that gravitation plays in the systems with which the astronomer is concerned.

N

" Between matter, which is the atom, and non-matter, which is radiation, the electron stands ", it has been said, " as the connecting link, since it forms part of the structure of the atom on the one hand, and by its movements in the atom gives rise to radiation on the other hand." The nucleus, with the exception of the nucleus of hydrogen (called a proton), is not, like the electron, indivisible, nor is it merely a collection of protons ; there is strong evidence that it is a collection of protons and electrons. When one thinks of the incredible swiftness of the particles thrown out in radio-activity by the nucleus, one realises what enormous dynamic agencies are concentrated therein. And when one thinks of what is happening in a single undisturbed hydrogen atom, of the electron spinning round its tiny orbit at a velocity of fourteen hundred miles a second, one is surely brought face to face with the fact that here we have work going on which, as Sommerfeld expresses it, is of a quite different order of magnitude from that of other physical processes. If this does not mean that stress, tension, strain, etc., are real factors belonging to the innermost structure of nature, one is at a loss to understand what it can mean ; to look upon it all as simply " the expression of the metrics of the world " seems to be like substituting mere formulae for concrete actualities.

I have tried to show the impossibility of conceiving of force as an independent existent, and in reference to that there is no difference of opinion among present-day scientists. Clerk Maxwell was equally convinced in regard to any independent existence of energy. " Energy ", he declared, " cannot exist except in connexion with matter ", and he would, there is no doubt, have likewise affirmed the truth of the converse of this proposition. But, in recent years, an attempt has been made by an influential school of physicists to conceive of energy as the one ultimate reality of physical nature. Their contention is that the notion of a material substance has been rendered obsolete by the electron theory, that the inertia of matter has been completely superseded by the inertia of energy, that an atom, as a system of protons and electrons, possesses no material but only " electromagnetic " mass. " It is ", says Professor Weyl, " not the electromagnetic field that requires matter as its carrier in order to be able itself to exist, but on the contrary matter is an offspring of the field." And he tries to show that an electron may be looked upon as an " energy-knot "—that is to say, as a region of the field for which the field-quantities and the electrical densities assume tremendously high values —which propagates itself in empty space in a manner no different from that in which a water-wave advances over the surface of the sea, that there is no " one and the same substance " of which, at all times, the electron is composed.[1]

The view seems to me untenable for several reasons. In the first place, an " energy-knot " in which " electrical densities " are concentrated is an excessively obscure notion which seems, at any rate, to suggest that we are being given back with one hand what has been taken away with the other. The very circumstance that this " energy-knot " can be pulled back by the action of the field in a way in which other parts of the field are not pulled back would appear to indicate that we have here something which is, to say the least, very different from the rest of the field. Density multiplied by volume in space gives us mass ; but, then, what is this density and how does it come to be there? In the second place, the chief argument that is relied on does not strike me as conclusive. It is argued, namely, that while the mass of a material substance would be unchangeable, it has now been proved that the mass of an electron is not unchangeable, but that it rapidly increases when the velocity of the electron approaches the velocity of light-waves. Now, the only ground for saying that the mass of an electron changes is that when its velocity is increased the field surrounding it exerts upon it a greater pull backwards. Yet surely it might quite well do that even though the mass of the

[1] op. cit., pp. 183-184.

electron did remain constant, because the greater pull backwards may, as Professor Sheldon has suggested, be due
simply to its increased velocity. In the third place, the
positive grounds already given for holding that force is inseparably combined with matter [1] seem to me applicable here
also. Assuming that electrons and protons are atoms in the
strict sense—that is to say, are indivisible—then an electron
or a proton possesses a *cohesion* which is not a characteristic
of anything else. If it moves, it moves as a whole, and no
part of it can move while leaving the rest behind. As we
have seen, what we mean by a material entity is just this
cohesion of parts. In the case of material *aggregates*—
chemical atoms, molecules, so-called " things "—such cohesion is relative only ; the parts can be torn asunder. In
the case of an atom in the strict sense, such cohesion is
absolute ; the parts can never be torn asunder. The parts
are charged with electricity of the same kind, and should,
therefore, repel one another ; yet none the less they are
irresolvably held together. And not only is there cohesion
of parts *ad intra*, there is also exclusion of parts *ad extra*. To
use again Professor Sheldon's phraseology, two electrons
never fuse into one, neither do two protons ; indeed, an
electron never fuses with a proton, although they mutually
attract each other. What explanation can be given of this
behaviour if the electron or proton be regarded as pure energy
and nothing else? Waves of radiant energy pass through
each other repeatedly ; one and the same portion of the
electromagnetic field may be occupied at the same time with
waves moving in various directions [2] ; but electrons and protons do not pass through one another. Again, it is this exclusion of parts *ad extra*, no less than the cohesion of parts *ad*

---

[1] See *supra*, pp. 191-3.

[2] I am not unmindful of the fact that the problem of radiation energy is,
in this connexion, thrust upon us and that the question might be raised
whether, then, it at least is not energy devoid of material substance. But
if radiation energy is in the form of undulatory motion the difficulty of
dispensing with some kind of material medium is notorious.

intra, that is characteristic of material substance. In short, atomicity—discreteness—differentiates *matter* from the space which it occupies.

"Yes," it will be objected, "but is not atomicity—discreteness—a determination, as we now know, of energy?" We shall be confronted, namely, with the quantum theory, according to which radiation energy is emitted, and would seem also to be absorbed, not continuously but in definite amounts. Radiation energy goes about, that is to say, in bundles or indivisible units, any one of which contains a specific store of energy and any one of which can liberate that energy and produce an effect, yet of which no fractions are possible. But there is, so far as I can judge, nothing in this discovery, when rightly interpreted, which at all conflicts with what I have been urging. For, as Professor J. W. Nicholson once observed, the one indubitable fact of the quantum theory is Planck's constant h, and this is not a constant of energy. While the theory constrains us to think of energy as present only in quanta, yet the quantum depends in each case upon circumstances. That is to say, in any system containing energy there is a "frequency", and the energy in that system is $h\nu$ (where ν is the frequency) or some whole multiple of it, so that the real constant is the quotient of energy and frequency, or product of energy and time, a constant of what is now called "action". And this "frequency" would seem to presuppose, in Professor Nicholson's phrase, "something structural".[1] In other words, what the constant ratio between energy and frequency appears to involve is not the discontinuous nature of energy as such, but the discontinuous nature of its emission and absorption by the atoms of matter, or rather by the electrons and protons of which such atoms consist. Moreover, what has sometimes been regarded as a difficulty in the quantum theory—the discrepancy, namely, between the dis-

[1] *Cf.* supplementary vol. iv of the Aristotelian Society : *Concepts of Continuity*, 1924, pp. 22-23.

continuous process by which energy is emitted from the atom and the continuous process by which it is transmitted in the form of waves—would then at once disappear.

The attempt to conceive of energy as dissociated from material substance and to picture it as an entity *per se* appears to me invariably to lead to one of two results, either of which is in truth inconsistent with the view in question. (*a*) The dematerialisation of matter, as it has been called, has meant in the hands of some physicists that while energy is declared to be the fundamental reality of which at any rate we are aware, the properties which it has been customary to regard as the properties of matter have been transferred to a hypothetical all-pervading ether in which electrons and protons are supposed to be strains or vortex motions or singularities of some kind. In order that it should be capable of fulfilling its functions there has to be assigned to the ether a whole host of mutually exclusive characteristics. That it should not retard the motion of the heavenly bodies, it must behave as a fluid with a density less than the lightest gas, while in the neighbourhood of electrons it must have a density that is truly enormous, and yet again, in order to transmit the transverse light-vibrations, its behaviour must be that of an elastic solid, endowed with extreme rigidity. Even Sir J. J. Thomson's hypothesis of a mass-producing material made up of particles all of the same kind and excessively small compared with even an electron, these particles moving with the velocity of light and the distribution of them depending upon the number or concentration of lines of force, would seem to be an ingenious effort to reintroduce the features of which the atom has been deprived. (*b*) The other alternative culminates in what has been named the materialisation of energy. The inertia of the electron is supposed to arise from the energy accumulated around it in the form of fields. The mass of the electron is taken to be due not to any material substratum which it does not possess, but to its own energy, which constitutes its only substantial reality. In short, energy is endowed with mass and with weight in proportion thereto and with structure ; it becomes to all intents and purposes a materialised body, although matter is supposed to be dispensed with. One is reminded of a procedure of a somewhat similar kind on the part of Leibniz, who, although he insisted upon disposing of the Cartesian notion of substance and substituting for it the concept of force, was yet constrained to bring back what he had discarded in so far as he had to recognise an element of passivity within the compass of active force itself.[1]

5

I will conclude by referring to certain consequences which have been thought to follow from the general theory of relativity. It has been maintained, namely, that if the general theory of relativity be interpreted strictly, the " forces of nature " turn out to be " illusions ", and reduce to nothing more than our subjective ideas of what are really special properties of the four-dimensional continuum in which we live our lives. Briefly, the contention, as I understand it, is based on considerations such as the following. Taking first the so-called " force of gravitation ", we are bidden, in accordance with relativity principles, to conceive of space in the vicinity of what is familiarly called " matter " as non-Euclidean in character. In other words, space in the neighbourhood of so-called material bodies is to be thought of as " warped " or " curved ", although the curvature is to be conceived as curvature in a four-dimensional continuum, in which time forms the fourth dimension. Wherever there is a " warping " or " curvature " of space, there is what we call " matter ", and, conversely, wherever there is " matter " there is a " warping " or " curvature " of space. In the presence of " matter " there must always be a gravitational field, a peculiar kink or twist in space, but " matter " is

[1] *Cf. infra*, p. 320 *sqq.*

rather an " outgrowth of the field " than the field a consequence of the existence of " matter ". Now, according to
Einstein's principle of equivalence, " a gravitational field of
force at any point in space is in every way equivalent to an
artificial field of force resulting from acceleration, so that no
experiment can possibly distinguish between them ". Hence
the conclusion is drawn that " gravitational force " is a pure
fiction, and what is really there is acceleration due to curvature inherent in the continuum. Having thus disposed of
gravitational force, it was natural to extend the method to
the other " forces " with which the physicist has to deal, and
to make an effort to explain these as likewise illusions
arising from our faulty mode of interpreting the special
metrical properties of the continuum. This, in fact, is what
Weyl tries to do in his brilliant and subtle work. He labours
to prove that the new curvatures which would be introduced
by further generalising the notion of a continuum are sufficient to account for the properties of electromagnetic fields
and electromagnetic forces as we are acquainted with them.

It is not possible to do more here than indicate in the barest
manner why intellectual constructions such as these strike
me as singularly unconvincing. At the conclusion of his
work Weyl has to acknowledge that " the problem of matter
is still wrapt in the deepest gloom " ; and it can hardly, I
think, have escaped notice how the writers who follow the
line of thought which I have very inadequately sketched are
constantly using phraseology which implies a theory of
material substance such as they would explicitly reject.
Thus, for example, Sir J. H. Jeans speaks of " the path of a
particle " in the continuum as being simply its " world line " ;
and of the curvature of path as being " thrust upon the particle by the nature of the continuum ".[1] But what are we to
understand by a " particle "? Is it a material entity of the
kind we have taken electrons and atoms and complexes of
them to be? If it is not, the reasoning would appear to break

[1] Art. " Relativity " in *Ency. Brit.*, twelfth edition, vol. xxxii, p. 266.

down ; if it is, the mere fact that the particle is moving would surely constitute it into an efficient agent of the very type that is repudiated as being illusory. Or, to put the point in another way, while a " particle " is continually being treated as though it were an occupant of the continuum and moving along geodesics in it, what the view really demands is that it should be a part of the continuum, which as such cannot step, as it were, outside the continuum and move along one of its paths.

But the main objection I am concerned to press is that the position I am criticising throws a burden upon what is described as " our subjective interpretation " which that faculty of ours, whatever it is, is wholly unable to bear. You cannot get rid of an awkward fact by the easy device of proclaiming it to be a subjective illusion. Even an " illusion " has a being of its own, and you are not entitled to treat it as belonging to a sort of no-man's land of which you need take no further notice. In the present instance, if the human mind invariably " interprets " changes in nature as due to the operation of forces, then, even though that interpretation be a misinterpretation, there must be in the objective world that which will account for the interpretation coming to be made and being what it is. And, on the theory before us, if it be understood literally, there is nothing in the objective world which by any conceivable manipulation could render such experience possible. The readiness with which the mind is supposed to be capable of creative functions when in the interests of a theory it is necessary that nature should be regarded as destitute of properties it seems to possess is certainly astonishing. For example, Sir J. H. Jeans, in the very able article to which I have alluded, after asserting that the apparent " force of gravitation " arises solely from acceleration and pointing out that acceleration results not only from changes in the amount of a velocity but from a change in its direction also, gives the following illustration to bring out his meaning : " A motor-cyclist riding in a circle at a uniform speed of 60 miles an hour will be the subject of an acceleration towards the centre of the circle. He knows that the apparent force so produced is just as real in its effects as gravitation, and to save himself from falling as a result of its influence he must incline the direction of his machine to the vertical." If, however, the " force " so produced is merely apparent (that is to say, as Sir J. H. Jeans implies, unreal and non-existent), how is it intelligible that it can give rise to effects so unmistakably " real " as those which are here depicted? Certainly, confronted with a theory of this sort, a poet may be allowed to protest :

> " If Nature be a phantom, as thou say'st,
> A splendid figment and prodigious dream,
> To reach the real and true I'll make no haste,
> More than content with worlds that only seem."

One of the distinctive features of Professor Whitehead's more philosophical rendering of the theory of relativity consists, I need hardly remind my readers, in his resolute rejection of the view of the non-uniform structure of the four-dimensional continuum, and his insistence upon the necessity of regarding it as homaloidal in character.[1] It would, therefore, be impossible for Whitehead to acquiesce in the attempt to reduce either matter or force to subjective interpretations of the special properties of the space-time continuum. On the contrary he expressly refuses to countenance any conception of psychic additions to the objects known in perception, any antithesis between nature as it really is and experiences of it which are purely psychological. For him our experiences of the apparent world are experiences of nature itself ; there is but one nature, the nature which is before us in perceptual knowledge. And he would, I take it, agree that just as " the nature which is the fact apprehended in awareness holds within it the greenness of the trees, the

---

[1] For the grounds of Whitehead's contention see *The Principle of Relativity*, chapters ii, iii and iv, and *cf.* his Address on " Uniformity and Contingency " (*Proceedings of Aristotelian Society*, N.S., xxiii, p. 8).

song of the birds, the warmth of the sun ", etc., so likewise it holds within it that which we denote by such terms as force, activity, strain, stress, tension and the like.   Indeed, in his emphasis upon " passage " and " process " as the fundamental characteristics of nature, he is meaning, if I mistake not, to include under these phrases the features with which I have been concerned.   I am afraid that the sharp contrast he seems to draw between " objects " and " events " will preclude his concurring with some of the things I have been urging, but I hope the main drift of my argument is not out of harmony with what he has taught us.

VIII

PROFESSOR EDDINGTON'S PHILOSOPHY OF NATURE

To attempt to examine critically the metaphysical views of a great man of science is for a philosophic inquirer always a thankless task. It will naturally be the scientific conclusions of the former that will be of main interest to those who are occupied in philosophical investigations, while to those engaged in scientific research his excursions into metaphysics will seem to be but deviations from the strict path of science which may be neglected by his fellow-workers, preferring as they mostly do to leave what they are wont to regard as "morasses of foolishness" judiciously alone.

But Professor Eddington's volume of Gifford Lectures[1] is a work of quite unusual significance and merits, I venture to think, respectful consideration on the part of the members of a philosophical society. It presents us with a well-balanced estimate of the stupendous changes in the scientific outlook on nature that have come about since the beginning of this century by one who has himself contributed in no small measure to the advance. "The theory of relativity and the quantum have", as he puts it, "led to strange new conceptions of the physical world", while the progress of the principles of thermodynamics has been making towards a more gradual, yet no less profound, modification of view. Professor Eddington[2] is of opinion that these scientific developments provide fresh material for philosophy. And of that there can be no question. The retrograde periods of

---

[1] *The Nature of the Physical World.* Cambridge : University Press, 1828.
[2] Now Sir Arthur Eddington.

philosophical reflexion have been invariably the periods in which an artificial separation was instituted between the general notions, attained by human reason, of the scheme of things and the facts brought to light by the patient labour of scientific specialists. In the latter half of the nineteenth century nothing influenced philosophical conceptions more markedly than the theory of evolution in the realm of life. The part played in this respect then by researches into the development of living organisms is being largely played now by researches of a more abstract character in the departments of mathematical physics and astronomy. Professor Eddington has made a resolute effort to convey to us some idea of the bearing of these researches so far as it is possible to do so without the aid of abstruse mathematical formulae, and philosophical students everywhere will be grateful to him for the vision he has given them of the present point of view of physical science and of the more speculative conclusions to which it appears to be tending.

In common, I presume, with most members of our society, I have been lately endeavouring to follow the lead of Professor Eddington through the various fields of inquiry within which he is so essentially at home. I have found myself often moving about in regions inhabited by entities the nature of which is puzzling to a stranger like myself but in regard to which I have been content to take the word of one who lives a good deal amongst them, and who is, therefore, speaking from an intimate acquaintance with their ways and peculiarities. With respect to a large number of the themes dealt with in these Gifford Lectures it would, of course, be not only presumptuous but foolish for one who is not a trained mathematician or physicist to vouchsafe an opinion ; but, at certain stages of his journey, Professor Eddington has been induced, and I, for one, am very glad he has been induced, to enter upon territory which is more or less familiar to me, and here, I confess, I feel less confidence in trusting to his guidance. When he gets into these provinces his argumentation seems to me to lack the coherency and cogency exhibited in the purely scientific portions of his work and fails, so far as I can see, to justify the conclusions that are drawn from it.

I have thought that I might in a short essay attempt to do two things. In the first place, so far as the treatment of mathematical and physical theories is concerned, I have no intention whatever of playing the part of a critic. This volume of Professor Eddington's is written, however, for the educated layman and not for the scientific specialist. One recognises the serious disadvantages under which the mathematician is labouring when he is debarred from using the instrument by which his results have been won. But it seems to me that it may be useful if, without calling in question the interpretations that are given of mathematical results, I try to state the sort of difficulties which, I think, the " plain man " will encounter in the effort to understand certain of those interpretations. It may well be that the fault lies all on the side of the "plain man ". Yet, even so, it will perhaps be helpful to the mathematician to realise what it is in his exposition that occasions difficulty. And, in the second place, so far as the treatment of philosophical problems is concerned, I conceive it will be legitimate to bring to bear such critical considerations as one would naturally bring to bear were the arguments in question set forth in an avowedly philosophical treatise. The fact that they are advanced from the point of view of an eminent scientific investigator lends to them undoubtedly a special interest, but it cannot be allowed to screen them from the scrutiny to which philosophical arguments are called upon to submit.

1

I propose, then, in this portion of the present essay, to assume the rôle not of a "prying philosopher" but of the " plain man ". I am going to select some few of Professor Eddington's illustrations and explanations in order to render manifest, if I can, why they fail to make clear to the " plain man " the import of the conceptions they are designed to elucidate.

(*a*) In dealing with the relativity of acceleration, Professor Eddington uses an illustration which I notice is employed by some writers on relativity and consistently avoided by others. We are bidden to think of a train passing through a station of the rate of 60 miles an hour. " Since the velocity is relative, it does not matter ", so the argument runs, " whether we say that the train is moving at 60 miles an hour past the station or the station is moving at 60 miles an hour past the train ". And, in like manner, we are bidden to realise that if I am travelling from Cambridge to Edinburgh it does not matter whether we say that I move to Edinburgh or that Edinburgh moves to me (p. 130). Now, to the ordinary common-sense mind this certainly wears the aspect of paradox and the question is whether it is, as a matter of fact, an apt illustration and not rather one that is calculated to cause unnecessary bewilderment and confusion.

The " plain man " needs not, of course, to be reminded that if, when he is seated in a moving train, he looks out of the carriage window, the ground and its contents will appear to be sliding away from him in a direction the reverse of that in which the train is moving, although that this is apparent merely he is very soon able to convince himself. But with reference to the illustration just mentioned, the " plain man's " difficulty is this. He feels in his bones that if the second statement is to be parallel with the first in each of the two cases it ought to have been differently worded. When the train is asserted to be moving, what is meant is that it is moving *over* the surface of the earth, which *relatively to it* is at rest. If, then, in a similar manner, the station is to be said to move that would imply that the station—its platform, its booking-office, etc.—is likewise changing its position relatively to other things on the earth's surface and is moving *over* that surface. So, too, in regard to the journey between

Cambridge and Edinburgh. The parallel statement to " Edinburgh moves to me " would be not that " I move to Edinburgh ", but that " Cambridge moves to Edinburgh ". And neither of these propositions expresses, I take it, what is actually intended.

I cannot help thinking that Professor Eddington deals with us somewhat unfairly in replying to the objection which he says was originally urged by Lenard. The objection is this : Supposing that an accident occurs to the train as it is moving through the station, and that its motion is in a few seconds brought to a standstill, can this change of acceleration be ascribed indifferently either to the train (relative to the station) or to the station (relative to the train), seeing that the persons in the train and not those in the station are injured? Professor Eddington replies that it is not the change of acceleration that does the mischief, but something that hits the train. " The train was bombarded by a swarm of molecules and the bombardment spread all the way along it. The cause is evident—gross, material, absolute—recognised by everyone, no matter what his frame of reference, as occurring in the train, not the station." Quite so ; but surely it is no less evident that the cause was not merely the bombardment of this swarm of molecules. If, instead of moving at the rate of 60 miles an hour, the train had been moving at the rate of a few yards an hour, it might still have been hit by the obstacle and been bombarded by a swarm of molecules, but the effect would have been very different. In fine, if it had been the station that had been moving and not the train, an accident would certainly not have been an unlikely occurrence, but quite obviously it would not have been *this* accident. And the purport of the objection is, I take it, to suggest that even though from observation of movement alone we should be in the predicament which writers on relativity are fond of depicting, yet there are numerous physical occurrences which do enable us to extricate ourselves from that predicament.

Or the point may be brought out in another way. Light-waves from Sirius, travelling at the rate of 186,000 miles a second, take eight years and nine months to reach this planet. When such waves pass our earth, is it a matter of indifference whether we say that they are moving at that speed past the earth or that the earth is moving at that speed past them? Clearly not, for it is one of the fundamental assumptions of the theory of relativity that no material body can ever travel as fast as light-waves, however great the force to which it is exposed and however long that force may act.

(b) I refer next to the way in which we are asked to conceive of " mass " and its relation to " energy ". In common with many other exponents of modern physical theory, Professor Eddington is of opinion that it has altogether discarded the notion of substance. Some writers have dismissed the notion as a survival of obsolete mediaeval metaphysics but Professor Eddington takes it to be one that has been reached by ordinary everyday experience. It is, he thinks, the notion of a solid, inert body which has qualities, and which offers resistance to the impact of other solid bodies. And this " solid substance of things " is, he contends, an illusion—a " fancy projected by the mind into the external world ". Physicists " have chased the solid substance from the continuous liquid to the atom, from the atom to the electron, and there they have lost it " (p. 318).

If this meant merely that modern physics has found the old conception of an atom as a hard, rigid, impenetrable particle altogether unworkable, no comment would be requisite. It has long been apparent even to popular reflexion that the dualistic view of physical nature as comprising two kinds of entities—the one kind ponderable, endowed with mass, weight and shape, the other imponderable, devoid of these characteristics and yet capable of being applied to and of acting upon the former—is a view that cannot withstand the slightest criticism. But this is not all that is meant. It is further meant that energy is the same thing as mass. Now,

o

it may well be, and apparently it is, the case that, under certain circumstances, measured energy and measured mass turn out to be indistinguishable—that is to say, in measuring the one you are likewise measuring the other, as in measuring the height of the mercury in a thermometer you are likewise measuring the temperature of the region in which the thermometer is placed. Yet surely we are not thereby entitled to conclude that the notion of energy is identical with the notion of mass, or that the connotation of the one term is similar to the connotation of the other. As a matter of fact, not only in ordinary language, but in the language of physical science, the *meaning* of the two terms would appear to be essentially different. When, for example, " mass " is declared to be " the inertia of matter " (p. 59), surely a distinction *is* being drawn between mass and energy. It has been shown theoretically, Professor Eddington elsewhere points out, that, since a charged conductor has to carry its electric field with it, additional force is necessary, simply on account of the charge in order to move or to stop it, and this property, he adds, is called inertia—the property, namely, of requiring force to set the field moving or to stop it. And, since the smallest separable particles of matter are very minute and carry charges, these charges may be responsible for the whole of the inertia detected in matter.[1] Be it so ; but, even then, the inertia or mass is a property of the electrical energy and is not the electrical energy itself. And when it is further pointed out that electrical energy which is not bound to electric charges *has* mass, that light-waves, for example, *have* mass, the distinction is virtually being recognised between something which has a property and the property itself. Now, that which has properties is probably the most ordinary way of describing what is meant by " substance ". So that it would appear, after all, that what the admission amounts to is that, instead of matter, energy is now to be regarded as a substance which is endowed (what-

[1] *Space, Time and Gravitation*, pp. 61-62.

ever that may mean) with mass, and consequently with weight
and other characteristics formerly attributed to matter.

It is worth while pursuing the subject somewhat further.
The relativity theory requires a distinction to be drawn between two kinds of mass—" invariant " mass, the mass that
is measured by an observer for whom the body concerned is
relatively at rest, and "relative" mass, the mass that is
measured when the body is moving relatively to the observer.
The former (m) is, we are told, a genuine property of the body,
which is not dependent upon the observer, and while not
strictly constant is approximately so ; the latter (M) has, on
the other hand, no physical significance, although from the
mathematical point of view it is of chief importance. Unless
the velocity be very great, M may be written as equal to
$m + \frac{1}{2}mv^2$, where, of course, $\frac{1}{2}mv^2$ represents the kinetic
energy. Accordingly, M may be said to consist of two parts—
the mass when at rest *plus* the energy of the motion. If it be
assumed that the term m represents a kind of potential or
" bound " energy, M can, it is maintained, be identified with
energy, and the increase of mass which it is now known occurs
with increase of velocity simply means that the kinetic or
" free " energy has been added on. What puzzles the non-
mathematical mind in an argument of this description is the
apparently cavalier manner in which the element m—evidently a very vital factor in the whole business—is handled.
You are out to prove that mass can be identified with energy.
Yet, in order to prove it, you take for granted a kind of mass
that you call " invariant " and simply show that if kinetic
energy be added to it the sum will equal the measure of what
you call " relative " mass. But your conclusion is not even
rendered so much as probable until, in some way, you have
shown ground for supposing that m is to be identified with
energy or a kind of energy. The suggestion that " the term
m represents a kind of potential energy concealed in matter " [1]
would seem to be almost a subterfuge. In the first place, the

---

[1] *ibid.*, p. 146.

potential energy of a body, as hitherto conceived, is not a constant quantity. And, in the second place, why " concealed in matter "? According to the theory, there is no " matter " for it to be concealed in. And the " plain man's " perplexity is enhanced when he is subsequently informed that " light has mass (M) of the ordinary kind, but the invariant mass (m) vanishes ".[1] If the invariant mass vanishes one would naturally conclude that kinetic energy alone remains. Now, how can this be " mass (M) *of the ordinary kind* " when the latter has already been declared to be expressible by the formula $m + \frac{1}{2}mv^2$? Moreover, Professor Eddington, in preparing the ground for a discussion of the quantum theory, refers to the experiments which appear to indicate that what the physicist calls light is not only an entity with the wave properties of spreading out, etc., but is simultaneously an entity with the corpuscular property of expending its whole energy on one very small target, and he suggests that in like manner electrons may possess simultaneously the properties of wave and particle and not be purely corpuscular in nature (pp. 201-3). Again, one feels embarrassment. If a " light wavicle " is similar to an electron in possessing the property of corpuscularity, would not that imply that, after all, it cannot be destitute of invariant mass, for it is presumably in virtue of its being a particle that an electron is possessed of such?

I will venture to indicate a further difficulty that will trouble, I imagine, not a few readers. In accordance with Einstein's general theory, Professor Eddington assumes that in the region of what we describe as matter, space is non-Euclidean. There is there " curvature "—endless hills and valleys, so to speak. " We do not ask ", he writes, " how mass gets a grip on space-time and causes the curvature. That would be as superfluous as to ask how light gets a grip on the electromagnetic medium so as to cause it to oscillate. The light *is* the oscillation ; the mass *is* the curvature "

[1] *Space, Time and Gravitation*, p. 148.

(p. 156). Since, then, mass and energy are taken to be identical, are we to say that " the energy *is* the curvature "? Apparently Professor Eddington would not hesitate to reply in the affirmative, for elsewhere he tells us that " action (*i.e.*, energy multiplied by time) is the curvature of the world ".[1] The difficulty of the " plain man " is not so much, I think, that he cannot " visualise this statement " as that he cannot attach any intelligible meaning to it. A live eel wriggles, and in wriggling is, no doubt, exerting energy, but to say that the wriggles *are* the energy seems simply nonsense. But let that pass. When you have got so far the problem is manifestly staring you in the face to give some clue as to the status to be assigned in such a scheme to radiant energy. In the regions of space-time where there is no matter, space is, *ex hypothesi*, not curved, yet periodic occurrences (light-waves, etc.) are everywhere present, and these are modes of energy. How, then, is it possible to identify energy or action with curvature?

(*c*) The last-mentioned difficulty leads me to notice another which continually, I think, baffles the " plain man's " efforts to grasp the significance of the new conception of gravitation. The point I want to emphasise is that, in every attempt to popularise the notion of non-Euclidean space, the difference between space and occupancy of space is slurred over and the illustrations are invariably taken from the latter, whereas the treatment is supposed to be of the former. Professor Eddington does not, it is true, employ the crude example which has frequently been used. He does not ask us to picture a room in which marbles dropped anywhere on the floor always move towards the centre, because the floor is curved, and to think in an analogous manner of the planets moving towards the sun because the space round the latter is curved. Nevertheless, most of his illustrations are drawn from the behaviour of space-occupying bodies or particles (see, for instance, p. 127 *sqq.*). But surely if you want to

[1] *ibid.*, p. 148.

convince us that " particles " are " ridges in the four-dimensional world where it is gathered into a pucker " it won't do to keep on speaking of these " particles " as moving about in the four-dimensional world like minnows in a pond. Indeed, in one passage, Professor Eddington goes further and assures us that space-time is a four-dimensional manifold " embedded in as many dimensions as it can find new ways to twist about in ". And he adds " actually a four-dimensional manifold is amazingly ingenious in discovering new kinds of contortion " (p. 120). Are we, then, to conceive of space-time as something that occupies, well, another space-time of more than four dimensions, and so on *ad infinitum*? Or do we ever come upon a space-time which is not embedded in something else, and which is so far in conformity with the ordinary notion of Euclidean space. One thing, at any rate, would seem to be certain. Space, Euclidean or non-Euclidean, cannot be conceived as a mere manifold ; in order to be space at all it must be continuous. And the question which puzzles the " plain man " is this : if so-called material bodies or " particles " are, in truth, parts or curvatures of such a con-tinuum, how can they project themselves out of it, so to speak, and move along geodesics in it, as though they were not parts but occupants of it?

(*d*) Professor Eddington is very confident that we have an intimate acquaintance with our own minds, that they are much less mysterious to us than either our bodies or the external world. No one can, he thinks, deny—what, I take it, well-nigh every psychologist would deny—" that mind is the first and most direct thing in our experience, and all else is remote inference " (p. 281). But for the " plain man ", if he be ever so little of a psychologist, the surprising thing will be the notion of the mind which this " direct self-knowledge " is thought to yield.

The mind is pictured, namely, as like an editor sitting in his sanctum receiving through the nerves scrappy messages from all over the outside world, and making a story of them with a good deal of editorial invention (p. 100). Can this, by any stretch of imagination, be said to be the information which direct and infallible self-knowledge affords? " We are ", it is asserted, " acquainted with an external world because its fibres run into our consciousness ; it is only our own ends of these fibres that we actually know ; from those ends we more or less successfully reconstruct the rest as a palaeontologist reconstructs an extinct monster from its footprint " (p. 278 and *cf.* pp. 317-18). Could any account of the mind and its operations be more diametrically opposed to what self-scrutiny reveals? So far as can be discovered no mental life has so much as the faintest glimmering of an acquaintance with the ends of fibres running into it, and if it had, to what conceivable use could it apply this modicum of insight? The palaeontologist can reconstruct an extinct monster from its footprints because he brings to bear a vast amount of knowledge of animal organisms. The unfortunate human mind is, however, taken to be in the pitiable plight of knowing only the ends of certain nerve-fibres. How, in the name of common-sense, can it be supposed to " reconstruct " from them anything, let alone the rest of the external world? Elsewhere, indeed, code messages are said to be transmitted along the nerves into the mind's sanctum (p. 240). Again, one is bound to protest that self-knowledge fails altogether to disclose the reception of such messages and once more one has to ask, of what possible avail could they be, even granting their advent? Code messages may be of service enough when the recipient possesses the key to their interpretation, when he is already familiar with the things which they signify. But delivered to a consciousness entirely destitute of any knowledge either of the source from which they come or of the entities to which they refer, code messages would be as meaningless as is the Greek alphabet to an infant. Yet a third version is outlined for us of mental activity. Consciousness is represented as weaving or spinning out of the impulses in the brain the various qualitative characteristics

—colours, sounds, odours, etc.—and as " projecting " these into the external environment. The difficulty is the same as before. Introspection, " direct self-knowledge " furnishes not the slightest indication that the mind performs either of these curious and enigmatical functions. If it does, it does so in total ignorance of what it is doing, and is operating no less mechanically than the looms and spinning-wheels with which it is compared.

It has not seldom been a favourite device of the physicist, when he has found numerous features which are apprehended as features of the external world awkward to deal with, to dismiss them from his purview as " images " or " illusions " of the mind. But neither direct self-knowledge nor psychological analysis lend the least countenance to ascribing to the mind a nature of this sort. And when one proceeds to inquire into the way in which these mysterious psychical effects are supposed to be produced the procedure invariably turns out to be of so fantastic a character that one is left simply to marvel at the ease with which such ideas can be seriously entertained.

2

I turn now to the more strictly philosophical portions of Professor Eddington's work. In the later chapters an interesting and resolute attempt is made to advance from the point of view of modern physics to what, I suppose, must be called an idealistic interpretation of nature. The position reached differs widely from that of Mr. Bertrand Russell, on the one hand, and from that of Professor Whitehead, on the other. Physical science has, Professor Eddington thinks, made it evident that the familiar world of everyday experience is very largely, at any rate, a creation of the mind. Not only are secondary qualities essentially subjective, but a large number of other ingredients of the familiar world are no less so. The mind weaves its own impression of " force " out of nerve-impulses transmitted to the brain. The element of permanence which we take to be in the objective world and denote by the term " substance " is regarded, as we have seen, as a mental construct. Not only so. The mind's facility of " world-building " is, it is held, likewise exemplified by the way in which, out of the scantiest supply of material, the physicist is enabled to frame a mathematical scheme of the scientific world, and thus to lay bare the fundamental structure underlying it. And the line of thought which Professor Eddington seeks to develop is that, if the human mind evinces itself as thus continuously creative, there would seem to be at least some justification for surmising that the " background " which the physical world, in order to render it actual, demands is of one piece, so to speak, with these human minds of ours, that consciousness is the avenue of approach to the reality and significance of the physical world, as it is the avenue of approach to all scientific knowledge of that world.

(a) Let us look, first, at the process of " world-building " which the expert mathematician is depicted as effecting—a process which is to result in the representation of " a physical world which will give a shadow performance of the drama enacted in the world of experience " (p. 230).

The primitive material which must be provided at the start consists of relations and relata. The relata are to be simply the meeting points of relations, and relations are simply to subserve the function of uniting the relata. In order to distinguish the latter from one another certain marks composed of four numbers, ultimately to be called " co-ordinates ", are to be assigned to each, the choice of four being justified by the circumstance that " ultimately the structure can be brought into better order that way ", though why this should be so is unknown to us. Moreover, we are to postulate that the relations are comparable, or in some measure like one another. And, by a process of argument which I will not try to summarise, the conclusion is reached that " to allow for all combinations the required mathematical formula contains

4^4 or 256 numerical coefficients ", and that " these coefficients give a numerical measure of the structure surrounding the initial relation ". The 256 measures of structure, it is then found, may be considerably reduced in number, first by omitting duplicates and then by the elimination of a great deal of " useless lumber "—that is to say, of elements that will not form part of a building which will shadow the things of common experience. In the end, we are left with sixteen coefficients for each relatum—ten of them symmetrical, out of which it is possible to construct geometry and mechanics, and six of them antisymmetrical, out of which it is possible to construct electromagnetism.

I have sought in vain to determine what these relata are. But we are told so much about them. They, with their coefficients, enable the mathematician to construct the physical world so far as field-physics is concerned, or, in other words, to include in his construction the metrical, gravitational and electromagnetic properties. On the other hand, they do not enable him to get at the laws and phenomena of atomicity ; the discontinuities of physics, such as quanta, electrons and protons, remain beyond his ken. There is, we are left to infer, no other way of arriving at a knowledge of the microscopic structure of the physical world than by the empirical methods of experimental physics.

But the difficulty I have with regard to this process of " world-building " is that it seems not only to presuppose the very thing it is professing to account for, but also to presuppose other things which it leaves completely in the dark.

The start is avowedly made from the everyday world of ordinary experience. The abstract theory of structure, together with the relata and the comparable relations, is suggested by what is found to hold between specific entities in that world. And which of the 256 measures of structure are useless lumber has to be decided by the question whether they will aid in forming an erection that will " shadow the things of common experience ". So that the world of com-

mon experience is both the datum from which the mathematical physicist sets out in his process of " world-building "
and the criterion by which he determines whether at the end
his efforts in that direction have culminated in success.

What, then, is the outcome of the process? A scheme or
representation of external nature from which all reference to
the qualitative has been rigidly excluded. Its connexions
are all quantitative ; even those relations that have usually
been regarded as causal are interpreted as quantitative
identities. " The whole subject-matter of exact science consists of pointer readings and similar indications " (p. 252).
" Although we seem to have very definite conceptions of
objects in the external world, those conceptions do not enter
into exact science and are not in any way confirmed by it."
Before the mathematical physicist can begin to handle any
problem, these conceptions " must be replaced by quantities
representing the results of physical measurement " (p. 253).
" Science has nothing to say as to the intrinsic nature of the
atom. The physical atom is, like everything else, a schedule
of pointer readings " (p. 259). Now, no one would question
the legitimacy of all this so long as its due limitations are
recognised. The mathematician knows his own business,
and if it be necessary, as it obviously is necessary, for a mathematical treatment of the physical world to make abstraction
of qualitative distinctions, such abstraction is, *eo ipso,* justified. But it is the function of philosophical criticism to insist
that the more the quantitative aspect of the physical world is
emphasised, and for certain purposes rightly emphasised,
the less adequate does the resulting scheme become for
expressing the *whole* truth of that which we have before
us in the physical world. As Lotze once said, the more
abstractly our symbols are conceived the more they pass
into *notiones communes* which do indeed apply fairly well
to everything, but give us no adequate knowledge about
anything. And, under no circumstances, is it ever possible
simply to identify physical nature with the abstract scheme

of quantitative relations ; at the best it can only be descriptive of the *form* of physical facts. Unfortunately, however, there is often a tendency to take the abstract scheme as faithfully representing existing entities, and this tendency I find illustrated in Professor Eddington's work. While in some passages he recognises that mathematical formulae are but symbols describing the physical world, in numerous others he speaks of the physical world itself as symbolic, as consisting of symbols, and writes as though this symbolic world which " shadows the things of common experience " had, within the whole realm of what we must call " reality ", a separate and independent being of its own. " Modern scientific theories have broken away ", he tells us, " from the common standpoint which identifies the real with the concrete " (p. 275). He speaks of " the formal and symbolic character of the entities of physics " (p. 280), of " the physical world " as " restricted to a complex of metrical symbols " (p. 288), of its being " the world of pointer readings " (p. 311). Carbon is said to *be* " a symbol definable only in terms of the other symbols belonging to the cyclic scheme of physics " (p. 269) ; and the question is raised whether " the symbols which the physicist has scattered through the external world are adequate to predetermine the future " (p. 308).

These are only a few of the many instances that might be cited. It would, of course, be easy to urge that phrases such as these are merely metaphorical, and ought not to be interpreted in any other sense. But that line of defence will not do, and it will not do for the following reason. Professor Eddington fully recognises that " experience comprises more than can be embraced in the physical world, restricted as it is to a complex of metrical symbols " (p. 288). He maintains that it requires a " background " (whatever that may mean), and that this " background " is of the nature of consciousness. The very reason, however, for assuming the " background " to be of the nature of consciousness is that a " schedule of pointer readings " requires to be supplemented by a " spiritual substratum " (p. 282) of the nature indicated, in a way in which the physical world of the Victorian physicist did not seem to require such supplementation (see, *e.g.*, p. 259). Just because the physical world is not what the older physicists took it to be, just because of its purely metrical character, we are warranted in supposing it to be embedded in something that has a nature capable of manifesting itself as mental activity (p. 260). If, then, that argument has any legitimacy, it follows that what is thus " embedded "— namely, the complex of metrical symbols—must have a being of its own.

It requires, I think, but little scrutiny to discover that the argument in question will not bear the weight which is imposed upon it, and that, in spite of his argument, Professor Eddington is himself virtually assuming that the physical world, *quâ* physical, is much more than a complex of metrical symbols. For, according to him, as we have seen, the mathematician is not the only " world-builder ". The world of common experience has likewise been built by the human consciousness—no small portion of it apparently by that of our ape-like ancestors (p. 81). We, or our ape-like ancestors, have put into nature well-nigh everything that we discern there. Colours, sounds, temperatures—the warmth of the air, the scent of the grass, the stir of the breeze, the solid substance of things—these are " fancies " which the mind has " projected " into the external world. In short, while the scientific world is " objective " the familiar world is " subjective " (p. 94). This view seems to me quite untenable,[1] but I am not now concerned to contest it. What I am concerned to point out is that, admittedly, even to weave images and illusions, we need to be endowed with sense-organs, with nerves and brains and cerebral systems. It is necessary to postulate that air-waves, light-waves, etc., produce " impressions " on the sense-organs, that " impulses " or " code messages " are being conveyed by the nerves and

[1] *Cf. supra*, pp. 31-3.

transmitted to the brain, and that we are acquainted with this " subjective world " because " fibres " of the objective world " run into our consciousness " (p. 278). Even " so relative and elusive a thing as force " cannot be built out of " entire nothingness " (p. 137). There is " stress " in our muscles which somehow we " feel ", and we have got to suppose that our bodies are being " continuously and vigorously buffeted " by rapidly moving molecules (p. 113). What, then, follows from all this? Surely one conclusion at least, that the physical world is *not* restricted to a complex of symbols, that it is not, even for the physicist, a world of mere pointer readings. It is admitted that descriptions of the phenomena of atomic physics have an extraordinary vividness. " We see the atoms with their girdles of circulating electrons darting hither and thither, colliding and rebounding. Free electrons torn from the girdles hurry away a hundred times faster, curving sharply round the atoms with slide slips and hairbreadth escapes ", and so on (p. 290). You may say that all this carries you no further, that it is only when " numbers are scattered freely in the description " that you can get along (p. 291). But the fact is that it does carry you an immense way further. Without a mechanism of this sort, or of something like it, your whole account of the " familiar world " as purely subjective, which formed the basis of your building a complex of metrical symbols, and which that complex has to " shadow ", would not have a leg to stand on. Admittedly, it is at the beginning and not at the end of the quest that a " reality " which is not merely conventional has to be found for such entities as atoms and electrons (p. 287). In other words, the theoretical physicist is himself constrained to recognise *in the physical world* a vast array of qualitative material, the nature and laws of which fall outside the scope of his quantitative scheme, in order that the latter should have any meaning or significance at all. He may protest that he knows nothing of the inner structure of, or of the occurrences within, an electron ; yet, on account of the effects to which it gives rise, and which he does know, he is all the while assuming that it has certain qualities and that these are *physical* qualities.[1]

(b) So long as the physical world was conceived as made up of atoms and molecules according to the Democritean model, even with the ether thrown in as a medium for the transmission of radiant energy, it was natural, Professor Eddington thinks, that scientific reflexion should have appeared to culminate in some form of materialism. If the whole of consciousness be viewed as reflected in the dance of molecules in the brain, then all the features of consciousness would seem to be phenomenal of what in the last resort would be matter in motion. Modern science has, however, changed all that. The recognition that the physical world is "entirely abstract", that physical entities are "only an extract of pointer readings", transforms, it is maintained, in a fundamental way the outlook of the physicist. He is bound to conceive of the schedule of pointer readings as attached to some "background", apart from which it would lack "actuality". For the most part he has no means of forming any conception of this "background". But in one case—in the case of the pointer readings of his own brain—he has, it is argued, an insight which is not limited to the evidence of the pointer readings, and that insight shows that they are attached to a "background" of consciousness. Consequently, he may not unreasonably conclude that the background of other pointer readings is of a nature continuous with that revealed to him in this particular case, although it does not follow that the more specialised attributes of consciousness are invariably characteristic of it.

One of the many difficulties involved in this argument is due to the fact that the physicist, even though it be granted

---

[1] After having urged that "science has nothing to say as to the intrinsic nature of the atom " (p. 259), Professor Eddington writes : "We have two chief ways of learning about the interior of the atom. We can observe electrons entering or leaving, and we can observe light entering or leaving " (p. 306).

that he has a " self-knowledge of that which is in his own con-sciousness " (p. 334), has no such insight into what is going on in his brain. That is completely hidden from him. From what physiologists have ascertained about other people's brains he may perchance construct an imaginary schedule of pointer readings of his own, but that is all. See, then, his predicament. In the case of other people, his schedule of the pointer readings of their brains will be on a par with his other schedules, but the assumed " background " will be hidden from him ; in his own case he will have awareness of the " background ", but no means of obtaining a schedule of the pointer readings of his brain. How, then, he can be said to have " insight " that these are " attached " to his conscious-ness it is hard to discern. But this by the way.

The metaphysical theory we are invited to consider is that ultimately the world consists of what is described as " mind-stuff ". This " mind-stuff " must be thought of as something more general than our individual conscious minds, but as not altogether foreign in nature to the feelings in our consciousness. The view in question is, we are told, practically that which was put forward by W. K. Clifford in the later years of his life. When, however, the two views are closely inspected, it becomes, I think, evident that they are by no means identical. Clifford's doctrine was essentially atomistic. Briefly, his argument consisted of two main steps. In the first place, he tried to show that every particle of matter, even inorganic matter, is correlated with feelings, or rather with " those remoter elements which cannot even be felt, but of which the simplest feeling is built up ", just as the elements of that particular portion of matter which he would have it I " perceive " as your brain are correlated with a vastly complex network of feelings constituting, as he held, your mind. And, in the second place, he tried to sustain the contention that the mind-stuff which he had at first spoken of as " *going along with* " the material object *is* neither more nor less than *the* reality of the material object, the material object being merely phenomenal ; that, in other words, the universe consists exclusively of bits of mind-stuff, some of which are, while some are not, woven into the complexes which we call minds. Now, so far as I can gather, Professor Eddington would agree that there must be supposed to be mind-stuff of an extremely rudimentary kind, that " only here and there does it rise to the level of consciousness ", although " from such islands (of it) proceeds all knowledge " (p. 277). But, unlike Clifford, he seems to be assuming that this mind-stuff, while in some way it must be capable of being " differentiated into parts ", is yet essentially continuous in nature, that it is, so to speak, all of one piece. So much so that he discerns the possibility of finding in it not only our own personalities, but a greater personality. " The idea of a universal Mind or Logos would be ", he writes, " a fairly plausible inference from the present state of scientific theory ; at least it is in harmony with it " (p. 338).

In relinquishing Clifford's atomism, Professor Eddington has no doubt relieved himself of an insuperable obstacle in the way of the theory which has been made manifest by several of its critics. But the question is whether in getting rid of one obstacle he has not exposed himself to others that are equally formidable.

To refer first to some minor points. I am at a loss to understand why the term " mind-stuff " should have been employed, seeing that confessedly what is thus designated is neither exactly what is meant by " mind " nor at all what is meant by " stuff ". What is necessary in order to render the abstract physical world " actual " is, *ex hypothesi*, linkage not to mind-stuff but to consciousness, and consequently consciousness is to be restored to a fundamental position, instead of being regarded as an unessential complication occasionally met with in the midst of inorganic nature at a late stage of evolutionary history (p. 332). Unless the " background " be of the nature of consciousness it will not serve the purpose for which it is postulated. How, then,

P

does it help us to discover a region of sub-consciousness, and beyond it "something indefinite but yet continuous with our mental nature" (p. 280)? A realm of "mind-stuff" below the level of consciousness (whatever that "stuff" might be) would be as unavailing as the material substratum of the physics of former times, and yet it is to this, apparently, that a vast part of the physical world is supposed to be linked. Again, the mind-stuff is said to be "the aggregation of relations and relata which form the building material for the physical world" (p. 278). These, as we have seen, are essentially quantitative in character. Yet we are at the same time told that the "spiritual substratum", in so far as it is known to us in consciousness, is "essentially non-metrical" (p. 282), that it is "unamenable to metrical specification" (p. 323). By what justification, then, can it be described as "the aggregation of relations and relata"?

But the crucial difficulty that besets this entire way of thinking seems to me to be that, while it was impossible for Clifford to make so much as intelligible how a sum of isolated feelings or mind-atoms could ever by themselves become a consciousness, it is, on the other hand, equally impossible along the lines of the present theory to find any room for atoms or electrons or quanta in the scheme of nature. Admittedly, the field-laws, which are held to be imposed by the mind upon nature, are characterised by continuity, "whereas the laws to which the mind as yet lays no claim are characterised", it is thought, "by atomicity" (p. 246). Indeed, we are informed that "the physicist is unconcerned as to whether atoms or electrons really exist ; he usually asserts that they do, but existence is there used in a domestic sense, and no inquiry is made as to whether it is more than a conventional term" (p. 326). Yet, apart from other considerations, the existence of atoms and electrons is, as we have seen, being all the while tacitly assumed in order to account for the fact of the appearance to us of the "familiar world". The theory is, therefore, committed to recognising that atomicity is no less a reality in nature than continuity. Whether, in spite of the divergence of his view from Clifford's, Professor Eddington still means to suggest that in the long run electrons and atoms may be specks of mind-stuff, I do not know. In any case, such a result would be unavailing. Mind-stuff is not, it is asserted, to be conceived as " spread in space and time ". It would, therefore, be preposterous to speak of particles of it " darting hither and thither, colliding and rebounding ", moving through space at enormous velocities, impinging upon the sense-organs, and " hammering on the soles of our boots ". There is absolutely nothing to be gained by christening entities " mental " or " spiritual " if every function they have to fulfil is precisely that which is the function of entities that in contrast to mental entities we have been wont to describe as physical or material.

(c) I have left myself but little space to refer to one portion of Professor Eddington's doctrine that has awakened a good deal of popular interest, his contention that in consequence of the latest development of the quantum theory we seem driven to the conclusion that the laws of physics are not strictly causal, that there is no strictly causal behaviour anywhere. He thinks that with the discovery of what he calls the principle of indeterminancy (the principle, namely, that we cannot know accurately both the velocity and the position of a particle at any one moment) the physicist is being led to abandon the conception of the invariably predictable character of a series of events in the physical world. In particular, the laws that have been ascertained respecting the microscopic elements of that world—individual atoms, electrons, quanta—do not enable us to make definite predictions as to what the individual will be up to next, but merely to recognise several possibilities and state the odds on each.

I must confine myself to a single observation. Professor Eddington allows that " the quantum laws for individuals are not incompatible with causality " (p. 303), and an

obvious consideration confirms, I think, that judgment.
The jump of an individual electron from one quantum orbit
to another seems to be arbitrary ; no definite cause can be
assigned for its jumping to State 1 rather than to State 2.
Now, if this arbitrary behaviour of the electron were spor-
adic, if it occurred only here and there, and if usually it
obeyed ascertained causal laws, the argument that in such
cases it was acting in a way that was not amenable to causal
explanation would doubtless have considerable weight,
although, of course, even then, it would not be conclusive.
But if this apparently lawless character of the electron's
behaviour is happening, as it is happening, on a perfectly
gigantic scale, if whenever light is being absorbed or emitted
it is occurring, the case is otherwise. The probability would
surely seem to be that the apparent lawlessness is due to
conditions of which we are ignorant rather than to arbitrary
freaks on the part of the electrons themselves.

IX

IS THE MIND A COMPOUND SUBSTANCE?

1. *Nature of the Theory to be discussed.*
2. *Comparison of it with Kant's theory of the " empirical subject ".*
3. *The Notion of " Emergence ".*
4. *The " bodily " and the " psychic " factors.*
5. *The Hypothesis of a universal " psychic factor ".*
6. *What is meant by the term " Mind ".*
7. *The Unity and Continuity of the Conscious Subject.*
8. *The Doctrine of " Traces ".*
9. *" Entelechies " and " Psychic Factors ".*

THE purpose of this discussion is to consider a theory of the mental life which has been propounded, so far as I know for the first time, by Dr. C. D. Broad in his stimulating and original work *The Mind and its Place in Nature* (London : 1925). I shall be destined to play, in the main, the part of an adverse critic ; but not seldom the criticism of a view, deemed to be untenable, may, when that view has been ably and thoughtfully presented, prove to be a helpful means of getting at the truth.

1. Dr. Broad describes the theory in question as a " modification " of what he calls the Instrumental Theory (p. 535)—the theory, that is, according to which the mind is a substance that is existentially independent of the body, and which seems to him, for various reasons, if not wholly untenable, yet excessively difficult to reconcile with the known facts.[1] The new theory is, in short, that the mind is a compound of two factors, neither of which in and for itself has the intrinsic properties of a mind but which, when combined, form a whole that does exhibit mental properties. These constitu-

---

[1] I should have thought, however, that, instead of being a "modification ", what we have before us amounts to an entire rejection of this view, and to substituting for it an absolutely opposed conception of the nature of mind.

229

ents are named the " bodily factor " and the " psychic factor " respectively. And an analogy is found in what we can assert of chemical compounds. Certain chemical compounds, namely, have properties which we are unable to deduce from those that are displayed by their elements, taken either in isolation or when met with in other compounds. The characteristic properties of sodium chloride (NaCl) cannot, for instance, be deduced from what we know of the properties of sodium or of the properties of chlorine, or from what we know of other compounds of sodium or other compounds of chlorine. So, too, nothing that we know about oxygen by itself or about hydrogen by itself would enable us to predict the distinctive chemical and physical properties of water. These properties which the complex possesses and which are not theoretically deducible from the properties and arrangements of its constituents, properties which belong to a complex as a whole and not to its parts, are, then, " emergent " properties ; and the theory is that mentality is likewise an emergent property of a compound composed of a living body, possessed of a nervous system, *and* of something else, a " psychic factor ", which, although it is not a mind, does possess some features that have usually been thought only to characterise a mind.

The considerations which have weighed with Dr. Broad in formulating this theory are mainly such as are suggested by the abnormal phenomena that have been investigated by the Society of Psychical Research. He admits (p. 647) that if there were no facts to be taken into account except the normal ones he should regard as, on the whole, the most reasonable view to take of the status and relations of matter and mind in nature that which he designates " emergent materialism "—the view, namely, that materiality is an attribute which is possessed by all substances and mentality an emergent characteristic of material aggregates of a certain kind and degree of complexity. But he is convinced that many of the abnormal features dealt with by psychical research cannot be dismissed as illusory, and that in perticular there is good evidence for holding that the phenomena described as those of " possession ", in which an entranced medium's body appears to be controlled by a dead person, have a basis in fact.   What is known about these phenomena does not seem to him either to require or to justify the hypothesis that the mind of a deceased person survives the death of his body ; they can be sufficiently explained, he thinks, by supposing that something has persisted for a certain period, that this something was an integral part of the mind of the deceased person, and that it is capable of affecting in a marked way the speech and bodily behaviour of a medium under favourable conditions.   I am not going to question Dr. Broad's estimate of the evidence furnished by psychical research.   He knows much more about it than I do.   So far as I am familiar with it, it certainly does not appear to me to have the degree of cogency that he claims for it.[1]   For the purpose, however, of the present discussion we may, I think, be content to accept Dr. Broad's judgment on that point.

2. That the mind is a compound of two heterogeneous factors is not in itself a novel view.   In a sense, I suppose, it might not unfairly be said that the Kantian theory of the " empirical subject " would amount, if it were pressed, to some such conception.   The two functions of sensibility and thought were often so sharply contrasted by Kant that they would seem to be two absolutely disparate constituents of mind, which are only brought together through means of a *tertium quid*.   It is true that Kant speaks of sensibility as a capacity of obtaining presentations through the mode in which we are affected by objects.   But it is difficult to see what, on his view of the " empirical subject ", such " affection " could be other than bodily " affection ", and, indeed, in his posthumous work, he repeatedly asserts that sensations are

---

[1] I think I may legitimately refer to Mr. Frank Podmore's two works, *Spiritualism : A History and a Criticism* (1902) and *The Newer Spiritualism* (1910), in support of this judgment.

due to the action of " the moving forces of matter " upon the sense-organs. Certainly, however, his view of the nature of the other constituent is totally different from Dr. Broad's ; and the notion of mentality as an emergent characteristic is foreign to Kant's way of thinking.

3. As regards the conception of " emergence ", I will content myself with laying stress here upon one consideration. " I know no reason whatever ", Dr. Broad says, " why new and theoretically unpredictable modes of behaviour should not appear at certain levels of complexity, or why they *must* be explicable in terms of elementary properties and laws of composition which have manifested themselves in less complex wholes " (p. 73). Nor do I. But it is, I take it, implied in this assertion that the appearance of these new modes of behaviour is *in some way* dependent on and conditioned by the complex in question, that it is not, in other words, a pure matter of accident that the emergent qualities appear in connexion, or in correlation, with a particular complex, or that they might have appeared here, there, or anywhere, independently of such complex. If, however, so much be granted, there remain several alternative ways in which the notion of " emergence " might be interpreted. (*a*) It might imply that the constituents of the complex have properties —" latent " properties, if one may use an ambiguous term— which do not evince themselves save when the constituents are brought into specific combinations, and that would mean that these constituents are, in truth, even in isolation, much more than we regard them as being. Or (*b*) it might imply that the constituents have no properties other than those which evince themselves, or could evince themselves, in those constituents in isolation, but that the way in which the constituents with these properties can in combination give rise to new properties is, through lack of knowledge, indeterminable by us. Or (*c*) it might imply that the complex is more than the sum of the constituents that we have taken account of, that these constituents cannot, in fact, be isolated from

their environment, and that in the complex these related factors are involved. Or (d) it might imply that what we are calling the " new " property is not a resultant of the coming together of the constituents in the complex at all, that it does not, in fact, arise as a new creation consequent on that event, but that it was already present in the universe, and in virtue of certain conditions hidden from us manifests itself in a particular form in conjunction with the specific complex in question.   Either of these alternatives is possible, and obviously the contention that mentality is an emergent characteristic would assume a different aspect according as one or the other of these interpretations be accepted.

4. I turn now to the specific question we have to discuss. " We have ", writes Dr. Broad, " a set of facts which point to the dependence of mind on body. One explanation is that mind depends on nothing but body, *i.e.*, that mental events either *are* also bodily events, or that at any rate they are all *caused* wholly by bodily events, and do not in turn affect either each other or the body. The present explanation is that the mind is a compound of the body and something else, and that mental events and mental characteristics belong to this compound substance and not to its separate constituents " (p. 538).   With this passage in view, I will plunge at once *in medias res*.

In the first place, the compound is declared to be a " substance ".   Going back to an earlier part of the book (pp. 22-23), we learn that that which is a substance must have (a) the " substantial attributes " of duration and of standing in causal relations, or of appearing as enduring and causally related, (b) *some* special or " differentiating attribute ", which is not essential to substance as such, which is a determinable that is not itself a determinate under any higher determinable, which if it belongs to any complex as a whole must belong also to all its parts, and which must be a simple attribute.   It at once becomes questionable, I think, whether a mind can be said to be a substance in this sense.

In the second place, one of the constituents of this compound is taken to be " the body ". By " the body " is evidently to be understood the *living* organism, for obviously no combination of the other constituent with a body whose life has ceased will give rise to mental events and mental characteristics. Presumably Dr. Broad conceives of life or vitality as one emergent characteristic and mentality as another (see, *e.g.*, p. 582) ; but, as he frequently speaks of the mind as *animating* the body, even when it is not " controlling " it (*e.g.*, pp. 393 and 400), one would gather that he regards the mental life as a specific mode of life, that mode of life, namely, which we mean when we speak of the life of the body as a whole. It is admitted that " we never find highly developed organisms without minds, any more than we find minds without organisms " (p. 660). A living organism, in the case, at any rate, of the higher organisms, is virtually always an organism that possesses mental life, so that the bodily factor will in this respect be analogous to those groups that are referred to (p. 56) as familiar in organic chemistry, radicals such as CH_3 and C_6H_5, which hitherto have not been found to exist in isolation (although I understand it is not altogether impossible that they might do so at very low temperatures) but which play, nevertheless, an essential part in determining the characteristic behaviour of certain compounds. Elsewhere the bodily factor is described as a " living brain and nervous system " (p. 651), but again we find no brain and nervous system that functions as a whole without also being the seat of mental life. Accordingly, it would appear that the union with the other constituent must occur when the bodily factor is in the embryonic stage and either before or at the moment of birth. I will not attempt to work out the consequences of such an assumption, though some of them would, I imagine, be of a perplexing character.

In the third place, as regards the other constituent, the " psychic factor ", it is more than difficult to obtain from Dr. Broad's account so much as the vaguest idea of its nature.

Admittedly, any characterisation of it must be extremely hypothetical ; but still certain positive statements are made about it which I have struggled without success to combine into a coherent view. In the passage cited above, it is definitely asserted that neither mental characteristics nor mental events belong to it. Nevertheless, from other passages one would gather that it is doubtful whether so much can be laid down. "There is at present", we are told, "no reason to believe and strong reason to doubt that it has the higher factors of mentality". It may possibly have some of the lower factors of mentality, such as sentience ; but from the facts there is nothing to be gleaned that requires or suggests this hypothesis (p. 651). In any case, however, whether it has any of the factors of mentality or not, it must be capable of persisting for a period, at least, after the death of the body with which it has been conjoined ; and it must be capable, when thus separated from that body, of carrying "traces" of experiences which happened to the mind of which it was formerly a constituent. In other words, it must comprise what is elsewhere (p. 391) called a "mnemic mass", which consists of "traces" and "dispositions". Now, one of the things that baffle me in regard to the conception before us is this. It is expressly maintained that there are no known grounds whatsoever for assuming that "traces" and "dispositions" are "mental states" or "mental events" (pp. 358 and 389) ; and, so far, the ascription of "traces" and "dispositions" to a "psychic factor" to which neither mental characteristics nor mental events belong might, perhaps, be allowed to pass unchallenged. But Dr. Broad works out an elaborate theory of "traces" (p. 465 *sqq.*)—and either it or a physiological theory of them he is, I gather, inclined to favour—according to which a "trace", though not itself a mental event, is "a characteristic modification in the qualities of mental events or in the relation which binds contemporary mental events into a single total state of mind". The theory requires us to picture the mental life as having no real gaps in it, and the apparent gaps as filled up by non-introspectible mental events that are of the same general nature and have the same kind of mutual relations as those which we can introspect. And the " trace " will be the characteristic modification of quality or structure imposed on each total state by the total state immediately preceding it. It is, no doubt, perfectly conceivable that certain qualities of the mental events of one total state of mind should be transmitted to the mental events of the next total state of mind, and so on. What, however, I utterly fail to understand is how either the qualities of mental events or modifications in the qualities of mental events or in the relations of mental events can be transferred to an entity which does not consist of mental events at all, and how they can persist there, ready to help in constituting other mental events when a suitable organism is available. If qualities of mental events or modifications in such qualities are to " persist " in an entity other than that in which they originally appeared, surely it is requisite that the entity in question should, at any rate, contain mental events to serve as the bearers of these qualities or modifications. The bare possibility is, indeed, allowed that the " psychic factor " may possess sentience ; but, apart from the fact that, of all mental characteristics, sentience would appear to be most of all dependent on bodily conditions, and, therefore, least capable of persisting when these bodily conditions are withdrawn, it would still be extraordinarily hard to conceive how qualities or the modifications of qualities of the higher mental processes can persist in mental processes that are of the lowest type of all. Nor do I think that the perplexities of the situation would be in any degree lightened if the alternative theory of " traces " were chosen, and they be interpreted as purely physiological phenomena. In that case, " traces " would have to be regarded as " simply modifications in the minute spatial or spatio-temporal structure of our brains and nervous systems, which are propagated from one state of the brain and

nervous system to the next state " (p. 468).   Such modifications could clearly not persist in a structure which, whatever
it be, is, *ex hypothesi*, totally different from the structure of the
brain and nervous system.   It is true that Dr. Broad does not
exclude the possibility of the " psychic factor " being a
material entity, but he admits that if it be material, the
matter must be matter of a peculiar and unusual kind—
matter, namely, that does not produce ordinary physical and
chemical effects, and which does not manifest itself to sense-
perception (p. 561).   How, then, could it carry " traces " of
the kind just indicated?   In short, it seems to me clear
that the " psychic factor ", conceived in any of the ways suggested, would be utterly incapable of fulfilling the functions
which it is required to fulfil, in order to justify the assumption
of its existence at all.

5.   But let us now look at the theory more in detail.   If the
mind be a compound substance of the kind depicted, and if
mentality be an " emergent " characteristic, it is evident, I
think, that the analogy which Dr. Broad endeavours to constitute between this compound and certain chemical compounds very soon breaks down when the comparison is
pressed a little further.   The characteristic properties of
sodium chloride cannot, it is true, be deduced from what we
know of the properties of sodium and of the properties of
chlorine.   The " emergent " qualities arise, in some way
which we cannot fathom, through the combination of these
apparently heterogeneous elements.   But both of these elements have existed before in isolation, and we have no reason
whatever for supposing that the characteristics of either of
them are dependent on the prior existence of the compound.
The case, however, is quite otherwise with respect to the
constituents which, according to the theory we are considering, are to be thought of as composing a mind.   On the
one hand, the " bodily factor " has grown and developed
only through being a constituent of the compound called the
mind ; the entire evolution of the bodily organism from its

rudimentary stage in the amoeba to its highly complex structure in the man would have been in no other way possible ; and had there been on the earth no minds, it is safe to assert there would have been no brains and nervous systems for " psychic factors " to unite with. On the other hand, it is equally certain that the " psychic factor ", so far, at least, as its essential characteristics are concerned, can only be an entity whose structure has been gradually formed in and through the development of mind. As we descend the scale of mental evolution and attempt to contemplate the nature of the primitive mind, it becomes increasingly embarrassing to assign any function whatsoever to this so-called " psychic factor ". Dr. Broad evidently finds himself not a little nonplussed with the problem that confronts him in respect to such fairly evolved creatures as earwigs, and he suggests that perhaps for the whole tribe of earwigs there may be only one " psychic factor ", the very trivial differences between the mind of one earwig and that of another being due simply to differences in their bodily organism (p. 538). I do not know whether it is meant that this one " psychic factor " would still contain " dispositions and traces " ; but, however that may be, there would evidently come a stage for which it would be necessary to postulate a " psychic factor " altogether destitute of them, a sort of primitive " psychic factor ", I suppose, for all the primitive modes of mental life. And what its nature could conceivably be Dr. Broad has certainly most effectively shut himself off from any possibility of determining. In another connexion, he has occasion to observe that the hypothesis of universal sentience seems to him " rash to the last degree " (p. 645). Yet apparently the hypothesis of a universal " psychic factor " that is neither mental nor, in the ordinary sense of the term, material, that is neither sentient nor conative, that possesses, in short, none of the features which are usually described as psychical, does not strike him as open to a similar charge.

6. I confess I am in grave doubt as to what exactly Dr. Broad intends to have understood by the term " mind ". He seems to me to be using the term in more senses than one. I do not mean, of course, merely that he is admitting the possibility of various *theories* as to the nature of mind being true. I mean that when he is engaged in working out what he judges to be the most likely view, he appears to employ the term now with one significance and now with another. A mind, we are told in one place (p. 390), must have a peculiar kind of content and a peculiar kind of structure. Its content consists of the kind of events which we call " mental ", and which we observe in introspection. Its structure is characterised by the ways in which these mental events are interconnected, and among such relations an important place must be given to mnemic relations. Now, when it is said that the mind *is* a compound of the body and something else, one would naturally interpret this as implying that the compound substance is at once material and mental, and that the events which make up its content are both mental and material. For it can scarcely be supposed that the material constituent loses its material character when it enters into combination with something else. Indeed, it is admitted (p. 625) that emergent materialism does imply that the events in question are both material and mental ; and, after a survey, in the last chapter, of the seventeen possible types of theory, the conclusion is drawn that " some form of the Compound Theory which is compatible with Emergent Materialism " is that which best accords with the available evidence (p. 625). And an attempt is made to show that, while there is no direct empirical evidence that what has mentality ever has also materiality, yet there is likewise none to support the proposition that the presence of mentality in an object entails the absence of materiality from it, nor any indirect way of proving this proposition. But, in other portions of the work, so violent a contrast is drawn between mental substances and material substances that the

inference would seem to be inevitable that the " mind " and " mental events " are certainly not also material. " A mind, as such, does not seem ", it is argued, " to be a spatio-temporal whole ; we can, therefore, hardly talk of *its* spatio-temporal structure. If we want to talk of spatio-temporal structure in this connexion, we have to desert the mind and start talking about the brain and nervous system " (pp. 438-39). Quite so ; but it is only the *living* brain and nervous system that in this case will serve our purpose, and the living brain and nervous system must already contain, according to the Compound Theory, the " psychic factor " which *should* constitute it a mind. Yet it is more than once asserted that " in many respects an organism is a kind of half-way house between an inorganic material substance and a mind " (*e.g.*, pp. 438 and 464). The fact is that here, as in various other places, Dr. Broad seems to be regarding the mind not as identical with the compound, but as made up of events which are distinct from the events that make up the compound, although doubtless caused by those events or existentially dependent upon them. And how the " psychic factor " of the compound can become the receptacle of the " dispositions " and " traces " of the mind is, then, if possible, still more of an enigma than before.

7. Whichever of these two conceptions be selected, I think Dr. Broad's treatment of the mind and its processes suffers from the defect that he is constantly on the search for analogies in the physical world. I sympathise entirely with his effort to withstand the tendency towards representing body and mind as two utterly disparate series of events, which somehow come into combination. I agree that whatever independence we may be induced to assign to either of them must not be absolute independence, and that, ultimately, both must form portions (if, for the moment, I may be permitted to use a vague term) of one interconnected real process. This consideration ought not, however, to blind us to the fact that mental events differ fundamentally from mater-

ial events. I leave out of account, meanwhile, what Dr. Broad calls " unowned mental events ", because, if there are such things, admittedly we can know nothing about them. Confining attention, then, to events that are " indubitably mental " (p. 305), I think we can say of them that they exhibit a unique double-sided aspect, a duality of nature, as contrasted with what may be described as the singleness of aspect presented by material events. Each distinguishable phase of the mental life is, namely, *at once* a mode of being aware of a certain content *and* a mode of what, for want of a better expression, one may designate " being for self ". The content may be confused and indistinct enough, the reference to self may be merely contained in an obscure stirring of feeling, but both are there as characterising and defining the mental state in question. And the form of unity that is peculiarly characteristic of mental life rests, it seems to me, on the fact that in each of its states or modifications the mind or subject is thus in some way and to some extent aware of self, although, of course, it is a long road from the obscure self-reference of the primitive mind to the self-consciousness of the mature mind. In other words, when the mental life is described as a unity, it ought at once to be recognised that we are employing a term which will not, on account of the very nature of that to which it is applied, have the significance which it bears in reference to material objects. The unity which we ascribe to a material object is based largely on artificial considerations, and involves a mode of connexion among the parts to which the mental life, so far as I can see, offers no analogy. Dr. Broad divides all theories about the unity of mind into two groups—namely (*a*) centre theories and (*b*) non-centre theories ; but I cannot find that either do justice to the facts of the case. On the one hand, a " pure ego " which either *has* its states or *to which* mental events happen would be, as Dr. Broad himself points out, more or less analogous to a region of absolute space in which sometimes one quality, sometimes several qualities,

Q

and sometimes, perhaps, no qualities inhere (p. 590). On the other hand, the theories which seek to explain the unity of mind by the ways in which the mental events, of which it is assumed the mind consists, are related to each other appear to be obviously framed on the analogy of the manner in which the parts are taken to be related to the whole in a physical thing. If we must have an image or picture for such general idea as we can form of the whole mental life, I suppose that of a continuous flow or stream would be the least misleading ; but we cannot adequately represent the unity and continuity of the mental life by anything drawn from the image of a physical stream or flow, because such unity and continuity as the latter possesses is more for the external observer than for the stream itself. But a conscious subject is not in a position to be himself an onlooker at the temporal flow of his own mental states ; unity and continuity cannot, therefore, have for him the significance they would bear for a supposed external spectator. The conscious subject describes himself as *one*, because in all the variety of his experiences he is, in some measure and to some degree, aware of himself. As Lotze put it, " our belief in the mind's unity rests not on our appearing to ourselves as such a unity, but upon our being able to appear to ourselves at all ". The conscious subject regards his mental life as *continuous* because of certain features exhibited by the contents of his actually present experience, of what, at the moment, he is actually aware—the fact, namely, that such contents always more or less involve and imply a reference beyond themselves, a reference to the past and, it may be, to the future. There is no unity or continuity in the process of cognising, feeling and conation which is not essentially dependent upon the unity and continuity of what is cognised or felt or sought. And, as regards this kind of unity and continuity, it would stand in no conflict with what an outside observer might describe as periods of unconsciousness. It may well be the case that since our mental life is bound up with bodily conditions, of the relations of which to it we know little or nothing, there will frequently be on its current, as viewed from without, gaps or pauses ; and I can see no need for recourse to the hypothesis of a " pure ego " in order to conceive of those gaps or pauses as being somehow bridged over. Nor does it seem to me that the phenomena of multiple personality need occasion in this respect any real difficulty. For there is exhibited in each of these apparently disconnected mental lives the same internal unity and continuity that we find in conscious experience generally. I am prepared, then, to say that the mind *is* its mental states, rather than that it *has* them ; but I am not prepared to say that an aggregate of mental states, externally interrelated, is the mind. Indeed, Dr. Broad himself doubts " whether anyone except a philosopher engaged in philosophising believes for a moment that the relation of ' himself ' to ' his toothache ' is the same relation as that of the British army to Private John Smith " (p. 484). That the mental states of a mind, no less than the contents apprehended through them, are related to one another, and in a very intimate fashion, is, I take it, unquestionable ; but the relation need not be of that nature which is exemplified in the relations to one another of physical events. The unity of an individual mind is, as Professor Stout has skilfully expressed it, " the unity of a complex whole, which is indivisible inasmuch as its partial ingredients have not an independent existence of their own, such that the whole could conceivably be constituted by taking them separately and then combining them". A unity of this kind is, as Stout further points out, likewise to be found in organic life, although in the mental life " it is, beyond comparison, most fully developed and most clearly recognisable ".[1]

8. What I have just said will enable me to add a word or two upon the doctrine of " traces " which figures so prominently in Dr. Broad's treatment of the mind. He does not, of course, lend his countenance to the crude view that has

[1] *Studies in Philosophy and Psychology*, p. 119.

often been prevalent in popular psychology. He acknowledges that we know nothing with certainty about the intrinsic nature of " traces " ; he will assert little more of them than that they are " mnemic persistents " which last for a long while and fill the gaps between transient states of mind. The grounds on which he feels constrained to assume the existence of " traces " are, so I gather, the following. He holds that as physical events are causally connected, so also are mental events. He holds further that while regular sequence is not what we *mean* by causation, it is one of the signs by which we judge that the causal relation is present. In itself, however, it is not an adequate sign. There must be in addition a certain temporal continuity between the sequent events ; all the independently necessary conditions of an event must either be continuous with it or immediately precede it. Now, in the case of a present memory of a past experience, this requirement is not fulfilled, if it be supposed that the past experience and a present stimulus are the complete cause of the present memory. The temporal gap between the past experience and the present stimulus must be filled with persistent conditions that stretch right up to the beginning of the effect. It is true that one general persistent condition (*e.g.*, the general integrity of the brain and nervous system) might conceivably suffice ; but, while he will not definitely rule out the possibility that a merely general continuity is sufficient, yet, for certain reasons which I need not go into, the more likely supposition seems to him to be that there are special persistent conditions for different experiences. Whether these special persistent conditions, or " traces ", are purely mental or purely physiological or both, he will, again, not undertake to decide. If they are physiological, they will be modifications in the minute spatio-temporal structure of the brain and nervous system, which will be propagated from one state of that structure to the next state, and so on. If they are mental, and if the assumption of a " pure ego " be discarded, the account we shall have to give of them will be more complicated. We shall then have to suppose that the apparent gap between an original experience and the revival of it in memory is filled up by unconscious or non-introspectible mental states and processes ; and that these have characteristic qualities and stand in characteristic relations to each other. And, as I indicated above in another connexion, the " traces " will not be these unconscious mental events themselves, but certain qualities of them that are handed down to subsequent mental events, or certain of their relations which are " impressed upon " the mental events succeeding them, and so on indefinitely.

As regards the theory last mentioned, it is evident that if unconscious mental states and the " traces " which they are assumed to carry are to be postulated at all, it will have to be on a prodigiously lavish scale. There would appear to be no end to the countless varieties of experiences that would thus leave behind " traces " of themselves ; and we should be compelled to conceive of the mind of every normal human adult as an enormous storehouse of unconscious mental events, in comparison with which the conscious portion of the mental life would be infinitesimal indeed. The question whether an individual mind could endure so burdensome a load can hardly be dismissed as a trifling question. It would no doubt be urged that the innumerable " traces " within the compass of any one mental life are not to be pictured as merely subsisting side by side ; that they are rather to be thought of as forming vast and elaborately organised systems. Yet, even so, the magnitude of the mechanism that will have to be assumed will still remain overwhelming ; and in addition there will be the further problem of accounting for the fact of so complicated a process of organisation being effected in the region of the " unconscious ". Now I know, of course, the sort of rejoinder that an objection of this kind is sure to meet with. It will be contended that the devices of nature are, as a matter of fact, infinitely varied and that we need not, therefore, be staggered by the complexity of the

" mental structure " that is here called into requisition. But this contention does not, I confess, in itself impress me ; it could be used to bolster up any theory, however fantastic, that might be advanced to explain phenomena the conditions of which are unknown to us. And I have an uneasy feeling that the mechanism we are bidden in this case to contemplate is an extraordinarily clumsy one, suggestive rather of the mode of procedure of an unskilled craftsman or of the theory of epicycles of astronomers before Copernicus than of what we actually know of the mind's method of working. Not only so. No attempt is made to show *how* these assumed persistent factors subserve the function for which they are declared to be necessary. Dr. Broad is emphatic in asserting that what persists is not an experience itself but the " trace " of that experience. " And ", he writes, " there is no more positive reason to suppose that the trace of an experience resembles it or any other experience than to suppose that persistent deafness resembles the attack of scarlet fever which left it in the patient " (p. 359). Be it so ; in what way, then, does the presence of a " trace " assist me in recognising that a man whom I chance to meet to-day is the same individual with whom I was conversing (say) a year ago? Apparently what the " trace " when it is " excited " by the present stimulus has got to do is either (*a*) to produce the awareness of a memory-image resembling the past event, or else (*b*) to make me cognise directly the past event which left the " trace " (pp. 444-45); but not so much as the remotest hint is given as to the manner in which it is supposed to operate in contributing to the accomplishment of either of these things.

But, it will be maintained, in order to justify the " trace " theory, one is not called upon to exhibit the way in which the " trace " when it is " excited " by the present stimulus actually gives rise to the memory. If it be granted that the memory is causally produced, and that in such case all its independently necessary conditions must immediately precede its occurrence, then the existence of " traces ", whatever

be their nature, has been virtually conceded. I should meet
this contention by raising at once the question whether it is
at all possible to apply the notion of causal connexion within
the sphere of subjective experience and to the mental events
that condition subjective experience. The difficulties in the
way of carrying out what no doubt represents our first
natural mode of interpreting the facts has repeatedly made
itself felt, and certain philosophers have been led to distinguish two types of causality—causality such as is manifested
in physical nature and causality as it is manifested in the
mental life. Thus, for example, Wundt would differentiate
between physical and psychical causality, aud Mr. Russell
between natural and mnemic causal laws. I would, however, go
farther, to the extent, namely, of urging that to employ the term
" cause " in this twofold sense is an error, and that we are
bound to inquire whether we are at all warranted in viewing
the two kinds of connexion—that between material events
and that between mental events—as being on the same level.
I cannot see that we are. Not only does the conception of
causation as used in physical science presuppose a certain
identity in essential nature of the entities that are said to be
causally connected, but I think it involves the additional
thought that the entities or events in question are exclusively
objective phenomena. I must not attempt here to defend
this position ; I will note simply that, if it be defensible, it
affords a ready means of determining where a limit to the
application of the notion of " cause " should be drawn.
Wherever, namely, the entities or events under consideration
cannot be treated as objects merely, but can be construed
only in a fashion other than what is appropriate in the case
of objects, there the application of the thought of causal
nexus is illegitimate. Now, it seems to me that in Dr.
Broad's discussion of the problem there can be found abundant reasons for concluding that the proposition just stated
is not devoid of justification. It is true he tries to show that
comparable to the fundamental causal characteristics of

matter, such as inertia, gravitational attraction, etc., there are certain general " mental powers ", characteristic of all minds—*e.g.*, the power of cognising, the power of being affected by past experiences, the power of association— where, if I am right, there is no such comparability. Yet he is compelled, all the same, to recognise many striking and crucial differences. For one thing, a mind in the course of its development is continually acquiring new and extremely determinate powers, while there is nothing analogous to this in the case of matter. And, more important still, he draws attention to the circumstance that " it is characteristic of modern science as contrasted with mediaeval science to correlate causal properties with minute spatial or spatio-temporal structure, and not to take them as ultimate facts " (p. 434), whereas a mind does not seem, at any rate, to be a spatio-temporal whole, nor to be composed of unobservable minds as a material substance is composed of bits of matter (p. 439).[1] I should be prepared, then, to take my stand on the last-mentioned difference, and to insist that it alone ought to suggest a doubt as to whether the mode of connexion between mental states is at all comparable to the mode of connexion between physical events.

The upshot of the matter is that while I do not wish to maintain that there are no persistent conditions involved in the structure of the mind, I am not by any means convinced that we are driven to a theory of " traces ", such as Dr. Broad has delineated. From what we know of the nature of mind, I do not think we are entitled to lay down the dogma

[1] In the later chapter on " The Unity of the Mind " the force of this admission would appear, however, to be weakened. The attempt is there made to show how it would be possible to take the notion of a material event as fundamental and to construct the notion of material substances out of it, without assuming absolute space in Newton's sense. And, then, an effort is made to show the possibility of likewise taking the notion of mental event as fundamental and the notion of mental substance as derivative. But for the latter undertaking it is necessary to assume that every mental event has not only a determinate temporal position but also a determinate " mental position " corresponding to the " spatial position " of material events (p. 599), although as to what the term " mental position " is supposed to signify no help is afforded for determining.

that all the independently necessary conditions of a memory *must* be present in the state of things immediately preceding it. And, in particular, I am more than sceptical in regard to the existence of *special* persistents on the huge scale which the " trace " theory would seem to necessitate.

9. Let me revert, in conclusion, to the doctrine of the mind as a compound substance, or rather as a compound substance of the kind which Dr. Broad takes it to be. The doctrine seems far more allied to the biological doctrine which he has called " substantial vitalism " than to that which he names " emergent vitalism " ; and, in criticising the former, he has himself supplied us with arguments (pp. 57-58) that can be pressed against this doctrine of his own. It is objected, namely, to the explanation of vital behaviour in terms of entelechies, in the first place, that no entelechy, or anything like one, has ever been isolated, that an entelechy is a *purely* hypothetical entity in a sense which a hitherto unisolated chemical element is not. That statement is clearly equally true of the assumed " psychic factor ". It is objected, in the second place, that whereas we can pass a chemical group, hitherto unisolated, from one compound to another, and note how the chemical properties change as one compound loses such a group and another gains it, there is no known analogy to this with entelechies. " You cannot pass an entelechy from a living man into a corpse and note that the former ceases and the latter begins to behave vitally." So, in precisely similar manner, it can be urged that you cannot pass a " psychic factor " from a living man into a corpse and note that the former ceases and the latter begins to behave mentally. It is objected, in the third place, that since entelechies are supposed to differ in kind from material particles, and it is doubtful whether they are literally in space at all, it is hard to make out what is meant by saying that a living body is a compound of an entelechy and a material structure. But, and for exactly similar reasons, is it any easier to understand what is meant by saying that a mental life is a compound of a

" psychic factor " and a material structure? Indeed, I am not sure that what Dr. Broad further contends in regard to entelechies might not also be contended, with little change of terms, in regard to " psychic factors ". Entelechies, he thinks, seem plausible to some people because they modestly conceive of them as very inferior minds or as the inferior parts of the minds which animate organisms. Yet this modesty is, he insists, altogether out of place ; if the hypothesis is to explain anything, the entelechy must be thought of as either a superior mind or a superior part of the mind which animates an organism. I am inclined to press the very same consideration in reference to " psychic factors ". For consider the functions which these " psychic factors " have to discharge. The presence of a certain sitter " attracts " (whatever that may mean) the " psychic factor " of a dead man who was known to him. The man may have died in Bombay and the sitter may be in a séance in London, yet somehow or another the particular " psychic factor " that is wanted finds its way to the right quarters and communicates with the one medium with whom it is required to communicate (p. 54). Is it alleged that this is a pure matter of chance, and that the " psychic factor " behaves in a wholly arbitrary fashion, that it might equally well have been any one of a myriad other " psychic factors " that may be " blowing about the universe " ? I imagine that it would be difficult to reconcile such a contention with any numerical measurement of probabilities. I leave out of account many other perplexities of the situation (such, for example, as to how it comes about that *this* " psychic factor " contrives to oust for a while the " psychic factor " of the medium herself, and then to depart leaving the latter once again in possession), in order to enforce this one point. Such wonderfully alert " psychic factors ", that when separate from the bodies with which they have been conjoined are up to so much that is usually associated with intelligence, would certainly seem to be a little too modest in disclaiming the attributes of mind!

X

THE REFUTATION OF SUBJECTIVISM

THE volume entitled *The Theory of Knowledge and Existence*, published in 1932 by Dr. W. T. Stace of Princeton, is an able and stimulating work. My interest in it has not, however, been due to any satisfaction I have felt in regard to the doctrines which its author is concerned to maintain. On the contrary, on almost all the fundamental issues of epistemological theory which he discusses I find myself in radical disagreement with him. My interest has been rather due to the fact that a view of the nature of knowledge and experience which I had thought the criticism of recent times had finally disposed of is here openly avowed and defended with no small amount of logical acumen and ingenuity. The arguments used have not convinced me ; they have not caused me to deviate in the slightest degree from a position which long reflexion has convinced me is based on grounds amply strong enough to bear its weight. But that a competent and judicious thinker should reach a result so diametrically opposite, and support it by arguments of an independent character, is perhaps a sufficient reason for reverting once more to problems on which, in former years, I have written much.

Let me, first of all, state as concisely as I can what I understand Dr. Stace's contention to be. He apparently holds that epistemology is a purely empirical science in which the structure and functions of knowledge are examined in a manner exactly similar to the way in which the structure of the bodily organism and the functions of its parts are examined in biology. So conceived, epistemology has, however, he thinks, implications with respect to the nature of

existence, and these implications may be said to be metaphysical in character. But it is important in this context to distinguish between empirical and transcendental metaphysics,
for it is only with the former, which takes the data of experience for granted without seeking to inquire as to how and
why they have arisen, that we have here to do. Yet it must
not be supposed that an empirical philosophy and a transcendental one necessarily contradict one another. They do
not ; they simply move on different levels. A disciple of
Hegel may consistently enough be at the same time a disciple
of Hume. Only he must recognise that in these two capacities
he is dealing with different problems.

Assuming, then, that knowledge must in some sense start
from experience, the question at once confronts us : *whose*
experience? And to that question there can, it is alleged,
be only one answer. Each individual must begin with his
own experience, and interpret the experience of others in
terms of his own. The method of empirical epistemology can,
therefore, be no other than that of setting out from the immediate data of one's own experience, the given elements in
one's knowledge, and, by working upwards from this basis,
attempting to see how the organised development of knowledge has taken place on that foundation.

Accordingly, the initial step will consist in disentangling
the " given " from the later accretions of knowledge, understanding by *the* " given " the particular " given " in the case
of a particular individual, and recognising that the " given "
does not imply any metaphysical doctrine as to how it
comes to be " given ". The classification of the given elements, which Dr. Stace has to offer, differs in several respects
from other classifications of a similar kind. In the first
place, the most obvious given elements of experience consist
in presentations or images, and under this general heading
are included (*a*) all sense-presentations, colours, sounds,
odours, tastes and so on ; and (*b*) all images of imagination
or memory, of hallucination or dream, which have the same

immediate character as sense-presentations. In the second place, the " given " includes what the author calls " extension-spread " and " duration-spread " ; but this is very far from saying that it includes space and time. On the one hand, the extension-spread which is part of the " given " is two-dimensional only—depth or distance is not " given ", but is a result of mental elaboration—and, on the other hand, empty space is not " given ", for it cannot be sensed, it is got at by means of later conceptual analysis and inference. So, too, duration-spread is not the " even flow " of Newton ; there is no empty time and no future time in the " given ". In the third place, while *all* relations are not " given ", there are *some* relations which are. The most important of the latter are (*a*) relations of position in the extension-spread, such as " to the left of ", " between ", and the like ; (*b*) relations of position in the duration-spread, such as " before and after " ; and (*c*) the extremely significant relations of resemblance and its opposite. In the fourth place, the " given " includes those mental activities on the basis of which self-knowledge becomes possible. Acts of mind, such as attending, feeling, willing, thinking, are just as much immediately presented as is the redness of red, and they are presented *as activities*. Not only so. The distinction between active and passive, which distinction is itself " given ", is the fundamental ground of the later division of the world into internal and external, mind and matter.

Such, in Dr. Stace's view, are the raw materials by means of which the edifice of knowledge is somehow to be reared. These materials are " given " and they consist in the phantasms and appearances which occupy consciousness within the self-enclosed area. In order to advance to knowledge of a public external world, it is necessary for the individual to issue forth from the privacy of his own ego into communication with other minds. Without such co-operation, the solitary mind would never come to a knowledge of an objective world. Its world would remain a private world of dreams. But, prior to the great step from a private world of each to a public world for all, it *is* possible for the solitary mind, shut up within itself, to elaborate a rudimentary kind of knowledge. No knowledge of any sort is, indeed, possible without concepts. Conceptual thought is the instrument with which even the solitary mind works upon the " given ". In itself, the given is a chaos of presentations and presented relations. This chaos the mind reduces to order by means of its concepts. *How* or *why* the mind conceptionalises we cannot say. That it does so is an ultimate fact, and that fact we have to accept with " natural piety ". The most elementary kind of concepts are, so it is maintained, what may be called " concepts of the given ", and these are possible for the solitary mind which has no awareness either of other minds or of an external world of objects. These concepts constitute the beginning, the first step of knowledge. They involve the smallest possible element of mental elaboration. Like all concepts they are founded upon the fact of resemblance, and they involve the mental act of comparing. Such a concept is, for example, the concept " red ". In this case, the mind notices the resemblance of two or more red patches, and identifies the red in them. *How* it does so is a question which cannot be asked. The *fact* that it does so is ultimate and unanalysable. It is itself " given ". Under the head of " concepts of the given " fall not only those of particular qualitative presentations, such as " red ", " loud "; " sweet ", etc., but even more general concepts, such as " colour ", " sound ", " odour ", " taste ", " sensation ", etc. Moreover, " concepts of the given " include concepts of those relations which are themselves given. " Resemblance ", for example, is such a concept, and so, too, is " unlikeness ". And such durational concepts as " before " and " after ", as also such extensional concepts as " beside ", " above ", " between ", belong to the same category.

So far, then, and no farther, may the solitary mind, as Dr. Stace conceives it, advance in the acquisition of knowledge.

There is, he insists, no way of escaping the conclusion that the initial position of every mind must be solipsistic. For the world from which we start is a world of mere presentations, along with its special and elementary concepts. And for each individual these presentations are his own presentations. My presentations are not your presentations, nor am I yet aware of your presentations or even of your existence. That is a later discovery. Each mind is, therefore, originally aware of its colour patches, its sounds, its scents and tastes, which come and go like images in a dream, and it is unaware of anything else. " It has no knowledge of the existence of any other mind. It has no knowledge of the existence of external objects in so far as these differ from mere presentations."

A distinctive feature of Dr. Stace's theory is that our belief in the existence of an independent external world depends absolutely on our belief in the existence of other minds. " The former belief ", he writes, " would be impossible unless we had first acquired the latter. The external world is a social product. The solitary mind, unaware of the existence of minds other than itself, is a mind necessarily confined to a world of private phantasms " (p. 169). How, then, does the solitary mind succeed in discovering the existence of minds other than its own? The reply is that the logical justification of my belief in the existence of other minds is by way of analogical inference. In the first place, I learn to separate out from the general mass of my presentations a certain group of presentations which I can never get rid of, which accompanies me about as a group and so becomes associated in my mind with myself, with my thinking, feeling, willing self. " My body is simply that portion of my presentations which forces itself upon me " (p. 189). Moreover, this group of presentations does not vary in size and shape, as other groups of presentations do ; it alone remains roughly constant. And lastly, it is specially associated with feelings of pleasure and pain. Thus the various visual, tactile and other presentations concerned first become thought of as a group instead of singly ; and then this group becomes associated in my mind with *me* as a thinking, feeling being—it becomes " my " body. The transition to the recognition of other minds is made through my coming to notice that there exist many groups of presentations which resemble the group which is " my " body. It is true that no one of the former is like the latter in the characteristics just mentioned. No one of them accompanies me about, or retains the same size, or is specially associated with my pleasure and pain. But I observe that these groups behave in the same way as the group constituting my body behaves. They laugh, cry out, run, smile and so on. So that their general similarity of shape and colour, more especially their similarities of behaviour, suggest to me by analogy that with them are associated minds like mine, and the inference to the existence of other minds is then complete.

The belief in the existence of an independent external world of things or objects is not, according to Dr. Stace, reached by inference, after the manner in which the belief in the existence of other minds is. It is not an inference, for there is nothing from which it could be validly inferred. But there are other logical steps possible besides inferences— namely, mental constructions. And the author's thesis is that belief in the existence of an external thing—or, indeed, the external thing itself—is formed by a series of such mental constructions. I find it, I confess, by no means easy to make out what exactly is meant here by the phrase " mental construction ". We are told, for instance, that " a construction is a fiction, a judgment invented by the mind, without any foundation in the " given " (p. 429). Again, " a construction is, among other things, an assumption which cannot be proved, *i.e.* cannot be shown to be logically necessary " (p. 433). Further, a construction is said to be " a work of imagination ", which uses always materials already supplied by the " given " (p. 111). The mind has

invented it as a fiction which suits its purposes (p. 105).
Nevertheless, we have somehow to distinguish between those
constructions which are true and those which are false.   In
order to be true, a construction must be internally self-
consistent, and it must be consistent with the system of
truths into which it is sought to embody it.   In reference,
now, to the so-called external world, we have to do with a
series of such " true " constructions.   Not only has the
human mind in the past explicitly gone through these stages
of mental construction, but each present-day individual
must do so somehow in the earlier period of his existence.
There are six such stages in all.   The first construction is
" that the presentations of one mind bear to the corresponding presentations of other minds the relation of resemblance ".   The second is " that the corresponding presentations of different minds are identical, and that there are
not many universes, but only one ".   The third is " that the
presentations of a mind may continue in existence unperceived by that mind, provided that some other mind perceives them ".   The fourth is " that presentations may exist
when no mind is aware of them ".   The fifth is " that there
exist ' things ' or ' objects ', which are not identical with
presentations ; that the presentations are ' qualities ' of the
' things ' ; and that the ' qualities ' may change while the
' things ' remain the same ".   And the sixth is " that with
the different senses we may perceive the ' same ' objects,
and that the worlds of the different senses are, in general,
identical with one another ".

It is, of course, impossible in a short survey to do adequate
justice to a theory which has been worked out by its author
in elaborate detail ; but I hope I have said enough to indicate
its general character.   I want now to try to state with equal
brevity some of the reasons that seem to me sufficient to
prove its untenability.

In the first place, then, I would call in question in the
present instance, as I have done in respect to other theories,

R

the initial contention that the individual mind starts with a world, or rather a chaos, of mere presentations. It is true that Dr. Stace refuses to describe presentations as mental; and that he frequently uses the term to signify simply the "given". Yet he insists upon sharply differentiating " presentations " from " objects " ; he maintains that the *esse* of the former is *percipi* ; he speaks of them as " appearances " or " phantasms " ; he pictures the mind as originally confronted only by a procession of fleeting colour-patches, detached sounds, isolated odours and so on ; and in a curious manner he asserts that " I cannot experience anything except *my own* experience ". Now, in this context, I would urge that to suppose presentations, as thus distinguished from " things " or " objects ", are directly apprehended entities is absolutely contrary to what can be gathered from even a cursory inspection of actual experience. On the one hand, in *mature* sense-perception what we are *immediately* aware of are certainly not presentations of the kind just indicated. Sitting in front of my study-table, I am certainly not *immediately* aware of fleeting colour-patches, of appearances of shininess, of smoothness, of an oblong shape and so on. What I am *immediately* aware of is a single unified object, possessing a variety of characteristics, which, when I am challenged, I can enumerate in detail, but which are never presented in isolation. It is, for example, only by a deliberate and sustained effort of attention, and through the aid of artificial devices, that I apprehend colour-patches in and for themselves at all. Ordinary perception is so dominated by what is misleadingly called " the reference to externally existing things " that visual presentations are not as such contemplated by us, but do duty merely as signs. If, then, the term " immediate " be used in reference to our mature experience, it is of *things* that we are immediately aware, while presentations, simply as such, are not *immediately* cognised. On the other hand, in regard to the primitive mind, the point I am pressing is still more apparent. If there be any truth which genetic psychology can be said to have established, it is that experience does not advance by a gradual building up of concrete objects from originally isolated and detached presentations. The individual mind does not start with the apprehension of fleeting colour-patches, with isolated presentations of hardness, smoothness and the like, and out of such definite appearances *construct* the complexes which are designated "things". On the contrary, the individual mind starts with an environment the characteristics of which are but dimly and confusedly apprehended, and the parts of which are but crudely and vaguely recognised as distinguishable from one another. And conscious intelligence advances by a continuously growing capacity of discriminating differences at first undis-criminated, of distinguishing features previously undis-tinguished, of holding elements apart that were formerly confused together. In short, at no stage in the history of the mental life, and least of all in the earlier stages, can there be said to be immediate awareness of detached and isolated presentations. Such awareness as we have of these is always attained through a process of abstraction, and cannot, there-fore, be "immediate" in the sense that is claimed for it. The conclusion, then, to which the facts upon which I have been dwelling assuredly leads is this—that sense-appearances presuppose, as the condition of their possibility, real existing things which appear, that the appearances are dependent upon the actually real objects, and not the objects upon the appearances.

In the second place, I venture to submit that the account offered by Dr. Stace of the way in which the individual comes to discover the existence of other minds is wholly unsuccessful. It is true he admits that the inference from analogy, on which he relies, does not and cannot yield cer-tainty ; there are no means, he allows, by which I can be absolutely *certain* that any mind exists except my own. The argument by analogy goes as far as is possible, he thinks, towards proving the real existence of other minds ; but, as in the case of all analogical reasoning, it is a probable conclusion only. It seems to me, however, that on the premises put forward it is not even a remotely probable conclusion. For let us scrutinise these premises a little more closely. The group of presentations which is my body is associated with my mind ; and I come to think that its modes of behaviour generally are caused by special kinds of mental content. Further, I also perceive certain other groups of presentations almost exactly like the group I associate with my own mind. These groups behave in the same manner as my group does. Therefore, they suggest to me by analogy that with them are associated minds like mine. But, in what conceivable way can these groups of presentations be associated with minds like mine ? That might be the case if these groups of presentations which I am supposed to be observing were actually presentations of *other* minds. That, however, is exactly what they can never be. They are *my* presentations, and how a group of *my* presentations can be associated with *your* mind in a manner similar to that in which another group of my presentations is associated with *my* mind remains, certainly, an inexplicable enigma. My presentations and yours are said to exist in different universes which are absolutely cut off from one another. The consciousness of each of us is a separate world. " It is not merely a physical impossibility for me to see your red ; the difficulty is a logical one. If I could see your red, your red would have become mine, and, in so far as I saw it, ceased to be yours." Now, what is here said of your red must hold of *your* group of presentations associated with your mind. I cannot get at *those* presentations ; whereas *my* group of presentations of your body is simply not associated with *your* mind. I contend, therefore, that the assumed analogical inference is entirely invalid, and affords not the slightest justification for the belief in the existence of other minds. Indeed, I think we must go further and affirm that the determination that another mind exists and has experience qualitatively identical with our own is possible only in so far as we have effected for ourselves the distinction between perceiving as an internal state and the perceived object as independent thereof.

In the third place, even allowing for the sake of argument that we do discover the existence of other minds in the way alleged, yet the mode in which belief in an independent external world—not to mention the being of that independent external world itself—is declared to be constructed appears to me, I confess, more like a fairy tale than a veritable piece of philosophical analysis. To suppose that the primitive mind actually performs the elaborate process of imaginative construction I have described strikes one as an hypothesis so grotesque as scarcely to need refutation. Take, for instance, the first of the six constructions we have noted. Why does the primitive mind make the assumption that when it and another mind are looking at a green book—not, be it noted, at the presentations of a green book—their two presentations are similar? Because, we are told, it thereby avoids a perfectly unnecessary complication ; and it will naturally adopt the simpler of two alternatives. But can anyone seriously suppose that this is the sort of reflexion that somehow goes on at the beginning, more or less, of an individual's history? Or, take the third construction, that the primitive mind, while admitting that its presentations may continue unperceived by it, will still insist that they must be perceived by some other mind. " Even this partial admission of an unperceived existence is ", we are told, " plainly a paradox. The existence of *my* presentation obviously consists in the fact that it is presented to *me*, that I am aware of it. And to say that it goes on existing when I am not aware of it is like saying that it goes on existing after it has gone out of existence. But either *A* and *B* must swallow this paradox, or they must give up their common world. They cannot have it both ways. Faced with this dilemma, they decide to swallow the paradox. They will not give up their common world. The convenience it introduces into thought and action is too great to be sacrificed. And it is not unreasonable to suppose also that having found companionship with each other, they fear the sense of loneliness and isolation which would result from their going back to their separate self-enclosed universes." A primitive mind that could ponder thus would certainly have no occasion to fear comparison with even the highest products of intellectual development! The vital objection to this whole attempt to trace the genesis of our belief in an external world is, however, that it is all the while being taken for granted that the so-called " constructs " are *not* merely results which we gradually come to assume, but are, on the contrary, veritable sources or conditions of the coming to be of our presentations themselves—that they have, in other words, actual existence, and are capable of exerting causal efficiency.

The study, then, of Dr. Stace's volume has served only to confirm my conviction that if we start from a subjectivism, such as he inculcates, there is no mode of effecting a transition to a knowledge of objective reality. I am aware, of course, that many writers have contended that there is no logical method of showing that solipsism, as it is called, is a false doctrine, however absurd it may seem to common-sense. " Solipsism ", so a modern Oxford writer informs us, " is intellectually quite an entertaining doctrine, and not *logically* untenable ; it is only practically uncomfortable. Anyone madly logical enough might always insist that he was the sole and omnipotent creator of his whole experience." But it must be acknowledged that it would be for philosophy somewhat of a scandal, if it were unable to provide a logical means of escape from what is confessedly a palpably absurd and ridiculous position. I want, then, now to try to show that philosophy is not in this predicament.

Let me start by quoting a sentence which in one form or another has been widely affirmed. " We *know* ourselves ", it has been said, " and we *know* around us an impenetrable wall of sense-presentations." Substitute the singular for the plural pronoun here ; and you have the proposition upon which it has been maintained solipsism might entrench itself without fear of being logically refuted. " I *know* myself, and I *know* around me an impenetrable wall of sense-presentations." This proposition I am going to argue *is* self-contradictory ; and is not, therefore, logically tenable.

The contradiction consists, to put it briefly, in this—that if there were around me an impenetrable wall of sense-presentations, that very fact would preclude me from knowing *myself*, or from speaking in any intelligible sense of " *I* " or " *me* " or of " *my* " presentations at all. In order so much as to formulate his position, a solipsist must assert that he is aware of his own existence. But, in laying down the proposition just quoted he is assuming *both* self-knowledge *and* a limitation which, according to his own showing, would render such self-knowledge impossible. Let me try to make this clear. Sense-presentations are taken to be entities within my own consciousness, affections of my own mind. Now, my mind is admittedly not one of its own affections. It is assumed, no doubt, that presentations or ideas are creations of the mind ; yet, even so, the presentations thus created, and the agency that creates them, cannot be identified. The contents of knowledge, so we are to understand, consist of the ideas or creations of the self : how, then, can this knowing, how can this creative, self be at the same time a content of knowledge? It is a question, this, which those who argue in the way I have been indicating never really face ; and one can only conjecture the kind of answer that might be attempted. So far as I can see, one of two, and only two, alternative answers is conceivable, and neither of them will avail for what is required. It may be argued, namely, *either* that the conscious ego constructs a presentation or idea of *itself*, in addition to the presentations it constructs of *things, or* that it has an awareness of itself through some other channel than that of presentations or ideas.

Consider the former alternative, that the conscious ego constructs a presentation or idea of itself. In that case, it will be *this* presentation or idea that I shall be aware of when I am said to know myself, and there will be a precisely similar antithesis between *this* presentation or idea of self *and* the assumed real self as, according to the theory, there is between a presentation of a thing and the assumed real thing. The existence of the real self, that is to say, will be, so far as knowledge is concerned, an inference from the presentation of the self, of which alone there is immediate awareness. But, if the individual self, as an existing entity, can only be inferred from the presentation of it, on what plea can it be alleged that the process of inference can be trusted in this instance, in spite of the fact that it is judged to be untrustworthy in making the transition from the presentation of an external thing to the actual existence of that external thing ? Is it not evident that the doubt which it is asserted pertains to the existence of so-called external things pertains likewise, in that case, to the existence of the *internal* thing, which is called the self ; and that thus the very proposition upon which it is claimed solipsism can be securely rested turns out to be a transparent fallacy.

Take, now, the other alternative—that the ego is aware of itself through some medium—say, through intuition or feeling, or what not—other than the medium of presentations or ideas. Then the question forthwith arises, how is this immediate awareness of self related to the other immediate awareness, that, namely, of presentations or ideas? If this question be not evaded, it will have to be acknowledged that, presuming such awareness of self is what is meant by immediate or direct awareness, then the awareness of presentations or ideas is *not* immediate or direct, but that, as contrasted with the immediately known self, presentations are external and independent entities. And *if* the fact of their externality does not preclude them from being known, why should the fact of the externality of what we name material things preclude these latter from likewise being known? In other words, the self-same argument by means of which it was sought to prove that external things are in themselves unknowable would prove also that presentations or ideas are likewise unknowable ; and thus, once more, the assumption of solipsism turns out to be self-contradictory.

That assumption has, however, so insidious a way of creeping into our reflexion that I may, perhaps, be permitted to add a final consideration. Even so scrupulously careful a writer as Professor Volkelt expressed himself as follows : " All the acts claiming to constitute objective knowledge are inseparably united to the individual consciousness of the knower, they have really existence primarily and immediately nowhere save in the consciousness of the individual, and they are perfectly incapable of extending beyond the conscious- ness of the individual and of grasping or entering the field of the real that lies beyond."[1] Now, the essential point of the argument I have been pressing may be brought out by em- phasising that there is, in this contention of Volkelt's, deep- rooted confusion between two propositions resembling each other, it may be, in verbal form but totally different from one another in meaning, the one of which is true and the other of which is false.

The true proposition is that knowing, as a state or con- dition of the individual mind, must of necessity be subjective in character. Even in the case of a consciousness that was capable of perfectly complete knowledge, it would still be a fact that knowing would be subjective in the sense of being an act or process of the mind in question. As Lotze, in a very valuable section of his *Logic*, conclusively showed, it is absurd to demand of knowledge that it should be something other than knowledge—that it should, namely, transcend *the* antithesis between knowing and the known which is implied in the very notion of knowledge itself. The proposition that knowing, as a condition or modification of consciousness, is

[1] *Erfahrung und Denken*, p. 4.

necessarily of the nature of consciousness ; and, therefore, subjective in character, is, then, I say, obviously a true proposition.

The false proposition with which the true proposition just referred to is often confounded, as I think it was by Volkelt, is the following : that knowing is not only co-existent with consciousness in its range as knowing, but has consciousness, and nothing but consciousness, for its apprehended content. For that proposition I can find absolutely no warrant. It may, indeed, be doubted whether we ever have knowledge of consciousness as such—whether, that is to say, consciousness can ever be presented as an object. But, waiving this point, it is clear that nothing is gained, so far as knowledge or certainty is concerned, by drawing a distinction in this respect between *intra-subjective* and *trans-subjective*. In and through the process of knowing, I can be no more certain of what is *in my* consciousness, if one may employ for the moment a purely metaphorical mode of expression, than of what is *beyond my* consciousness. In the case of so-called introspection, for example, the knowing is, like knowing of all kinds, a process of mind, but here the known is also a condition or process of mind, yet the latter fact gives no additional certainty whatsoever to the resulting cognition. On the contrary, we know a great deal more about tables and chairs, or even about planets and suns, than we know about our own mental states.

Or, to put the point in still another way, it is a delusion to suppose that, in the genesis of knowledge, we begin with the awareness of the contents known as being subjective in character, and then come to refer these contents, or rather certain of them, to the trans-subjective. There is, it may be safely asserted, no such procedure as that occurring in actual fact. As Edward Caird once concisely expressed it, if we start with the merely subjective, " it is as much a problem how we get *into* ourselves as how we get *out* of ourselves." Neither logically nor chronologically does the awareness of the subjective precede the awareness of the objective. The conception of the self comes into being only in correlation with the conception of what is other than the self ; psychologically, the development of the two conceptions proceeds strictly *pari passu*—there would be no recognition of the one without a corresponding recognition of the other.

XI

THE PHILOSOPHICAL RESEARCHES OF MEINONG

1. *The Nature and Aims of Philosophical Inquiry.*
2. *The Hume-Studien. Abstract Ideas and the Theory of Relations.*
3. *" Object " and " Content ". The Subjectivist Interpretation of Relations.*
4. *Gegenstandstheorie.*

To venture upon giving some account of Meinong's contributions to philosophy is a rash undertaking. For the task is
one of peculiar difficulty. Had Meinong made any attempt
to think out or develop a comprehensive metaphysical
theory, it would have been comparatively easy to sketch the
main features of that theory, and perhaps to indicate where
it seemed exposed to attack. But his speculative genius lay
not in the direction of system-building ; and I suspect he
distrusted the attitude of mind which system-building frequently betokens. His published work, and it is amazingly
voluminous, is all of it of an extremely detailed kind ; its
value largely consists in its resolute thoroughness, in the rare
combination it shows of unprejudiced observation with
acute inference, and in the minute care with which he tried
to see all round and to get to the roots of the problems he
handled. Moreover, the themes he selected for treatment
were almost always those at the growing-point of philosophical inquiry ; he had an extraordinary facility of discerning precisely that which required to be wrestled with in
order to make headway in philosophical research. As a
writer he was lucid and clear ; but his very persistency in
tracking a subject through its ramifications gives to his mode
of exposition a certain prolixity, which those who like to have
their philosophy served up to them in imagery and metaphor
will be ready enough to decry as dullness. Yet his intellectual

honesty in describing the data with which he was concerned, his subtlety of analysis, his keenness of criticism are sufficiently exemplified in everything he wrote.

In spite, however, of its difficulties, there is more need of such a task as I have undertaken in the case of Meinong's work than in the case of that of most philosophers. For it is true to say that the different investigations upon which he was engaged, independent of one another though at first sight they appear to be, are not in fact unrelated, and that his various lines of reflexion have principles in common which it would certainly be worth while to drag to light. I can hardly hope to succeed in doing so ; but I may perhaps contrive to furnish such an outline of Meinong's ways of thinking as may be serviceable to those who have not as yet made acquaintance with his writings. Of their importance no one who is familiar with them can be in doubt ; they are important as profound inquiries into the most fundamental of philosophical questions ; they are important no less as illustrating the method by which philosophic truth is won.

By way of preface, I prefix a few words of biographical import. Alexius Meinong was born at Lemberg on 17th July, 1853. His family was of German extraction, and his father had settled on Polish soil on account of his professional duties. Meinong's student years were all spent in Vienna. After being six years at a private school there, he became a scholar of the academic gymnasium ; and it was due in particular to two of his teachers in the latter institution that, contrary to the original plan of his parents, who had destined him for the law, and despite a strong inclination on his own part to devote himself to music, he decided in the end upon a scientific career. He entered the University in the autumn of 1870, matriculating in the Faculty of History. In the summer of 1874 he took his degree, having submitted for it a dissertation on Arnold of Brescia. From his gymnasium days he had, however, imbibed an interest in philosophy ;

and he chose philosophy as his *Nebenfach*, offering himself for examination in the first two of Kant's *Kritiken* which, in blissful ignorance of their pitfalls, he had striven to master by his own unaided reading. The results of his criticism of Kant, animated, he tells us, by a very naïve radicalism, must, he confesses, have been primitive enough ; but, without suspecting it, he had thus commenced his life's work. For a while he attended lectures on law ; but early in 1875 he resolved to give himself entirely to philosophy. He sought naturally the guidance of Brentano, then at the height of his influence. That guidance was unstintingly placed at his disposal ; and Meinong never ceased to speak in the warmest terms of his indebtedness to his teacher,[1] although he had occasion to disclaim the description of himself and Ehrenfels as belonging to the Brentano school. The first of the *Hume-Studien* was the outcome of a line of investigation which Brentano had proposed to him ; and it served as *Habilitationsschrift* by which he became a *Privatdozent* in the Philosophical Faculty of Vienna in 1878. In that capacity he continued in Vienna four more years, during which period Höfler, Ehrenfels and Oelzelt-Newin were his pupils. He was appointed in the autumn of 1882 (when the second of the *Hume-Studien* was published) Professor extraordinarius of Philosophy at Graz ; and in Graz he remained for the rest of his life, refusing repeated calls to larger fields of labour (such as Kiel in 1898 and Vienna in 1914), because it seemed to him that here he would best succeed in accomplishing the scientific work he had prescribed for himself. He started at the University in 1886, through apparatus provided by private means, experimental research in psychology ; and in 1894 there was instituted in Graz the first psychological laboratory established in Austria. In the spring of 1889, Meinong was

---

[1] For instance, in the last of his publications, he wrote : " Was etwa das Leben nicht mehr zu schlichten vermochte, das hat der Tod geschlichtet, und vor dem Auge meiner Erinnerung steht als unverlierbarer Besitz, wie einst, die Lichtgestalt meines verehrten Lehrers in durchgeistigter Schönheit, übergoldet durch den Sonnenglanz seiner und meiner Jugend."

appointed Professor ordinarius ; and in the autumn of that year he married. During the thirty years that followed, an extensive series of investigations occupied his activity—investigations some of which had to do with fundamental epistemological issues, others that were of a psychological nature, and others again which belonged to the field of ethics, more especially to the theory of value, to which his yearly recurring lectures on practical philosophy had, in a certain measure, afforded the stimulus. Only by degrees (scarcely, he tell us, before 1900) did he come to realise that in all these researches he had been moving in a direction which was new and of vital philosophical significance. To the bulky volume that was issued in 1904 in celebration of the tenth anniversary of the Graz psychological laboratory, Meinong contributed an introductory essay in which he definitely formulated, and endeavoured to determine the scope of, what seemed to him entitled to be called a distinct department of philosophical science, clearly demarcated from either metaphysics, or epistemology, or logic, or psychology ; and to it he gave the name of *Gegenstandstheorie*. After 1904, much of his strength was concentrated upon what he regarded as problems of this new field of inquiry, and upon urging its claims to recognition. In 1914 he was elected a member of the Austrian *Academie der Wissenschaften* (he had been a corresponding member since 1906) ; and to its *Proceedings* several of his latest papers were contributed.[1] He died at the age of sixty-seven on 27th November, 1920, of an ailment which for months he had patiently borne, continuing his academic and scientific labours until a few days from the end.

[1] Apart from the scattered papers now collected together in the *Gesammelte Abhandlungen*, the following are Meinong's chief publications : *Psychologisch-ethische Untersuchungen zur Werttheorie* (1894) ; *Ueber Annahmen* (1902 ; a second and greatly altered edition in 1910) ; *Ueber die Erfahrungsgrundlagen unseres Wissens* (1906) ; *Ueber Möglichkeit und Wahrscheinlichkeit* (1915).

1

One of Meinong's early writings [1] was partly devoted to a discussion of the nature and aims of philosophical inquiry and the position of philosophy in respect to the other sciences. Without unnatural limitation, he had there contended, philosophy cannot be taken to denote a single comprehensive science. It indicates rather a whole group of sciences, linked together by a common characteristic. And the characteristic in question is, he urged, that of being concerned, either exclusively or at least in certain essential respects, with inner experiences. Not only psychology itself, but likewise epistemology and logic, ethics and aesthetics, can readily be brought under this point of view, embarrassing though it may be to find an exact formula for the connectedness which is thus implied. Even metaphysics, in virtue of the very generality of its subject-matter, is constrained to bring non-psychical into relationship with psychical facts, in order to maintain an independent position alongside of the natural sciences.

It might seem, then, as though Meinong were here assigning to psychology a dominant position among the parts of philosophy as a whole ; and so in a manner he was. Any attempt to proceed in philosophical reflexion by leaving out of account the consideration of psychical processes is in itself, he argued, a sufficiently convincing demonstration of the inherent unnaturalness of such an endeavour, and no metaphysic elaborated without regard to psychological research and its results can be expected to stand.[2] Such was his contention to the last. But, as time went on, he came to draw a very sharp line of demarcation between psychology

---

[1] *Ueber Philosophische Wissenschaft und ihre Propädeutik*, 1885.

[2] On the other hand, he was equally strenuous in maintaining that the psychology, be it never so experimental, which ruthlessly brushes epistemological and other philosophical considerations aside is bound to become entangled in crudities and absurdities, which, in the long run, will mean its undoing.

and psychologism, and to express himself as virtually in accord with Husserl's well-known polemic against the latter in the *Logische Untersuchungen*. Within the circle of a certain set of problems it is, Meinong declared, sufficiently easy to see what is meant by the term psychologism ; it simply means psychological methods of treatment in the wrong place. Since knowing is a mode of experience (*ein Erlebnis*), epistemology cannot wholly dispense with psychological methods. Yet over against the act of knowing stands the known ; knowledge, in other words, has a double-sided aspect ; and whoever pursues an epistemological inquiry as though there were only the psychical aspect of knowledge, or persists in forcing the other aspect under the point of view of psychical event or occurrence, cannot escape the reproach which the term psychologism carries with it.

Nevertheless, I am inclined to believe that Meinong exposed himself to not a little misunderstanding by adhering as he did throughout to that early contention of his that in psychology is to be discerned the thread, so to speak, which binds the different parts of philosophy into such whole as they constitute. For he scarcely meant to imply more by the contention than that in the notion of *knowledge* is to be found the link of connexion between the several branches of philosophy, theoretical or practical. In other words, what, in truth, he was saying was that there is not one group of objects specifically entitled to be called the subject-matter of philosophy ; but that any part or the whole of what is vaguely described as the field of experience may be handled philosophically if treated from the point of view of its relation to the human thinking subject. What light can it throw on the relations in which the human mind stands to the surrounding reality ?—such was the fundamental question which philosophy has addressed to it. And then the special branches of philosophy would seem to be determined by the main differences of a general kind which disclose themselves in those relations. These differences would, for example, be

s

not inappropriately classified under the three heads : (a) cognitive, (b) practical and (c) aesthetic. So conceived, it is obvious that the treatment of knowledge in all its aspects must form the central portion of philosophical science. For it is only in and through the process of knowing that the human mind has a place at all in the scheme of existence ; and, although the practical and aesthetic activities are distinguishable from the knowing activity, they nevertheless imply the latter as an essential condition of their possibility. Clearly, the investigation of knowledge divides into two diverging lines of inquiry, according as it turns upon the question as to the validity of knowledge or upon the question as to the way in which knowing comes forward as a natural process in the life of the individual mind. Furthermore, inasmuch as in both these paths of inquiry the antithesis between the subjective and the objective presents itself, yielding, in the one case, the problem of what meanwhile may be described as that of the " correspondence " of our thinking with reality, and, in the other case, that of the way in which our mental processes are occasioned or influenced by external conditions, the final issue is bound to be raised which has been traditionally designated metaphysical. That issue may perhaps be expressed thus : What conception of real fact are we led to form in order to render intelligible, on the one hand, the attainment of truth by human thinking, and, on the other hand, the conjoint co-operation of mental and external conditions in the natural world?

Such, at any rate, in broad outline, is what I take to have been the essence of Meinong's view in respect to the function and scope of the philosophical sciences. Most of his publications between the years 1882 and 1904 had to do with questions which could not be exhaustively dealt with either from the point of view of psychology alone or from that of epistemology alone. And Meinong came gradually to see how both modes of investigation could be combined, and combined without committing the blunder, which can only lead to hopeless confusion, of prematurely mixing up the two methods and of drawing upon the one while ostensibly engaged in carrying on an inquiry under the other.

2

It was a fortunate circumstance that Meinong had been induced to devote himself, at the beginning of his career, to a thorough study of Hume's theory of knowledge. The outcome of his patient examination of that theory was not only a valuable piece of genuine philosophical criticism ; it was also a clear discernment of the exact points in regard to which the adequacy of the empirical doctrine could best be tested. The *Hume-Studien* disclose, in fact, the way in which the crucial problems of knowledge originally shaped themselves for Meinong ; it is, therefore, advisable to look at these *Studien* somewhat in detail.

The first of them (published in 1877) is concerned with abstract ideas and the process of generalising. The treatment of the matter by Berkeley and Hume is submitted to a scrutiny far more searching and penetrating than that which T. H. Green, in his elaborate *Introduction*, had brought to bear. Attention is drawn, for example, to the totally different senses in which Berkeley employs the term " sign " when dealing with ideas and words respectively and to the fact that he leaves entirely unanswered the important question, how a general *name* is related to a general *notion*. Berkeley, it is argued, ought to have seen that he had not disposed of abstract ideas by disposing of Locke's account of their mode of origin ; for the very concessions he makes, obviously inconsequences in his exposition as it stands, would, if they had been followed up, have forced him to that conclusion. Indeed, in more than one place, Berkeley, it is pointed out, was on the verge of a psychological theory that could have been substituted for Locke's, in so far as he laid stress upon the consideration that in observing an individual fact it lies within our power to concentrate *attention* upon certain of its characteristics, and that thus its remaining characteristics are disregarded. Hume, it is shown, completely misconceived what he described as " one of the greatest and most valuable discoveries " made in his time "in the republic of letters ". But the nominalistic view, which he erroneously took to be Berkeley's, *was* the view which he himself tried to put " beyond all doubt and controversy " ; and, by examining in turn each of the negative and positive arguments employed in the *Treatise* for this purpose, Meinong exhibits, in a convincing manner, the failure of that attempt.

As regards the negative arguments, the very formulation of the thesis they are advanced to support is, Meinong bids us observe, in itself extraordinary. While Hume's intention is admittedly to deny *all* abstraction, what he actually tries to prove is that " the mind cannot form any notion of quantity or quality without forming a precise notion of degrees of each ", as though it were not evident, on the face of it, how many of the cases usually taken to be cases of abstraction are thereby left out of account. But, waiving this objection, no one of the three arguments by which the thesis was to be put beyond the range of controversy will bear examination. Take, for instance, the third of them. It will be granted, Hume avers, that everything in nature is individual, and that it would be absurd to suppose a really existent triangle which was without definite dimensions. And, if this be absurd in regard to existent reality, it must also be absurd in regard to ideas. Again, " to form the idea of an object, and to form an idea simply, is the same thing ". If, then, it be impossible to form an idea of an object that is not possessed of definite quantitative and qualitative degree, there must be an equal impossibility in forming an idea that is not limited in both these respects. Meinong has little trouble in convicting this argument of either a formal or a material fallacy : a formal fallacy if by " everything " be meant *jedes Ding*, for then the word " object " is equivocal, since it is used both for an existent thing and for a content of presentation ; a material fallacy if by " everything " be meant *alles*, for then it is false that everything in nature is individual. Furthermore, granted that it is absurd to suppose there can be a thing in nature without its definite degree of quality and quantity, granted that each thing must accordingly be perceived as in this respect a determinate thing, does it, then, in the least follow that each idea of that thing must necessarily represent all these determinations? An assumption of that sort would be no less ridiculous than to maintain that because an individual existent has an indefinitely large number of characteristics, the content of the notion of that existent must be indefinitely great. In short, an idea of an individual thing is far from being an individual idea ; and yet, except on the ground that the idea of an individual thing is an individual idea, no inference can be drawn from the individuality of things to the individuality of ideas.

The positive line of argument by which Hume sought to come to the assistance of what he took to be Berkeley's theory turns out, in Meinong's hands, to be no less unsatisfactory. First of all, he would have us notice the singular want of perspicuity characterising Hume's exposition. The problem was to explain how a particular idea attains in our reasoning an application such as it would have were it universal. The explanation offered is that we apply the same name to similar objects ; and, when that custom has established itself, the hearing of the name revives the idea of one of these objects, the one which happens casually to make its appearance most readily. Yet what about the other ideas, likewise associated with the name? " They are ", Hume replies, " not really and in fact present to the mind, but only in power ". But, asks Meinong, since when? Hume would appear to say, since the act of mentioning the name. A disposition to revive the ideas in question must, however, surely have been previously there if, eventually, through aid of the word, they are reproducible. The situation becomes the more perplexing when Hume goes on to assert that the

word raises up besides the idea a " certain custom ", and that
this custom produces any other individual idea, for which we
may have occasion. Are we, then, here to understand by
" custom " a permanent indispensable pre-condition of the
last-mentioned idea, and by " occasion " the immediate
cause of its appearance? If so, the whole theory stands or
falls with what can be made out with respect to this " occasion ". Nevertheless, Hume vouchsafes no information as
to whether such an " occasion " must always be present
whenever we hear that word, nor is it easy to see wherein the
necessity of its presence could be supposed to lie, although
in its absence there can admittedly be no question of generality. Hume's lack of precision just where precision is
necessary renders it difficult to come to close quarters with
the theory itself ; but the moment we try to do so it becomes
manifest, Meinong urges, how little mere association without
abstraction is able to achieve. We have before us, let us say,
a round piece of paper or a mill-stone (seeing that, *ex
hypothesi*, we cannot think of a circle *in abstracto*), and we
call this "shape". Now, it can safely be affirmed that it
would never occur to us, so soon as we happened to see a
square corn-field, to call to mind that " shape " and to give
the name "shape" likewise to the field. No doubt, if we
were in a position to think of shape *in abstracto*, all would be
plain sailing, but this is precisely what Hume is concerned to
deny. Naturally, the difficulty becomes the more glaring the
greater the generality attaching to the name. Moreover, as
Hume himself points out, the same thing may be called by a
great number of different names—*e.g.*, mill-stone, a round
thing, a heavy thing, a material thing, etc. Yet he has offered
no explanation of how, under such unfavourable circumstances,
it comes about that even the slightest appreciable association
between word and idea could be formed. Once more, and
assuming meanwhile that objections such as the foregoing
have been surmounted, no sooner is the effort made to see
how " general ideas ", formed in the manner supposed,

function *in propositions* than the theory breaks down hopelessly. A proposition, such as " wolves are mammals," it would have to be said, is in the first instance an assertion about words ; so far as actual things are concerned, the statement could only express the result of a perfectly general inference based on a similarity which association with the word " mammal " presupposed. But, since the same objects are also associated with many other words—*e.g.*, organic being—nothing would be gained by the knowledge of that similarity. Finally, if account be taken of all that is usually included under the head of abstraction, the inadequacy of the doctrine becomes strikingly apparent. We speak often enough of family traits, of natural types, of a literary style, and so forth ; and, in doing so, are referring to characteristics which several individuals have in common. The ideas of such attributes appear, therefore, as general notions, in regard to which scarcely any one would dispute that the common feature must first be recognised as such before a name can be given to it. Here, then, quite certainly the name acquires its generality through the notion, and not the notion through the name.

The two fundamental errors that, in Meinong's opinion, vitiate Hume's theory are (*a*) his failure to take account of the content or intension of a concept, and (*b*) his use of the doctrine of association to explain the way in which the concept acquires its extension or denotation. In ordinary usage, the terms general and particular have reference to the extension, and the terms abstract and concrete to the intension, of a concept. A concept that is or can be applied to many objects is general ; a concept that is obtained by an act of abstraction is abstract. Every concrete object is an individual object. But the presentation of a concrete object includes only such characteristics as can be apprehended by sense at any one moment ; consequently individual objects are known, for the most part, in a form that is more or less abstract. No doubt, it is as concrete that every empirical datum comes at first into consciousness ; and, in so far, concrete data furnish the basis of knowledge. Knowledge, however, is primarily concerned not with presentations but with their objects. In knowing, we seek to liberate that which we take to be peculiar to the object from the contingent features introduced into it by the act of apprehending. So that almost always just that which makes the presentation concrete will fall away from it. It follows, therefore, so Meinong argues, that while all general notions are abstract, not all abstract notions are general. In respect to the question whether a concept is universal or particular, the number of attributes constituting its content is quite immaterial ; not so, however, the quality of those attributes, because it will be according as, in view of such quality, the presence of individual objects, corresponding to the concept in question, be conceived as mathematically or physically impossible or otherwise, that the concept must be held to be individual or general. On the other hand, however, in respect to the question whether a universal concept is more or less universal, the amount of content may, under certain circumstances, be a relevant consideration, and the quality of the content always is ; but neither from the one nor the other nor from both *alone* can any answer be given to the question, because, in reference to extension, we are concerned with a *relation*, while the content gives us only one term of the relation, and the second term must be supplied by experience. Meinong insists, then, that the extension is not, like the intension, something definitely fixed or self-evident ; but that, on the contrary, the real extension of a notion is no less independent of our knowledge than is any fact of the external world. Consequently, to suppose that between general and individual idea an association must first be contracted in order that the latter should be subsumed under the former is, for this very reason, absolutely precluded. In fine, Meinong's argument is directed all through to bringing out what he conceives to be the truth that not association but the self-conscious activity of attention is the main function involved in abstraction and generalisation.

The second of the *Hume-Studien* (published, as already noted, in 1882), deals with the theory of relations, and is much more constructive than the first had been ; Meinong here elaborates a position of his own that, in view of his subsequent work, deserves special notice. His method, however, is still the same as before. He still proceeds on the basis of a critical discussion of what he finds in the writings of Locke, Hume and the later empirical thinkers. As he had formerly refused to recognise in Hume's nominalism a legitimate development of Berkeley's doctrine, so here he is inclined to defend Locke's common-sense treatment of the subject under consideration against Hume's psychical atomism. But he does not fall into Kant's mistake of supposing it was only in reference to cause and effect that Hume had raised the issue of necessary connexion ; indeed, it is not so much upon Hume's handling of causality as upon his handling of the more elementary relations of likeness and difference that Meinong's scrutiny is concentrated. And he maintains that Hume's whole theoretical philosophy is so essentially built upon his *Relationslehre* that an exposition of the latter, with any claim to completeness, would scarcely be justified in leaving a single portion of the former out of account.

At the outset, Meinong resists the view (the view of Mill and Spencer, but derived ultimately from Hume) that a relation, such as that of likeness, is explicable from the mere presence to consciousness of two or more presentations, in this case like or resembling presentations. He takes his stand at once on the principle laid down by Lotze. " Every comparison, and in general every relation between two elements, presupposes ", so Lotze had asserted, " that both points of relation remain separate, and that an ideating activity passes over from the one to the other, and at the same time becomes conscious of the alteration which it has experienced in this transition. We exercise such an activity when, for example, we compare red and blue, and thereby there ensues for us the new presentation of a qualitative similarity, which we ascribe to both."[1] Meinong points out that the existence of an activity of the kind indicated by Lotze had already been virtually recognised by Locke, when he described relations as complex ideas resulting from an act of comparison, although Locke had left the nature of the act which he thus specified undetermined. So much being granted, there is, Meinong argues, already determined what alone, in any intelligible sense, can be called the *fundamentum relationis* of the activity in question ; clearly it can be no other than the compared presentations themselves. No doubt, what, as a rule, we have given are not simple but complex presentations, complexes of presented attributes. If two dice, one red and the other blue, be compared and found to be different, the comparison, in the strict sense, has reference not to the shape but to the colour ; and, accordingly, only the actually compared features ought to be spoken of as *fundamenta*. Yet, in such cases, we are wont to say not merely that the two colours but that the two dice have been compared, with the qualification, perhaps, " in respect to their colour ". And in this usage may be discerned what Locke had in mind when he insisted that in a relation there is always requisite, on the one hand, the things to be compared, and, on the other hand, the " occasion " for such comparison. In the example just used, the dice are the things, the colour the " occasion ". Evidently, then, there can be no relation without a *fundamentum*, or more precisely two *fundamenta*. These may themselves be relations, for relations can, of course, be compared ; but we cannot go on making relations the *fundamenta* of relations indefinitely ; ultimately every relation has for its *fundamenta* presentations which are not relations, for otherwise there would be a comparison in which there was nothing compared. Hume's initial error, an

[1] *Grundzüge der Psychologie*, p. 23.

error that ruined his classification of relations, consisted in his confusing the notion of *fundamentum* with that of relation.

Two chief classes of relations are distinguished by Meinong —relations of comparison (*Vergleichungsrelationen*) and relations of compatibility (*Verträglichkeitsrelationen*). (*a*) Under the first class are included relations of likeness (*Gleichheit*) and of unlikeness or difference (*Verschiedenheit*). And here the view (*e.g.*, Mill's) that likeness is only a special case of resemblance (*Aehnlichkeit*) is decisively rejected. Resemblance, it is argued, may be present in all conceivable gradations, but in likeness there is no gradation—what is like is completely like, and what is not completely like is not like—so that it would be unnatural to bring the cases of likeness and certain cases of unlikeness under the head of resemblance, and the remaining cases of unlikeness under the head of difference. Not only so ; it would be difficult to imagine how, through determination of the notion of resemblance, the notion of likeness could have arisen. And finally, the usage of language is altogether adverse to the view in question, for in speaking of similarity one is almost invariably conscious of difference as being likewise involved. Resemblance, then, is always a special case of difference ; in so far as partial agreement or likeness is essential to resemblance, it is still only likeness *of elements*, while the resemblance is asserted of the whole. Spatial and temporal relations fall within this class. The *fundamenta* of the former are like and unlike space-determinations within the homogeneous space-continuum, and of the latter time-determinations within the homogeneous time-continuum. (*b*) Meinong was led to constitute relations of compatibility into a class by themselves through consideration of what Hume had meant by " contrariety " and Locke, in his familiar definition of knowledge, by " repugnancy." The notions compatibility and incompatibility are not, he maintains, constituted after the manner of the notions likeness and difference. The latter admit of no definition, and can only be explained by means of

examples ; the former do seem to admit of a kind of definition—compatible is what can subsist together, incompatible
what cannot. In the long run, the question of compatibility
can only be raised with regard to attributes of like time- and
space-determinations. Here we seem to be face to face with
an ultimate fact, and a fact which belongs not to the province
of presentation but to that of judgment. When it is said, for
example, that the " round " and the " square " cannot be
simultaneously in the same place, there is no new presented
content introduced by the phrase " cannot " ; it only
makes the statement an expression of a negative judgment,
and this judgment carries with it that peculiar, indescrib-
able, and familiar characteristic which it has long been
customary to describe as evidence. It would seem, therefore,
that relations of compatibility may be said, in a certain
sense, to be secondary formations, in so far as they are
based upon a special case of relations of comparison—
namely, on the case of like space- and time-determinations.
There is, however, a further feature to be noticed. The two
possibilities that come forward in regard to this second class
of relations do not stand independently side by side as likeness and unlikeness do. The one can only be characterised
as the negation of the other ; and, moreover, it is compatibility that is the negation of incompatibility and not *vice
versa* ; for compatibility seems to imply no more than that,
in a particular instance, one has before him a case where
evidence for an incompatibility of the kind indicated is
wanting. If it be asked why such different things as cases
of comparison and of compatibility should be grouped together under the title of relations between presented objects,
Meinong would here justify his doing so by pointing in the
first instance to the part played by the presented objects,
which seemed to him perfectly analogous in the two cases.
For these objects, the *fundamenta*, are invariably the basis
upon which rest, in the one case, the presentation of likeness
or difference, and the evident affirmation which attaches

itself thereto ; and, in the other case, the evident negation.
So that incompatibility and likeness may each be said to be
a relation between presented attributes.[1]

Meinong does not claim that his twofold classification of
relations is an exhaustive classification, although it does, he
thinks, cover *all* the seven kinds distinguished by Hume in
the *Treatise*.   There are, however, other relations, *toto genere*,
distinct from any that were considered either by Hume or
Locke.   For instance, in quite a legitimate sense, one may
speak of a relation between the act of presenting (*vorstellen*)
and its content, where we have to do not with presented
contents alone but also with the act in and through which
those contents have their being.   And this relation is not the
product of a new activity ; on the contrary, in the apprehension of it we seem to be no less passive than we seem to
be in regard to the data described as *fundamenta*.   So, too,
the relations between the elements of a composite presentation are not in the least analogous to the relations between
the presented parts of a physical object.   These, then, are
instances of what Meinong here calls " real relations "—real
because, seeing they are not outcomes of a new activity,
they must really belong to the data, otherwise there could
be no awareness of them.   At the same time, " real ", in this
context, must not be understood as referring to anything
extra-psychical, for obviously the relations in question are
between psychical data and are directly accessible to us in
a way in which relations outside the circle of psychical
phenomena never can be.   As contrasted with these " real
relations ", the relations previously considered may be
called " ideal relations "—ideal because they are the products
of a specific psychical activity, and do not belong to the data

---

[1] This contention was discarded in the later writings.   In them, Meinong
maintains that relations of compatibility are based upon Objectives (see
infra, p. 293 *sqq.*) ; and that, consequently, they are relations not between
presented attributes but between objects such as can only be apprehended
through judgments or assumptions (*cf., e.g., Ueber Annahmen*, 2te Aufl.,
p. 215 *sqq.*).

apart from such activity. But now, within the sphere of "ideal relations", a further line of demarcation requires to be drawn. Hume distinguished between relations that depend entirely on the ideas compared and those that may be changed without any change in the ideas. Through his failure clearly to recognise the significance of *fundamenta* for a relation, Hume was led wrongly to include contiguity and distance under relations of the last-mentioned kind. Yet his distinction itself is an important one and coincides with the distinction upon which Meinong thinks stress should be laid between primary and secondary relations. The primary relations, those of comparison and of compatibility, are recognised beyond question by an act of discrimination directed upon the given *fundamenta*. There are, however, secondary relations, combinations of special cases of primary ones, where relative determinations without *fundamenta* come more or less to the front. With respect to secondary relations the data accessible to us are not sufficient, and if we connect the assertion of such relations with these data, we must have grounds for doing so outside the data themselves. The two chief secondary or derivative relations are those of causation and identity, both of which have been acquired originally as the result of practical needs. Meinong's analysis of the causal relation is virtually in agreement with Mill's. He lays repeated emphasis, however, upon the consideration that with respect to causality (and the same is true with respect to identity) it is impossible to confine attention to presentations ; there is always involved a reference to external things, to actual existents. To ascribe causality to mere presentations would, he says, be like ascribing a true biography to a prince in a fairy tale. The relation of causality is invariably " carried over " into the external world. And he tries to show that there is nothing inexplicable in this reference to external existents. When one says, for example, of two feelings, that prior to the act of comparison by which they are judged to be different they were in fact different, there has already been such a " carrying over " of the ideal relation of difference from presented contents to actual entities. At the same time, primary relations may be said to be " pure relations " in the sense that an *Uebertragung* of this kind is not essential for their being as relations, whereas it is essential for the being of secondary or " empirical " relations. The pure relations are, therefore, *a priori*, and the judgments asserting them are *a priori* judgments. But no judgment about empirical relations can rest on a merely *a priori* basis ; and just as little can a judgment about pure relations do so when it has reference not merely to presented contents but also to external fact. It is further clear that none but " ideal relations " can be " carried over " into the domain of extra-psychical reality.

3

The foundation of Meinong's subsequent work is laid in these early *Studies*. In them almost all the problems to which later he devoted such unwearied intellectual industry are, in one form or another, indicated, if not distinctly formulated. Not a few of the positions which were here maintained came, it is true, in the course of time, to be abandoned, and others to be radically revised ; and the reasons that led to such changes often throw the clearest light upon the views that were finally adopted. I shall have something to say immediately upon some of the principal changes ; meanwhile I want to refer to one definite result which these investigations yielded him, and from which he found no occasion to deviate.

In his own way, Meinong had reached the principle which may not inappropriately be said to be the starting-point of the Kantian theory—the principle, namely, that knowledge involves a unique antithesis between knowing and the known and that any attempt, such as Hume had made, to dispense with the former term of the antithesis must inevitably prove futile and abortive. In other words, through grappling with the crucial questions which the work of Hume and Hume's followers had thrust upon him, Meinong came to see the necessity of insisting upon the consideration that an object known never can be identical with any act which is a knowing of it. And when once he had convinced himself that all knowledge involves recognition of relatedness among the parts of what is known, the existence of cognitive acts, as distinct from what Hume had called " impressions " and " ideas ", seemed to him to be indisputably established.[1] Even on the assumption that isolated contents, presentations, are given, as Hume supposed, the inference is irresistible that the simultaneous presence of these contents, their peculiarities, their changes, and so on, furnish a new set of conditions in response to which an inner activity of the mind must have taken place, if so-called ideas of relation forthwith make their appearance. In so far, Meinong was but reiterating Lotze's well-known contention ; and in this particular reference, I do not know that he ever advanced any considerable way from Lotze's position. He did not, I mean, ever call in question the view of presentations as so many separately given units, or ask himself whether the separateness, the singleness, the distinctiveness which presentations, we will say, come to have may not be due to that very activity which he took to be involved in the comparison of them and in discerning their relations. Had he done so, not a few of the obscurities that beset, as we shall see, even his mature view of cognition would, I believe, have been avoided, and he would have emerged completely from the subjectivism of his early days.

I pass now to consider the two main directions in which Meinong was led to see that the view of knowledge he had hitherto been taking required modification. These are not, in fact, disconnected ; so soon as the one advance had been made, it was well-nigh certain that the other would follow.

[1] *Cf.* what is said by way of illustration, *supra*, pp. 71-2.

(a) In the *Hume-Studien* no distinction had as yet been recognised between the " content " of an act of apprehension and the " object " (*Gegenstand*) of that act. Throughout, the former term had been employed as equivalent to the latter ; and the act of apprehending had frequently been spoken of as being " directed upon " the content. Meinong acknowledges that he was materially influenced in this regard by an exceedingly acute piece of psychological analysis by Twardowski, which was published in 1894.[1] With admirable lucidity, Twardowski pointed to the ambiguity that attaches to the term *Vorgestelltes*—an ambiguity in its way no less pronounced than that which admittedly attached to the term *Vorstellung*. An object may be said to be " presented " in the sense that, in addition to the many relations in which that object stands to other objects, it also stands in a definite relation to a cognising subject. And, in this sense, a " presented object " is a veritable object, just in the same way as an extended object or a lost object is one. But, on the other hand, by " presented object " may be meant what is a decided contrast to a veritable object—namely, a " mental picture " of an object—and then it is no longer a veritable object—is no longer, in fact, an object at all. That which is presented *in* a presentation is its content ; that which is presented *through* or *by means of* a presentation is its object—so Twardowski tried to bring out the contrast. In the paper (published in 1899)[2] in which Meinong himself first definitely insisted on the importance of the distinction, Twardowski's little book is specially alluded to and some of its illustrations are used. The considerations that had weighed with Meinong were, he tells us, such as the following. Nothing is more common than to represent (*vorstellen*) or to think of something which does not exist. We may think of something that is contradictory, a round square, for example, or of something that does not happen to exist as a matter of fact, a golden

---

[1] *Zur Lehre von Inhalt und Gegenstand der Vorstellungen*, Wien, 1894.
[2] *Ueber Gegenstände höherer Ordnung*, § 2, *G. A.*, vol. ii, p. 379 *sqq.*

T

mountain, say, or of something which in virtue of its nature cannot exist (likeness or difference is an instance), or of something which has existed or will exist but does not exist now. Nevertheless, in all these cases a *Vorstellung* exists, and exists in the present. Now, argues Meinong, no unprejudiced person would wish to maintain that the *Vorstellung* exists whilst its content does not. That, however, is not the whole story. " Content " and " object " differ not only in respect to existence, but in respect to their nature or character. That which is physical can be presented, but the content of a psychical act can only be psychical ; so, too, qualities such as blue, warm, heavy can be presented, but neither the *Vorstellung* nor its content by which these qualities are presented is blue or warm or heavy ; attributes of this sort evince themselves at once as totally inapplicable to the contents of mental acts. As regards the relation of the mental act to its content, the view which Meinong came to hold appears to have been that they are inseparable but distinguishable constituents of one existent fact or event. Whether it be a presentation (say) of a steeple or of a causal relation, in each case an act of presenting is involved, and these acts of presenting resemble one another. On the other hand, in so far as the presentations are presentations of different objects, these presentations do not resemble one another. And that wherein presentations of different objects are unlike one another, notwithstanding the circumstance that the respective acts of presenting are not unlike, is their content ; such content, no less than the act, being in each case a psychical existent in the present, whereas the object presented by means of it may be non-existent, not in the present, not psychical.

" The chief argument *against* contents ", Mr. Russell once declared, " is the difficulty of discovering them introspectively " [1] ; and it seems often to be supposed that whoever speaks of the content of a mental state is speaking of something purely hypothetical, of which there can be no direct

[1] *Monist*, vol. xxiv, 1914, p. 452.

experience. But, in Meinong's sense of the term " content ",
it would be nearer the truth to say that " contents " are the
only things which we do discover introspectively. For
mental states can become known to us introspectively not as
mere bare states or processes, but only as *specific* states—the
awareness of a blue colour, for example, as contrasted with
the awareness of a pain or the awareness of a want. And if it
be contended that the common element, awareness, can, in
all such cases, be distinguished from the specific elements,
the reply is : " No doubt it can, but only in the way in which
the common characteristic ' human ' can be distinguished
from the more specific elements that belong to particular
individual men—that is, by an act of deliberate abstraction ".
Now, whatever else it is, an act of introspection is certainly
not an act of deliberate abstraction ; and whoever is on the
search for mental states apart from their contents, or for
" contents " apart from the states whose contents they are,
may well find that of either or both he can find no trace.[1]
That, however, is due to the fact that he has been looking for
something which no one ever supposed to be there.

(*b*) Throughout the *Hume-Studien*, Meinong had evidently
been proceeding on the assumption that relations must be
regarded as products of mental activity. They might, indeed,
be thought of as " carried over " into the physical world ;
but their essentially subjective character was not thereby
called in question. It is in the article which appeared in
1891,[2] on Ehrenfels' view of *Gestaltqualitäten*, that Meinong
is to be seen for the first time freeing himself from this assumption. In that article he acknowledges that he had himself
fallen into the " psychologist's fallacy " of thinking that,

[2] As an interesting illustration, it is worth noting that, after having for
a long time been assured of the existence of "mental acts " (cf., e.g., *Problems of Phil.*, p. 65) and altogether sceptical of " contents ", Mr. Russell
is now persuaded of the existence of " contents ", at least in the case of
memory and thought, and cannot discover anything corresponding to acts
(cf. *Analysis of Mind*, pp. 17-18 and 20-21).

[2] *Zur Psychologie der Komplexionen und Relationen, G. A.*, i, p. 281 *sqq.*

because a psychical act is requisite for the apprehension of relations, it is necessary that reflexion should be directed on psychical states in order that relations should be presented. But he had now come to see that from an empirical point of view the attempt to conceive the presentation of a relation (such as that between a colour and extension) as based upon the inner perception of an act of comparison instead of upon the compared elements themselves is wholly unnatural and contrary to fact. More particularly is the futility of such an *Umweg* apparent when it is pursued with respect to relations of compatibility. To suppose, in the case of the round square, that it is not " round " and " square " but the " presentation of the round " and the " presentation of the square " which are judged to be incompatible is surely perverse and nonsensical. No doubt, under certain conditions, these presentations may be judged to be incompatible ; but " round " and " square " are found to be incompatible under the presupposition of like space- and time-determinations, whereas, to show that the corresponding presentations are incompatible, account would have to be taken of *their* mode of connexion. In the book that was published in 1907, in defence of the *Gegenstandstheorie*,[1] Meinong's rejection of the doctrine in question is still more emphatic. The most radical form of the subjectivist interpretation of the relations of likeness and difference would be, he thinks, that which took the former to *be* the possibility of confusing one thing with another, and the latter to *be* the absence of that possibility. Now, it may be quite true that likeness does really *indicate* the possibility of such confusion ; but little consideration is required to see that likeness only indicates and *is* not this possibility. In point of fact, one sees this neither better nor otherwise than one sees that a water-cart is not a mountain-tarn, or anything else that is obvious. And the best proof that likeness is not identical with " to find like " is simply

[1] *Ueber die Stellung der Gegenstandstheorie im System der Wissenschaften*, pp. 143-145.

what a direct inspection of the two things yields. But an indirect proof can easily be provided by the reflexion that red and orange (say) are still like one another when they are not being compared. The argument is carried further in the volume, published in 1906, on the empirical bases of knowledge,[1] where it is contended that relations possess not only validity for what are there designated " pure objects " but are transferable from the phenomenal to the real. While, in reference to our apprehension of relations, the influence of subjectivity need not be disputed, yet, it is argued, what we, as we are now constituted, are capable of knowing *a priori* is in no way rendered dubious through such subjectivity. We are justified, therefore, in asserting that things in themselves *are* like or unlike, etc., on precisely the same grounds as we are justified in asserting that colours are.

4

The two steps to which I have been referring having once been taken, the road to the elaboration of a *Gegenstandstheorie* was a fairly straight one. The next stage of Meinong's advance towards it consisted in his coming to recognise a class of objects which he called " objects of higher order ",[2] a conception, now sufficiently familiar, which was, in fact, only a further working out of the position that relations are objective in character. Objects of this class were found to be characterised by a want of independence, by a sort of incompleteness—such, for example, as attaches to the object " difference ", if the attempt be made to isolate it from the differing terms. These objects are built, so to speak, upon other objects as their indispensable conditions, the latter being the *inferiora* of the former and the former the *superiora*

---

[1] *Ueber die Erfahrungsgrundlagen unseres Wissens*, § 21 *sqq.*

[2] *Ueber Gegenstände höherer Ordnung, G. A.*, ii, p. 377 *sqq.* The phrase was not, of course, a new one. Meinong points out that Fechner had previously used it. But Lotze also spoke of *Vorstellungen* of higher order (cf. *Grundzüge der Psychologie*, iii, § 2).

of the latter. The class of objects in question comprises not only relations but also complexes ; and, in the case of complexes, the constituents, as in this sense analogous to the terms of a relation, play the part of *inferiora*. But a complex is more than a collection of its constituents ; it is not composed *merely* of a relation *and* its terms, for the terms in being related by the relation are at the same time related to it ; and, although this involves a regress, the regress is not a vicious one and so creates no difficulty.

The monograph just cited, published in 1899, may not inappropriately be said to be a preliminary survey of the ground which Meinong spent the last twenty years of his life in exploring. The preliminary survey was, however, sufficient to convince him of the enormous extent of the field. By " metaphysics " had usually been understood a comprehensive science having for its aim to form a conception of the nature and ultimate ground of the universe ; and numerous as the deceptive hopes that have been and are associated with the name may be, it is our intellectual shortcoming and not the idea of such a science upon which the blame for the deception must rest. Yet, in spite of the universality of its scope, metaphysics falls far short of being a science of objects. With the whole of what exists it has, indeed, to do. But the whole of what exists, including what has existed and will exist, is infinitesimal when compared with the whole of the objects of knowledge ; and the fact that this has been so easily lost sight of is due, so Meinong avers, to that " prejudice in favour of the actual " which has driven us to the extravagance of supposing that the non-actual is something too trivial with which to concern ourselves. How absurd this prejudice is Meinong's preliminary survey had already made clear to him. Among the objects of higher order, he had discovered a great sub-division of " ideal objects "—objects which, to use his phraseology, subsist (*bestehen*), and many of which are of tremendous moment for what exists, but which themselves can, in no case, either exist (*existieren*) or be actual (*wirklich sein*). Similarity and dissimilarity are, for instance, objects of this kind ; they may subsist between existent realities, but they are not themselves bits of existent reality. Nevertheless, that in knowing we are vitally interested in these objects goes without saying. So, too, number does not exist alongside of the counted things, supposing the latter to be existents ; and things that do not exist may be counted. Pure mathematics has, in fact, solely to do with ideal objects ; and our " prejudice in favour of the actual " leads here to the extraordinary, although, of course, not explicitly recognised, dilemma : Either that to which my knowing refers exists in reality, or it exists at least " in my presentation ". And the very word " ideal," in defiance of its history, has come to stand for the latter. What does not exist outside of us must, at any rate, exist within us—this we take involuntarily for granted, and it seldom occurs to us to reflect how futile and meaningless the subterfuge is.

Here, then, was a huge *Gebiet*, constituting, as it seemed to Meinong, that of a new science, of which only one portion, the department of mathematics, had hitherto had justice done to it. *Gegenstandstheorie* he defines as the science of objects as such, or of objects without limitation to the special class of those that exist, and of these latter only in so far as their nature (their *Sosein*), irrespective of their existence, is concerned. It has to inquire, one might, borrowing a favourite expression of Shadworth Hodgson's, say, what an object is " known as " ; about its " what " and not about its " that ". Or it may be said to be the science of what can be known *a priori* about objects, understanding *a priori* in the sense in which Meinong uses the term.[1]

What is meant here by *Gegenstand* ? A formal definition is, we are told, precluded, seeing that both *genus* and *differentia* are wanting ; *alles ist Gegenstand*. But etymologically the

---

[1] Judgments are said by him to be *a priori* when they (*a*) are grounded on the nature of their objects, (*b*) evince themselves as of self-evidencing certainty, (*c*) hold necessarily, and (*d*) take no account of whether their objects exist or not. See *Erfahrungsgrundlagen*, p. 10.

term *gegenstehen* furnishes, at least, an indirect characteristic. This term has reference, namely, to the experiences through which the *Gegenstand* is grasped or apprehended (*erfasst*), the experiences, however, not being looked upon as in any way constitutive of the *Gegenstand*. Every inner experience (*Erlebnis*), at least every sufficiently elementary one, has an object (*Gegenstand*), and in so far as the experience comes to expression, ordinarily in words and sentences, there stands normally over against such expression a significance or meaning (*Bedeutung*), and what is meant is the object.[1] In so far as all objects in order to be known must be grasped or apprehended (*erfasst*), it is true that what is grasped or apprehended (*Erfasstes*) and object are the same. What is apprehended can, however, either be thought of as such or only as object. In the former case, the relation in which the object stands to the apprehending subject is thought of along with it. Yet it is by no means necessary that it should be. What is grasped or apprehended can be thought of merely as object, for, not only is the relation in question not contained in the thought of the object, it belongs in no way to the nature of the object. Every object stands in relations to other objects ; the fact that along with these relations there is that of being apprehended by a subject gives to the object the character of being an *apprehended* object, but not that of being an *object*. An object can *be* when the presentation by which it would be apprehended *is not* ; and it can likewise *not be* when this presentation *is*.[2]

As the notion of object in general may in some measure be determined from the point of view of apprehension, so Meinong thinks the chief classes of objects may be character-

---

[1] Cf. *Ueber Annahmen*, 2te Aufl., p. 26.

[2] For several reasons it is, I think, unfortunate that Meinong should have used the term *Gegenstand* in this all-inclusive sense (see *supra*, p. 9). If he had employed the term " being " with the comprehensive denotation it has become customary to give to it, he might have spoken of " entities " instead of " objects ", and of a science of entities instead of a *Gegenstandstheorie*.

ised by reference to the chief classes of apprehending experiences (*der erfassenden Erlebnisse*). Accordingly, the four main classes of experiences—presentation (*vorstellen*), thinking, feeling and conation—may be said to have corresponding to them the four classes of *Gegenstände*—Objects,[1] Objectives, Dignitatives and Desideratives—only the peculiar character of these objects must not be assumed to be first constituted by the peculiar character of the experiences by which they are apprehended.

(*a*) The various species of Objects may be brought to light by different modes of division, but meanwhile I confine attention to the division of them into those which exist, those which subsist, and those which neither exist nor subsist.

That there are non-existent Objects—that is to say, Objects which only subsist—Meinong took to be indisputable. No one would assert that the difference between red and green exists as tables and chairs exist ; but equally no one would doubt the being of this difference. The difference between red and green is not, it is true, seen as the colours are seen, but, then, perception is not requisite for its apprehension; from the nature of red and green it is manifest that they *are* different.[2] Difference is, in fact, a *superius* which discloses itself in an *a priori* manner from the *inferiora* [3] ; it is founded (*fundiert*) through its *inferiora*.

Meinong was likewise convinced that a class of non-subsistent Objects must be recognised. Impossible Objects, such as a round square, do not subsist ; nevertheless they are Objects, so that we seem driven to the apparent paradox of asserting the being of that which has not being. Meinong's position in this reference is a difficult one ; but, then, the problem which he was here up against is extraordinarily difficult. He tried, however, to meet the various objections that were raised against his view. Little weight could, he thought, be laid on the argument that the Objects which he

---

[1] When translating the German *Objekt*, I use a capital O.

[2] Cf. *Erfahrungsgrundlagen*, p. 5 *sqq.*   [3] See *supra*, pp. 293-4.

regarded as non-subsistent must, in truth, be subsistent, seeing that they can be the subjects of true and, therefore, subsistent propositions. For obviously it is an argument which cannot be used by those who deny that there are non-subsistent Objects. If, as a matter of fact, a kind of being must belong to the round square, because subsistence cannot be denied to certain propositions based upon it, that is an argument *for* Objects such as a round square and *not* an argument *against* them. And to Mr. Russell's contention that the admission of impossible Objects involves denying the law of contradiction (the round square can be asserted to be both round and not round), his answer was that the law of contradiction had never been asserted except of the actual and the possible, and that whether it holds likewise of the impossible requires, at least, special scrutiny.[1] Meinong saw, at all events, that the problem is a real one and faced it seriously, whereas usually it is conveniently thrust aside as though it were no problem at all.

There is, however, a further difficulty with respect to this first class of objects, about which I should like to say a few words. It arises in reference to the primary division of them, of which I have not as yet spoken. What reason is there, on the view Meinong was taking, for supposing that we are aware of *Vorstellungsgegenstände* which not only subsist but exist? Meinong himself distinguished between these two kinds of being by pointing out that what exists must exist at some definite period of time, whereas what merely subsists is timeless, although existence as such is as timeless as subsistence.[2] And his pupil Ameseder, who usually follows

---

[1] *Ueber die Stellung der Gegenstandstheorie*, p. 16. In his review of this book (*Mind*, N.S., xvi, p. 439), Mr. Russell urges that the reply " seems to overlook the fact that it is of propositions (*i.e.*, of ' Objectives ' in Meinong's terminology), not of subjects, that the law of contradiction is asserted ". I do not see that Meinong's remarks give countenance to this supposition. He appears to me to be saying that to suppose that two contradictory propositions can both be true may not be inadmissible when their subjects are impossible Objects.

[2] *Cf. Ueber Annahmen*, 2te Aufl., p. 75.

him closely, adds the further differentiation that " that only is actual (or existent) which can operate causally ".[1] Meinong certainly seems to imply that what are now often called sense-data (*Empfindungsgegenstände*) are not existent entities. These " homeless objects " (so described because hitherto they had formed part of the subject-matter of no science) are, he insists, neither mental nor physical. Colours, for example, are not mental ; acts of seeing them are, of course, mental, and so, likewise, are the contents of these acts ; but colours are quite distinct from presentations of colours. Nor are they physical ; their substitutes in the material world are vibratory motions or modes of energy.[2] Ameseder definitely affirms that " since a colour is, like every other object of sensation, not capable of operating causally, its being is not existence ". Every sensation, he contends, has a cause, but this cause is never identical with what, through the sensation, is apprehended. The cause is physical, or, at any rate, not psychical ; what is apprehended through the sensation, the so-called sense-datum, is neither physical nor psychical and is not an existent.[3] What, then, are the existents that can be said to be, in Meinong's sense of the term, *Vorstellungsgegenstände* ? As instances of existents, Ameseder mentions a quantum of water and a psychical process. But the water, as distinct from the sense-data erroneously, as he thinks, ascribed to it, is not presented and can only be known, if at all, through perception, perception being, in Meinong's view, always an act of judging. Physical existents, one would gather, therefore, never can be presented Objects (*Objekte*). And the same would appear to be true of psychical processes, for they, too, according to the theory, cannot be presented. So that it would seem as though we were driven to the conclusion that for human knowledge, at any rate, there is no way of directly apprehending existent Objects.

[1] *Untersuchungen zur Gegenstandstheorie*, p. 79.

[2] *Ueber die Stellung der Gegenstandstheorie*, pp. 8-9.

[3] *Untersuchungen zur Gegenstandstheorie*, pp. 94 and 481-482.

It is here, I think, that we come upon one of the weaknesses of Meinong's doctrine of *Vorstellungen*.

(*b*) His view of Objectives has become sufficiently familiar from recent discussions of it. If by a " proposition " be meant not a form of words which expresses what is either true or false, but that which is expressed by the form of words, that which is true or false, then an Objective would be, to some extent, equivalent to a proposition. Meinong himself, however, preferred to say that a proposition (*Satz*) *is* an expression of an act of thinking (an act of judging or assuming) and *has* a meaning ; and that the meaning is the Objective, *i.e.*, the object of the act of thought. Just as it is a characteristic of every *Vorstellung* to present an Object, so it lies in the nature of every act of thought to think an Objective. By employing the term " Objective " Meinong wished to emphasise that what is judged or supposed is not an ideal *construction* on the part of the mind ; that it is not the content of an act of thought any more than a presented object is the content of a presentation ; that it is what thought discovers and not what thought may be supposed to make or manufacture. Objectives must clearly be " objects of higher order ", and as such they are founded (*fundiert*) upon other objects—that is to say, either directly or indirectly [1] upon Objects. Confining attention at present to acts of judgment (*i.e.*, omitting *Annahmen*), we may say that the Objective is what is judged (*was geurteilt wird*) and the Object what is judged about (*was beurteilt wird*). If, for example, it be asserted that the fire is bright, the Objective is " that the fire is bright ", and this Objective is founded upon the Objects " the fire " and " brightness ". Objectives are, of course, incapable of existence, but only false Objectives are incapable of subsistence. In his latest writings, Meinong was in the habit of saying that every object *has* being (or non-being);

---

[1] The Objective of one act of thought can, of course, be founded upon an Objective of another, *e.g.*, " it is certain that *A* is *B* ", where what is judged to be certain is neither *A* nor *B* but " that *A* is *B* ".

that there are, however, objects which not only *have* being
(in this widest sense) but also *are* being, and that these are
Objectives, while what *has* being, and *is* not being, is thereby
characterised as Object. Or, expressed otherwise, Objectives
attach to Objects, and Objects stand in Objectives. What
exactly is to be understood by the non-being of false Objectives is, he admitted, a matter that requires investigation. Naming it meanwhile *Aussersein*, what remains
undecided is whether this *Aussersein* is a determination
of being or whether it denotes simply deprivation of being.
The principle of Occam's razor and the circumstance that
Aussersein has no negative seemed to him to favour the
latter alternative, although he recognised the difficulty of
the position.[1]

Being, taken in the widest sense as that which comes
before us in every Objective, evinces itself either as being in
the narrower sense, expressed in the form " *A* is " ; or as
being so-and-so (*Sosein*), " *A* is *B* " ; or as co-being (*Mitsein*),
" If *A*, then *B* ". These correspond more or less to the distinctions recognised by traditional logic between so-called
existential, categorical and hypothetical judgments. [Whe-
ther there is any class of Objectives corresponding to the
disjunctive judgment of traditional logic Meinong considered
to be doubtful ; it would rather seem, he suggested, that we
have here to do with complexes of Objectives, such as may be
met with in each of the three classes mentioned.] Since both
Sosein and *Mitsein* necessarily involve a bifurcation of
inferiora, these *inferiora* exhibit themselves in characteristic
relations—the relation of predication in the case of *Sosein*,
that of implication in the case of *Mitsein*. *Sosein*, again,
falls into the sub-divisions of *Wassein* (*e.g.*, " the horse is a
mammal ") and *Wiesein* (*e.g.*, " snow is white ") ; and
Mitsein appears to be differentiated into the cases where the

---

[1] The difficulty is not, of course, peculiar to Meinong's view. On *no*
theory, so far as I can see, has any satisfactory explanation been given of
what Meinong called " false Objectives ".

inferiora stand in an " if-relation " and those where they stand in a " because-relation ".

Meinong held further that the peculiarity of the being of Objectives is manifested in nothing more decidedly than in the modal qualities which, as he maintained, belong to it. " Factuality " (*Tatsächlichkeit*), the property of being a fact,[1] can be ascribed only to Objectives, or to other objects only in a derivative sense. And, on purely empirical grounds, Meinong was convinced that when we are thinking of the factual character of an Objective we need not be thinking of the certainty and evidence in the judgment which grasps it. Certainty and evidence are subjective characteristics—the one belonging to the act of judging and the other to its content ; and although we may come to be aware of the factual character of an Objective by reflecting on the certainty and evidence of the judgment, we are usually aware of it by direct inspection. Possibility is, so to speak, " factuality " of a lower grade, " factuality " is the maximum of possibility ; so that the various degrees of possibility might be represented on a line the opposite ends of which would be " factuality " and " non-factuality ". So, too, necessity is a characteristic of many Objectives, a characteristic which is grasped, Meinong maintained, by what he called rational evidence, but which is in no sense constituted thereby. The characteristic of necessity, when it belongs to an Objective, is knowable in the most direct and immediate way [2] ; it is given as something essentially positive, so that the interpretation of it as the inconceivability of the opposite is ruled out on this account alone. Not only so. Necessity cannot be taken to be an enhanced degree of " factuality ", as the latter is an enhanced degree of possibility, for " factuality " does not admit of enhancement. And, on the other hand, it is, in strictness,

[1] By " fact " Meinong meant everything that is the case, whether it concerns the existent, or the subsistent, or entities which neither exist nor subsist.

[2] *Cf.* the opening pages of *Erfahrungsgrundlagen*.

no less absurd to speak of a decrease of necessity, out of which decrease " factuality " could, as it were, result. For even within the region of merely possible Objectives necessity is likewise to be found.[1]

(c and d) Presentation and thought are, however, far from being the only means by which, as Meinong conceived, objects (*Gegenstände*) can be experienced by a conscious mind. No doubt the capacity of feeling as a medium of knowledge falls a long way behind that of presentation. Yet when, for instance, we pronounce a degree of warmth to be pleasant, it is easily seen, he urged, how utterly foreign it would be to experience to interpret the quality pleasant as being an experienced feeling produced in us by the warmth. So, too, he contended, the heavens are called beautiful in no other sense than that in which they are called blue, save that the experience (*Erlebnis*) through which the former of these qualities comes to recognition does not play in the inner life *merely* the part of being a mode of grasping or apprehending. But, all the same, it *does* play that part ; and, consequently, there stand over against the feelings special kinds of objects, precisely as there do over against presentations and thoughts. These objects are always objects of higher order ; and are, therefore, akin to Objectives. Meinong distinguished four classes of feeling—namely, those accompanying (i) the act of presentation, (ii) its content, (iii) the act of thought and (iv) its content ; and he tried to show that to each of these a specific kind of object could be correlated—namely, the qualities pleasant, beautiful, true and good (provided that not only a cognitive but a feeling significance be ascribed to the term " true "). These values, then, are distinctively objects (*e.g.*. when we say " this ornament is pretty " we imply that it deserves to please, that it is worthy of being regarded as pleasure-giving) ; they are grasped through or by means of experiences, as all other objects are, but in their essence they are independent of such experiences ; and as

[1] *Ueber Möglichkeit und Wahrscheinlichkeit*, p. 122 *sqq.*

such they are what he designated Dignitatives. So, too, in desire, that which is desired is grasped through or by means of the content of the act of desiring, but it is not constituted thereby. To this class of Desideratives may be reckoned objects that fall under the heads of *Sollen* and *Zweck*.

In the manner I have thus tried briefly to sketch, Meinong contrived to map out broadly the province of *Gegenstands-theorie*, and to carry out in several of its departments researches of a far-reaching kind. It may be objected that a province of these dimensions must certainly be co-extensive with the whole of philosophy, if not with the whole of knowledge. Meinong thought otherwise. It is clearly possible, he maintained, to deal separately with the general properties of objects, to consider what can be ascertained *a priori* from their nature, without reference to their existence or non-existence. So regarded, it seemed to him that *Gegenstands-theorie* belongs to philosophy as an essential part of it ; and that it in no way encroaches upon those parts of philosophy already recognised.

XII

THE "MODES" OF SPINOZA AND THE "MONADS" OF LEIBNIZ

1. **Esse essentiae** *and* **esse existentiae.**
2. *Activity as the Principle of Individuality.*
3. *Stages in the Development of Individual Things.*
4. *The Relation of Finite Individuals to God.*
5. *Conclusion.*

" LEIBNIZ's philosophy is a metaphysic, and, in sharp opposition to the simple universal Substance of Spinoza, where all that is determined is merely transitory, it makes fundamental the absolute multiplicity of individual substances." The contrast which Hegel [1] here institutes between the systems of thought whose relations to one another in some aspects I propose in this essay to consider has become familiar enough in more recent expositions, and I do not deny that it has a certain measure of justification. I believe, however, the antithesis suggested is far more pronounced than any which a careful comparison of the philosophical conceptions in question will reveal, and that, notwithstanding the antagonistic positions from which they start, the results reached and the difficulties encountered by the two thinkers present a surprising amount of similarity. "Spinoza would be right", Leibniz once observed, "if there were no monads "; and he meant, no doubt, to imply that the theory of monads had entirely altered the philosophical outlook. I shall try to show that, as a matter of fact, it did not. But let it not be supposed, on that account, that I am wishful to disparage the work of Leibniz. To most of the branches of philosophy he made contributions of real value and importance, and these

---

[1] *Werke*, Bd. XV, p. 408.

retain their significance even though his solution of ultimate metaphysical problems turns out to be one of the numerous ways in which they cannot be solved.

In this connexion another remark may be permissible. Mr. Bertrand Russell has made himself responsible for the dictum that "monism must be pantheistic and monadism must be atheistic"[1]; and he appears to think that a coherent philosophy might have emerged from the labours of Leibniz, if from it there had been pruned away the inconsistencies due to the retention of the idea of God. This is a view which more than one writer has countenanced, and I am not at present concerned to ask how far it can resist criticism. One thing, however, is certain. A monadism of that sort would have had no affinity with Leibniz's monadism. He would have recognised in it little that was distinguishable from the atomism in opposition to which his speculative reflexion was one sustained polemic. The notion of God, as the ultimate ground of things, was no excrescence on Leibniz's system, nor did it play the part there of that convenient receptacle for the difficulties of thought—the unknown and the unknowable. On the contrary, it was intimately related to well-nigh every one of the general considerations which he brought to bear in his interpretation of the world and human life.

It is, of course, impossible here to do more than indicate in a summary manner the lines of consideration along which, as it seems to me, the two systems may be profitably compared with one another. If, in thus dealing summarily with great conceptions, I seem unsympathetic or even unfair, I plead the exigencies of a limited undertaking ; and protect myself by pointing out that judiciously balanced statements of the philosophies of both thinkers exist already in abundance.

I am well aware, for instance, that two opposing ways of regarding Substance are struggling for mastery in the *Ethics*, and that to do full justice to Spinoza one would have to take

[1] *Critical Exposition of the Philosophy of Leibniz*, pp. 172 and 185.

both these tendencies into account. I shall, indeed, have something to say about them later on. But in a short essay it is legitimate to lay stress upon what appears to be the actual effect of his reasoning rather than upon its effect as he himself was sometimes inclined to conceive it. To avoid misunderstanding, however, it is perhaps necessary to state, without attempting to defend, the view I should take upon one or two matters of disputed interpretation. In the first place, it seems to me clear that the guiding principle of Spinoza's philosophical method is the principle of ground and consequent, and that what he calls causation is identical with this relation. It is, so I understand him to mean, only when things are viewed from the standpoint of the imagination that they are conceived as connected in some other manner than that of logical sequence. From the point of view of reason, it is seen that if anything is a cause its effect must necessarily be deducible from it, must follow from it " by the same necessity as it follows from the nature of a triangle that its three angles are equal to two right angles ". Substance, therefore, is not for him a producing cause of the universe, or even of finite things, but the ground or reason thereof, that on which all else must depend, as the conclusion of a syllogism depends upon the premisses. In the second place, I cannot, largely on account of what I have just been saying, accept the representation of those expositors who take Spinoza to mean by " Attributes " lines of force or energy, lying at the basis of the divine activity. The doctrine of " Attributes " is notoriously a difficult doctrine even from the point of view of mere exegesis, but I find it wholly impossible to suppose that Spinoza, at least in the *Ethics*, intended to postulate a number of real powers or potencies, each existing in and for itself, whatever he may have done when he was more immediately under the influence of Cartesianism. That would have been palpably to contradict, *ab initio*, the very thesis he was setting out to establish. How could modes of energy each be infinite *in suo genere*? Admittedly, there is nothing in the definition of "Attribute" to support this interpretation. Spinoza I take to be defining "Attribute" as a way in which Substance is apprehended. At the same time, I do not think it is implied that the content thus apprehended is subjective in character. To our apprehension, it is true, Substance can present only some of its features, some of its essence, but so far as what is apprehended is concerned, no distinction is to be drawn between the content cognised and the real essence. Strongly as he emphasised the distinction between partial and complete knowledge, Spinoza recognised no antithesis between what is truly known and what is.

So much, then, by way of preface. I proceed now at once to the special themes I purpose to discuss. I propose to consider the sense in which particular things are regarded by the two thinkers as existing, the mode of being ascribed to them, the different stages of development they are thought to exhibit, and the relation in which they are conceived to stand to the ultimate ground.

1

Esse essentiae *and* esse existentiae

A long and intricate chapter in the history of thought remains to be written upon the transformations in meaning undergone by the term " substance " prior to its adoption by the Cartesians. Professor Pringle-Pattison is certainly justified in emphasising the fundamental difference between the Aristotelian conception of πρώτη οὐσία and the conception of substance as the self-subsistent.[1] It is worth while, however, reminding ourselves that Aristotle's use of οὐσία is by no means uniform, and that the prototype of the latter conception is also to be found in the *Metaphysic*. After defining οὐσία as that to which being (τὸ εἶναι), in the strict sense, belongs (*Meta.*, 1028, *a* 31), Aristotle does, no doubt,

[1] *The Idea of God*, p. 272.

usually interpret this to mean " that which cannot stand in a
judgment as predicate or attribute of anything else ". The
distinctive mark of a substance then consists in the fact of its
being a τόδε τι, a single individual thing with a determinate
nature (τὸ καθ᾽ ἕκαστον). It is not, indeed, the content apprehended by sense at any given moment ; it is the individual
entity which through all its changes preserves its indestruct-
ible form or essence and which can only be truly known by
grasping the form or essence which characterises it. All the
same, it does not consist of essence or form (εἶδος) merely ;
it is always an οὐσία σύνθετος, that is to say, the essence or
type as realised under conditions peculiar to each individual,
conditions which can be summarily expressed by the term
matter (ὕλη). Matter is equivalent, in short, to the totality of
conditions by which each individual concrete thing (σύνολον)
is determined as a unique existent and as finite. Yet, while
insisting that in the world of genesis only the concrete individual thing is substance, Aristotle is constrained (in Book
xii of the *Metaphysic*) to the admission that there must be an
eternal unmovable substance (ὅτι ἀνάγκη εἶναι τινα ἀΐδιον
οὐσίαν ἀκίνητον), because otherwise the universe would be
destructible. And this eternal unmovable substance he takes
to be pure essence without matter, and to be complete reality
(τὸ δὲ τί ἦν εἶναι οὐκ ἔχει ὕλην τὸ πρῶτον· ἐντελέχεια γάρ).
In other words, the divine being, as a self-dependent, eternally
complete and unchangeable essence, is an individual substance, and hence an individual existent, but in a sense
totally different from that in which concrete individual things
had been defined to be substances and existents. To put it
briefly, Aristotle is virtually saying that God is *causa sui*
whose essence involves existence, whereas in the case of finite
things their essence never does involve their existence. And
the irresolvable problem created by these two incompatible
positions would be one way of exhibiting the incoherent
character of Aristotle's speculative system. Aristotle, it is
true, conceived of God as standing outside the whole process

which, by his mere presence, he initiates in nature. But the fact that precisely the same irresolvable problem reappears in the speculation of Spinoza should be sufficient to show that the substitution of the notion of immanence for the notion of transcendence affords in itself no safeguard against the danger which so constantly besets metaphysical construction—the danger, namely, of finding ourselves stranded with two worlds which persistently fall apart and resist any possibility of rational connexion.

From the commencement of his literary activity Spinoza had resigned himself to admitting a twofold significance of the term "existence". In the *Cogitata Metaphysica* he defines being (*ens*) as "all that which, when clearly and distinctly apprehended, is found to exist necessarily, or at least to be capable of existing", and proceeds to the assertion that being may be divided into (*a*) being which in virtue of its own nature exists necessarily, or the essence of which involves existence, and (*b*) being the essence of which involves only a possible existence, indicating, at the same time, that this is equivalent to a division of being into substance and mode, not into that of substance and accident (i, 1). Then, in regard to modes, he goes on to explain that *esse essentiae* is "nothing else than the way in which created things are comprehended in the Attributes of God", while *esse existentiae* is "the essence of things considered apart from God (*extra Deum*) and in itself", seeing that "it is attributed to things after they have been created by God" (i, 2, § 3). Later on, in a chapter on the eternity of God, he contends that eternity is not to be conceived as indefinite duration. God's being is eternal in the sense of timelessness ; in it *nihil prius nec posterius dari potest*. Duration is an *affectio existentiae, non vero essentiae rerum*. No one would say that the essence of a circle or of a triangle, in so far as it is an eternal truth, has endured for a longer period than from the time of Adam. A created thing can be said to possess existence, because certainly existence does not belong to its essence ; but God cannot be said to possess existence, for the existence of God is God himself. Consequently, while created things may be said to possess duration, God can in no wise be said to possess it.[1] Writing to Meyer, about the time of the publication of the *Cogitata*, Spinoza urges that of the existence of substance we conceive in a totally different manner from that in which we conceive of the existence of modes. Hence arises recognition of the distinction between eternity and duration, for we can explain a certain measure of the existence of modes in terms of duration, but we can only explain the existence of substance in terms of eternity, in terms of the infinite enjoyment of existence or essence (*Ep.* xii, Vloten and Land's ed.). In the *Short Treatise*, the identity of God's existence and essence is laid down at the outset as fundamental. On the other hand, it is asserted that while " the essences of things are from all eternity and will remain to all eternity unalterable ", yet as existences particular things are constantly changing. And in several places it is certainly implied that, although the essences of all things are included in God, the existences taken on by particular things are not in like manner included therein. A similar line is followed in the *Ethics*. " The existence of God and His essence are one and the same " (i, 20). " The essence of things produced by God does not involve existence." Consideration of that essence, whether existing or non-existing, discloses that it involves neither existence nor duration. It cannot, therefore, be the cause or ground either of the existence of things or of their duration (i, 24). Essence and existence, that is to say, are to be distinguished as two different forms of being which in the case of God and the Attributes are in harmony with one another, even identical with one another, in the case of the infinite modes are in harmony with one another but not identical, while in the case of the finite

---

[1] A follower of Bergson might argue that in strictness the analogy required it to be maintained that God cannot be said to possess duration, because God is duration. But that, of course, is just what Spinoza denies.

modes they evince themselves as throughout in disharmony. Accordingly, it is contended that the being of Substance does not pertain to the essence, does not constitute the form, of a man (or of any finite mode), because then the existence of the latter would follow from the existence of the former, which would imply the absurdity of its being necessary existence (ii, 10). Finally, attention may be drawn in this connexion to the proposition (v, 23) that " the human mind cannot be absolutely destroyed with the body, but something of it remains which is eternal ". What remains is the essence ; as timeless, it cannot be affected by death, which is merely a change in the series of changes ; death affects only temporal existence. We feel that our mind, in so far, that is, as it is *mentis essentia*, is eternal. On the other hand, only in so far as it involves the actual existence of the body can the mind be said to possess duration—in other words, existence limited by a fixed time.

These passages, which might easily be added to, will suffice to bring out the kind of conception with which Spinoza was proceeding. He was trying to work together two ways of regarding the universe of particular things. It appertains to the nature of a finite mode, on the one hand, that it possesses an individual existence, a particular and determinate being, distinct from the being of Substance as the ground of this determinate being, distinct, also, from other determinate beings ; and, on the other hand, that it is yet Substance itself in a determinate condition, and in so far again one with the whole complex of other modes, so that things are not *realiter* but only *modaliter* separate from one another (*Eth*. i, 15 Schol.). Hence it is that a mode is described as " God *in so far as* He is modified in a determinate modification ", or " *in so far as* God is affected in a certain manner " (e.g., *Eth*. i, 28) ; hence it is that an idea is spoken of as " God *in so far as* God is considered as affected by an idea " (e.g., *Eth*. ii, 9), or that the human mind is spoken of as " God having such an idea *in so far as* God forms the essence of the human mind " (e.g., *Eth*. ii, 11). The

observation has often been made that the full stress of
Spinoza's problem comes to a head in the use he makes of this
relative particle *quatenus*. (*a*) In so far as " all things are in
God ", each particular mode is, *in a sense*, eternal and infinite.
As an " affection " of Substance, even its continuance in
existence is dependent upon Substance ; and its essence considered simply as contained in the whole modal system or
natura naturata involves its existence. But this " existence "
is not temporal existence, not duration, not existence
" abstractly conceived " (*Eth.* ii, 45) ; it is the timeless being
which the mode possesses as following from the necessity of
God's nature ; and we are not entitled to assume that, in the
being of God, the mode stands out as a *res singularis*. (*b*) In
so far as things have a distinctive nature of their own, each
particular mode exhibits characteristics which cannot be
traced back to its dependence upon Substance. " That which
is finite and which has a determinate existence cannot be produced by the absolute nature of any Attribute of God, for
whatever follows from the absolute nature of any Attribute
of God is infinite and eternal " (i, 28). Thus " determinate
existence ", or the existence of modes in the *communis ordo
naturae*, and the " existence " which modes may be said to
possess in virtue of their essence in the Attributes of God—
that is, as constituting *natura naturata* [1]—these are not only
different but fundamentally antagonistic.

The insuperable difficulties which are thus occasioned for
Spinoza's metaphysical theory come to light at well-nigh
every turning-point of its development. So far as necessary
" existence " is concerned it is, for example, clear that the
demonstration offered of the proposition that it pertains to
the nature of Substance to exist (*Eth.* i, 7) is a *petitio principii*.
Substance, according to the definition, is " that the conception of which does not require the conception of another

[1] Spinoza does not retain in the *Ethics* the distinction he had made in the
Short Treatise between *natura naturata generalis* and *natura naturata
particularis*, and I am following Professor Joachim's interpretation of *natura
naturata* in the *Ethics*. (See *Ethics of Spinoza*, p. 119 *sqq.*).

thing ". But, in that case, so the proof runs, it can have no cause outside of itself, for " the knowledge of an effect depends upon and involves the knowledge of the cause ". And, as Substance can have no cause outside of itself, it must be *causa sui* ; existence, therefore, must pertain to its nature. The argument, however, assumes just that which it purports to establish. For if Substance has no cause outside itself, it follows that it must have an inner cause *only* on the assumption that it *is* existent, and that such existence needs a cause, in accordance, indeed, with the dictum laid down in the Scholium of the next proposition, that " of any existing thing there must necessarily be some cause on account of which it exists ". In the immediate sequel, Spinoza appears, in fact, tacitly to allow that, by his proof, he has made no advance, for he proceeds to base the self-existence of Substance upon the bare definition (Substance is " that which is in itself and is conceived through itself ") and to maintain that he who has a clear and distinct idea of Substance and yet doubts whether Substance exists, is in the predicament of the man who says he has a true idea, but doubts whether or no it is false. And later on still (*Eth*. i, 20) it is definitely laid down that the existence and the essence of God are one and the same, from which follows that God's existence is an eternal truth. So far as determinate existence is concerned, Spinoza's embarrassment is no less manifest. Particular things, as they appear in the *communis ordo naturae*, cannot be regarded as following of necessity from the nature of Substance ; their existence as such is transitory and limited ; the occurrence of any particular thing or event here and now can only be traced backwards from one limited thing or event to another in a chain to which there is no terminus (*Eth*. i, 28). This chain of limited things is, that is to say, somehow in possession of that which can confer upon an essence what it cannot derive from infinite Substance. It is true an attempt is made to save the situation by means of the consideration that each of the causes in such a chain is " God or one of God's Attributes, in so far as it is modified by a modification which is finite and has a determinate existence ". Yet, here again, there is obviously being taken for granted the very thing, and, in this context, the only thing, that requires explanation. The question is, how it is possible that existence which is not identical with essence can arise in Substance whose existence is identical with essence. To reply that it arises in so far as Substance is already infected by an endless series of existences of the precise type about which we are inquiring, is but to ignore the problem and not to solve it. We are left, as Professor Joachim expresses it, with a world of bare existences standing over against the world of essences ; somehow certain of the essences or potentialities of things have stepped into the actualities of the world of temporal existence ; and, although they have thus become less real than those which remain *in posse* as mere essences, they have yet acquired a distinctness and an individuality and a power of activity, of which, as mere essences, they were destitute.[1]

Turning now to Leibniz's way of handling the problem we have had before us, our object will be to discover whether the theory of monads enables him to avoid the *impasse* just indicated. Leibniz repudiates emphatically enough " the view of Spinoza and of other similar authors, who will have it that there is only one Substance, namely God, who thinks, believes and wills one thing in me, but who thinks, believes and wills quite the opposite in some one else " (Gerhardt, vi, p. 537). He reverts to the Aristotelian definition of substance as that which can only be the subject of a proposition and never a predicate. But this definition, he contends, is not sufficient, and is in itself merely verbal. Every true predication must have a basis in the nature of things, and even when the predicate is not explicitly contained in the subject, it is still necessary that it should be implicitly contained in it. The content, then, of the subject must always include that of the predicate in such a way that, if one understood perfectly

[1] *Cf.* Joachim, *op. cit.*, pp. 224-5.

the subject-concept, one would know that the predicate necessarily belongs to it. The concept, therefore, of any individual substance includes, once for all, everything which can ever happen to that subject ; and, in contemplating this concept, a perfect intelligence would be able to discern whatsoever can be truly said about such individual, just as in the nature of a circle it would be able to discern all the properties which can be derived therefrom. Each monad is, in this respect, a substance, and in so far an entire world, or a mirror of the whole world which it represents in its own fashion. " The universe is in a manner multiplied as many times as there are substances." Thus, it may, in a sense, be said that just as Spinoza had maintained that everything can be deduced from the one Substance, so Leibniz maintains that everything is deducible from the notion of any one of the multitude of substances. So far the contrast between the two ways of thinking seems to be a marked and decided contrast, although even here it is, I think, more apparent than real. His next step, however, brings Leibniz back, almost at a bound, to the standpoint of Spinoza. For he is constrained to introduce the all-important distinction between primary or original substance and derivative or created substances ; and, in so doing, accepts, without recognising the significance of the acceptance, the doctrine of a twofold mode of existence. The ultimate ground of things must, he argues, be a necessary substance, in which the variety of particular changes exists only " eminently " as its source ; and this supreme substance, unique and universal as it is, nothing being independent of it, must be illimitable and contain as much reality as is possible (*Monad.*, §§ 38 and 40). Derivative substances, on the other hand, are contingent entities, dependent upon the ultimate ground just as their own states are dependent upon themselves, essentially limited in character, their limitation constituting, in one sense, their individuality[1] (*ibid.*, § 42).

[1] *Cf. infra*, pp. 320-1.

Here, then, we see the water trickling in that was destined to overflow the house. Since the ground of any existing being can only be sought in an existing being, there must, it is contended, be one being which has metaphysical necessity, and whose essence is identical with existence. In other words, there must exist a being bearing in itself the reason of its own existence, and different from that plurality of beings, the world, which has no metaphysical necessity. If, now, it can be shown that such a being is possible—that is to say, is not self-contradictory—we are entitled to affirm its existence, because, since the essence of anything constitutes its possibility, it follows that to exist by its essence is the same as to exist by its possibility. And that the being of God is possible can, Leibniz thinks, be conclusively shown. For God is by definition pure affirmation, absolute perfection, without limit or negation ; there can, therefore, be no contradiction involved in the notion of God's being. Accordingly, for Leibniz just as for Spinoza, a radical difference of kind is to be constituted between existence in an absolute sense and existence in a relative sense. The essence of an infinite being involves its existence because it is unlimited, because there is nothing to hinder that need of existence (*exigentiam existentiae*), or that tendency to exist, which all essence, as he curiously puts it, carries with it. It is, in fact, the prerogative of the divine nature to have need only of a possibility or an essence in order actually to exist, and this is precisely what is meant by *ens a se*. The essence of a finite being, on the other hand, does not involve its existence, because such essence is limited by other essences ; and only by adaptation to other essences, so as to form along with them the best possible world, does it involve even the possibility of existence.

In the case, therefore, of the dependent monads, existence implies, in Leibniz's view, something over and above essence. The position may be briefly formulated thus :

Possibility + a supplement, x, = Actuality.

The supplement is that, whatever it is, which is needful to raise possibility into actuality. What, then, is the nature of this x? Such answer as can be extracted from Leibniz strikes one as singularly ineffective. According to his well-known doctrine, there hovered before the understanding of God innumerable images of compossible universes, each of them so ordered in point of detail as to be consistent with certain eternal laws of truth. The monads were called into existence by the divine will, which is to be distinguished from the divine understanding, and which is morally determined by the principle of the choice of the best. But how does that account of the matter help us in regard to the vital point we are considering? We need to know what new factor is constituted for God or for the world by this fiat of creation, we need to know what has been added to that world of compossible essences which is now more than a world of images, in order that it should have stepped forth into existence outside the divine mind. The mere empty notion of an act avails us nothing, unless the x which has accrued through the act can be indicated. The contention might, I suppose, be advanced that the supplement in question was for Leibniz precisely the element of activity which he regarded as the fundamental factor in existent reality. I do not, however, envy the task of anyone who undertakes to render explicable the manner in which activity can be added to essences. Nor would the contention be in keeping with Leibniz's own statements. He is repeatedly asserting that " in possibility or essence itself there is a certain aspiration to exist ", that " essence by itself tends to exist ", so that it would appear that activity is already involved in the being of essence. Moreover, the choice of the best is, as Professor Latta put it, " rather a negative release into existence than a positive creation " [1]; for it is pictured as a liberating of the essences in question from the counteracting influences of opposite essences, as a removal of hindrances to their inherent power of development. In

[1] *Mind*, N.S., vol. viii, 1899, p. 347.

some way, through the act of creation, the monads become " windowless ".

2

Activity as the Principle of Individuality

" I maintain ", says Leibniz, in opposing his own view of substance to that of Locke, " that substances cannot be conceived in their bare essence without any activity, that activity is of the essence of substance in general " (Gerh., v, p. 58). It is a slippery notion, that of activity, and all too easily interpreted in a quasi-psychological fashion, into which fashion, indeed, Leibniz's descriptions of it not infrequently tend to fall. But Leibniz makes, at any rate, the attempt to form a conception of activity as contrasted with a mere picture of it. " By force or power (*puissance*) ", he writes, " I do not mean the capacity (*pouvoir*) or mere faculty, which is nothing but a mere possibility of acting and which, being as it were dead, never produces an action without being stimulated from without, but I mean something between the capacity (*pouvoir*) and action, something which iucludes an effort, an act, an entelechy, for force passes of itself into action, in so far as nothing hinders it " (Gerh., iv, 472). Leibniz's doctrine may be expressed briefly thus. The characteristic feature of every individual substance is unity—a unity which is not conceivable after the manner of a merely presented object. Just as it requires more than the notion of extendedness to explain the nature of a material fact, so it requires more than the notion of being merely an object to explain the nature of an individual substance. We need to call to our aid the very different conception of power or energy, a permanent principle of change and action, in order to give definiteness to the thought of individuals as substantive realities. Not only so ; the same line of reflexion enables us to define more explicitly the kind of force which is requisite in order that an individual substance should maintain its numerical identity. It is not a force in any way dependent for its mode of being upon spatial relations—in other words, it is non-material in character. Moreover, since the unity of an individual real substance must be a unity which connects together the various changes that constitute its states, the activity which is its essential quality must be of a kind that is capable of uniting multiplicity of relations with singleness of being ; it must, that is to say, be a one in many, or a many in one. And the only activity which can fulfil a function of that sort is the activity or force of a soul or mental life. Monads are active *per se*, and in them perception implies representation of the external in the internal, of the compound in the simple, of multiplicity in unity, which, again, involves appetition, or the tendency to pass from one perception to another. If, then, the contention of Dillmann[1] is to be allowed, that " the most important concept of Leibniz's monadology is the concept of representation ", the proviso must be added that representation is not merely perception but also striving tendency, that it is a spontaneous power of development no less than a reflecting mirror of the universe.

But the other side of the shield must be displayed. Think out the notion of activity, Leibniz argues, and it will be seen to involve what at first sight appears to be diametrically opposed to it, namely, passivity. Activity is the way in which an individual manifests its individuality. It is, however, not only in virtue of this positive quality that individuality is constituted ; an individual not marked off from others, not negatively characterised as being exclusive, would be a contradiction in terms. Activity which simply flowed forth would give no manifestation of itself, just as little as an elastic force which met with no resistance. Every monad must, then, be at once active and passive ; active in order to exist at all, passive in order to exist as distinct from the other members of the universe. Accordingly, passivity in the monad is the element of limitation, of incompleteness, of

[1] *Neue Darstellung der Leibnizischen Monadenlehre*, p. 304.

finitude ; and since the position of each monad in the whole system is determined by its degree of finitude, its passivity may be said to be that element which constitutes its relatedness to the other monads. Furthermore, each monad, in so far as it is active, has clear and distinct ideas, and apprehends the true nature of reality ; in so far as it is passive, its ideas are obscure and confused, and what is obscure and confused *seems* foreign to it, *seems* other than itself, *seems* to be external and material. Matter, in short, although an essential feature in the life of the monad, is but the phenomenal appearance of that which in truth is non-material.

In all this, it would look, at first sight, as though we had left the " modes " of Spinoza far behind ; but, as a matter of fact, Leibniz has been largely engaged in making explicit what is more or less implicit in the *Ethics*. For Spinoza, no less than for Leibniz, the individuality of determinate existences consists in activity. Already in the *Cogitata* (ii, 6) it had been maintained that the principle of life should be attributed to all things, both corporeal and mental. And by life was to be understood the *vim per quam res in suo esse perseverant*—a force which, although differently represented in different things, each thing may be said to possess in varying degree. But in the *Ethics* the conception is expanded in significance so that it comes to stand for a measure of self-dependence on the part of particular things.

In the first place, it followed directly from the doctrine of Attributes that all *res particulares* are at once corporeal and ideal in character ; regarded from one point of view they are modes of extension, regarded from another point of view they are modes of consciousness. In fact, were it not for the limitation of our understanding, we might apprehend each particular thing as a mode of any one of the innumerable Attributes which constitute the essence of God. Individual things are all of them *animata*, although in different degrees[1] (ii, 13).

---

[1] Cf. *Short Treatise* (ii, 22). " There can be nothing in nature of which there is not in the soul of that same thing an idea."

x

What, therefore, can be said generally concerning the human mind may be said regarding the mind of any other thing. Yet this affords no reason for denying that minds or souls differ from one another as their bodies do, and that one contains more reality than another. In other words, the kind of life or soul animating a particular thing will depend upon the number of qualities characterising it, or upon its power of acting or suffering.

In the second place, particular things are modes of God's Attributes which express those Attributes in a definite and determinate way (*certo et determinato modo*). Each thing, that is to say, manifests God's nature or essence in a manner peculiar to itself, and as no other thing manifests it. All things derive their essence, and in one sense their existence, from God ; but, apart from the fact that they thus follow from the necessity of the divine nature, they have, in virtue of their relation to a fixed time and place, a certain relative independence or modal distinctness. The difficulty or impossibility of reconciling this contention with the trend of thought pursued in the earlier portions of the *Ethics* is patent enough. But it can hardly be questioned that at this juncture of his reflexion Spinoza does speak as though there belonged to particular things, even though the negative element which he had taken, formerly, to distinguish them from the Absolute be disregarded, a certain individuality which, as contained in God, is still positive, and can be known through God.

This affirmative, self-assertive factor which the essence of a particular thing appears to involve is what Spinoza calls its *conatus*, its tendency or striving towards preservation.[1] Everything strives to maintain itself in existence, and to resist whatever threatens to encroach upon, or destroy, its being. Thus the existence of any individual thing cannot be terminated from within itself ; on the contrary, " each thing strives, so far as in it lies, to persevere in its own being "

[1] *Cf.* Leibniz's assertion that force is " that from which activity follows when nothing prevents it ; it is effort, *conatus* ". *Lettre à M. Pelisson* (1691).

(*Eth.* iii, 6). The *conatus* is, in fact, it is now declared, the given or actual essence of the thing itself ; and it is, therefore, not conditioned by time ; it is independent, that is to say, of the reciprocal determination of one thing by another. An inorganic thing manifests its *conatus* by resisting and repelling whatsoever would tend to alter its condition of motion or rest. A plant has its own way of striving to maintain itself against ill-adapted surroundings, and of using its environment to subserve the continuance of its growth and life. In the animal the *conatus* takes the form of appetite or impulse (*appetitus*), and in that form new scope for its exercise is provided. Finally, the *conatus* in the case of man becomes, or may become, an object of his consciousness ; he not only strives to persevere in his own being, but he may be aware of such striving. *Appetitus* assumes the aspect of *cupiditas*. It is true that Spinoza makes the curious reservation that the presence of self-consciousness makes no difference, for " whether a man is conscious of his appetite or no, the appetite still remains one and the same " (*Eth.* iii, App., § 1). But I do not think we are entitled to conclude from this that Spinoza meant to imply that the *conatus* which expresses itself in man is a blind unconscious force, a mere will-to-live which uses man as its instrument, whilst the consciousness of it is but an accident of its operation. As Mr. Duff points out,[1] what Spinoza is saying in the passage just quoted is not that there is no difference between appetite in general and human desire, but that there is no difference between a human appetite and a human desire. And I think Mr. Duff is right in his contention that, according to Spinoza, all human striving is *cupiditas*, whether it be called a *conatus*, an appetite, or a volition, and that of every *cupiditas* a man is, or at least may be, conscious.

The activity, then, upon which Leibniz lays such stress as constituting the essence of individuality was equally recognised by Spinoza ; and was, in fact, not less strongly em-

[1] *Spinoza's Political and Ethical Philosophy*, p. 78 *sqq.*

phasised by him. Whether he regarded it as playing the important part in perceptive experience that Leibniz claims for it is not easy to determine. But, at any rate, he leaves us in no doubt as to its unique position in the higher intellectual life. " Whatever we desire through reason is nothing else than the desire to understand. And since this striving of the mind (*mentis conatus*), by which the mind, in so far as it reasons, endeavours to preserve its being, is nothing but the striving to understand, it follows that this striving to understand (*intelligendi conatus*) is the primary and sole foundation of virtue " (*Eth.* iv, 26).

Equally, too, Spinoza had discovered what seemed to him elements of passivity in the development of individual experience. The various *imaginationes* of vague experience, when the order of their occurrence is not regulated by the conscious subject—so long, that is to say, as the mind perceives things as existing in the *communis ordo naturae*, or, in other words, is determined from without to apprehend this or that—are *passive* in character ; and in describing these as fragments, or as torn, mutilated portions of ideas, Spinoza was on the verge of formulating the doctrine that sensations are confused concepts. And one need do no more than refer to the elaborate analysis of the " passive emotions " in the third book of the *Ethics*, where the notion of passivity carries with it similar implications.

That Spinoza, on the basis of his view of Substance, was legitimately entitled to make use of the conception of *conatus*, as the essence of an individual thing, may well, indeed, be doubted. Activity is introduced by him *ex abrupto* and no serious attempt is made to justify its introduction. It is true we are vaguely told at the beginning (*Eth.* i, 11) that to be able to exist is power (*potentia*) ; but it is in the descent from the realm of the Unconditioned to the realm of the Conditioned through means of the infinite modes that activity first becomes prominent. The infinite modes, *motus et quies* and *intellectus absolute infinitus*, are just the Attributes of

Extension and Thought *plus* the element of activity. But as
to how this supplementary factor is supposed to emerge from
the undifferentiated wholes of Extension and Thought,
Spinoza leaves us in the dark. He seems to be taking the
notion of " depending on " as equivalent to that of " following from ". Obviously, however, the identification of these
two notions is illegitimate. Motion no doubt depends upon
extension ; but in no sense can it be said to follow from
extension. Yet it is evident, I think, that Leibniz, too, is in
the long run confronted with no less obstinate a difficulty.
The transition from the pure undifferentiated activity of God
to the myriad finite centres of activity in the created universe
is hardly easier to render intelligible than the transition
sought to be effected by Spinoza.

3

Stages in the Development of Individual Things

It is impossible here to do more than briefly indicate the
various stages recognised by Spinoza and Leibniz in the
development of particular existences. The notion of evolution was, of course, more deeply imbedded in the speculation of Leibniz than in that of Spinoza. The general principle of continuity was never for long absent from Leibniz's
thought. Though at first formulated by him with reference
to the nature of quantitative changes, it was soon extended
to the whole range of reality. It led him rapidly to the conclusion that any absolute qualitative difference between one
entity and another, such as was involved in the Cartesian
antithesis of consciousness and extension, calls to be rejected.
If there are to be real individuals, and if these individuals are
to be parts of one and the same system, no differences of kind
must be allowed to obtain among them. In its ultimate
nature, reality must be continuous. Any amount of difference there might be, provided such difference be difference of
degree only. From this to the further determination of the

ultimate elements of reality as psychical in character was but a short step for a speculative genius of the subtlety of Leibniz. The step was taken by help of the consideration that an individual being must be conceived as that which unites in itself a manifold, and that in a sphere of mere extendedness a unity of the kind in question would be precluded.

The individuals, then, of which the universe consists are mental in nature and distinguishable by differences in the degree of completeness with which the combination of a manifold in unity is represented by them. Taking the human individual as our point of departure we find, on the one hand, the lower types of life exhibited in animals and plants, and, on the other hand, we are entitled to contemplate forms of life higher than our own, culminating at length in the life of the supreme Monad. There is one power common to all these individuals—the power, namely, of representing in various degrees the universe, of mirroring it each from its own point of view. The mirroring activity up to a certain stage may be called "perception", the process of including the many in a unity ; beyond that stage it may be called "apperception ", that is to say, perception which has become self-conscious. " Life is a perceptive principle ; the soul is sensitive life ; mind is rational soul." And what distinguishes one stage of representation from another is just the degree of clearness and distinctness of apprehension. At the one limit dim, obscure, confused perception ; at the other full, clear, adequate apperception—between these lie all the stages of psychical development. Naturally, Leibniz's chief obstacles lie at the two extremes of the scale — at the lower, he has to make the leap from the unconscious to the conscious ; at the higher, that from imperfect to perfect self-consciousness.

Beginning, then, at the lower end, the principle of continuity has to serve as justification for regarding the unconscious as simply a low degree of the conscious, for regard-

ing unconsciousness as infinitely minute consciousness. The
start is made from those " naked monads ", as Leibniz called
them, whose condition is comparable to the condition of a
dreamless sleep. When the stage is reached where differentiated organs appear, the organic world arises, and in the psychical life of the animals we have something resembling our
own life in dreams. The psychical equivalent of an organ of
sense is what is ordinarily called sensation. Sensations are
ideas in their primitive and most undifferentiated form ;
they constitute " the vertigo of the conscious life ". Flooded
with ideas of everything in the world which has any relation
to its body, the animal soul has distinct ideas of nothing.
Advance consists not in putting these sensations together—
thereby confusion would become more confounded—but in
distinguishing them, in getting clearness to emerge out of
confusedness, in finding out what they mean. The self-
conscious monad, having thus acquired knowledge of necessary truths, can represent the universe with more or less
adequacy and distinctness. But, looked at from the point
of view of psychical development, rational truths are in
the long run percepts developed to the full degree of distinctness and clearness ; thinking is perceiving clarified and
developed.

Now, although Spinoza did not work out in detail his conception of the different stages of *animata*, it needs little
ingenuity to see that he was practically distinguishing the
stages which Leibniz describes. Starting with the dictum
that all the individual things of nature are living, he was
clearly committed to the position that below the level of
organic beings there were modes in which consciousness was
present in a dull, crude, weak form. Everything had its soul-
side. And in regard to organisms, what Leibniz designates
" perception " is coincident with what Spinoza designated
" *experientia vaga* " or " imagination ". In crude experience,
as represented by Spinoza, an enormous number of presentations come pouring in ; and " running together ", they appear

blurred and confused, so that the mind is overwhelmed with the multiplicity of impressions and images. Modes entirely at the mercy of these would be at the stage of the animal life as it is delineated by Leibniz. Then Spinoza proceeded to trace the way in which from these vague undiscriminated presentations there come to be formed, in human experience, the first primitive universals which serve to guide the actions of ordinary men. The manner of their formation is through the more or less mechanical process of association, and that process varies according to the level of development attained. When, however, the grade of *ratio* is attained, we acquire knowledge of the kind which Leibniz specifies by the term " apperception ". "Universal notions and adequate ideas of the properties of things "—ideas which are shared by self-conscious intelligences and which express features common to vast numbers of things—come then to be used. The ideas of imaginative experience are inadequate—that is to say, partial, fragmentary, incomplete and, therefore, confused and indistinct ; the ideas of reason are adequate—that is to say, contain within themselves the marks of truth, clearness and distinctness, self-sufficiency and consistency of content. Spinoza, as is well known, differentiated yet a further stage which Leibniz hardly does more than hint at, *scientia intuitiva*, " that kind of knowing which proceeds from an adequate idea of the formal essence of certain attributes of God to the adequate knowledge of the essence of things ".

It is true there is less explicit recognition by Spinoza than by Leibniz that these stages represent differences of degree only. But I am by no means convinced that Spinoza definitely regarded them as different in kind. Certainly, if he did, it would be difficult to render consistent his account of *scientia intuitiva*. And, on the other hand, it has to be remembered that in one very important respect Leibniz departs from his doctrine of degrees. He finds it hard, he says, to conceive that there is a natural means of raising a

sensitive to the rank of a rational soul, and suggests that God
has given reason to this soul by a special act, a kind of *trans-
creation* (Gerh., vi, p. 352).

4

The Relation of Finite Individuals to God

Almost all writers on Spinoza have drawn attention to the
wavering in the *Ethics* between two radically inconsistent
conceptions of Substance—the one abstract, according to
which Substance is the blank unity, mere being in general,
which is the presupposition of all that seems to be real ; the
other concrete, according to which Substance is the absolute
totality of things, regarded, indeed, as in some sense a unity
in which particular existences are contained and subordinated.
On the one hand, Spinoza was working with the principle that
every determination is or involves negation, and that it is
only when the fictitious differences introduced by the imagination are eliminated that Substance can be truly conceived.
" Substance is considered in itself—that is, truly—when we
set aside all its modifications (*depositis affectionibus*)."
Along this line of reflexion, the notion is reached of the
Unconditioned as simply indeterminate being, which can be
characterised only by denying of it whatsoever we may assert
of the limited and the determinate. So regarded, no predicate can be applied unequivocally to the absolute and to the
relative ; the former differs from the latter, not only in
existence, but also in essence (*Eth*. i, 17 Schol.). The essence
of finite beings involves privation, want of being; the essence of
the infinite is pure being simply. Evidently from such a bare
abstraction there is no possibility of advance ; from pure
affirmation merely to the determinations that are necessary
in order that Substance should be real there is no road. On
the other hand, working rather with the principle that each
finite thing expresses God in a definite and determinate way,
Spinoza conceived of Substance as *ens realissimum*, the

collective sum of all possible predicates, a being that cannot be exhausted in any one attribute, and containing all perfection and reality. Obviously, these two conceptions are incompatible and cannot both be combined into a coherent view. The former, the notion of logical ground, yields no explanation of that which constitutes the difference between the logical ground and the particular ; a universal can never be contemplated as in its own nature that from which the concrete individual has proceeded. The latter, the notion of *ens realissimum*, yields no means of reaching what Spinoza was desirous of reaching, an ultimate ground to which the particulars stood in a relation of dependence. The notion of *ens realissimum* has been attained through means of the category of reciprocal determination ; and, valuable as this category is in enabling us to systematise the realm of nature, it is inapplicable to the Unconditioned, it has no relevancy when extended beyond the sphere of finite particular things. Viewed either in one way or the other, the notion of Substance can in no sense serve as the notion of a matrix from which all determinate differences have arisen, as the notion of the one ultimate being of which everything else is a partial manifestation.

The nature of the difficulty which besets Spinoza's whole way of thinking comes prominently to light in one portion of his work which has not, perhaps, received the attention it deserves. The human mind is treated by him as the sum of those determinate modes of consciousness, ideas, which unite to form an individual subject, just as a group of determinate modes of extension may unite to form an individual physical object through the relation of action and reaction. But now Spinoza recognised that the determinate modes of mind involve at once a relation to modes of the body as their objects and a relation to the subject or the self. " The idea of the mind is united to the mind in the same way as the mind itself is united to the body " (*Eth.* ii, 21). When a man perceives (say) a table or chair, there is (i) a certain mode of consciousness having for its object certain affections of the body of the percipient—the sensations of vision, touch, etc.—and (ii) the idea of that perception, for every mode of consciousness has itself also for its object, or involves the idea of itself. Here, however, the question at once presents itself—is this idea of itself, an idea which appears to be thought of as an aspect of each mode of consciousness, the uniting synthetic act whereby self-consciousness is constituted? And does the centre of reference lie in the individual mind or does it lie in God? So far as I can judge, Spinoza wished to locate it in God (*Eth.* ii, 21, Schol.), while at the same time he was compelled to allow a species of self-consciousness to the individual mind. Yet, whether the centre of reference be located in God or in the individual mind, it is clear that Spinoza utterly fails to do justice to the peculiar fact involved. Throughout he treats all modes, whether of consciousness or of extension, as though they had to one another only the relations of separate, isolated parts—as, for example, the parts of extension have to one another—and hence he naturally looked upon the centre of reference, in this case, as lying external to the elements united. Obviously, however, external relation of that sort is not compatible with the nature of consciousness ; and had Spinoza followed out the conception of the human mind as involving a unity, a centre of reference, internal to itself, he must of necessity have been led to see, on the one hand, that the notion of Substance is altogether inadequate to render intelligible what here lay before him ; and, on the other hand, that it is not possible to maintain the absolute identity of the universe as consisting of entities which are at once modes of consciousness and modes of extension. For if modes of consciousness be treated after the manner of modes of extension, they are deprived of just that reference to a uniting centre which is essential to their nature, while if such reference be given to them, the conception of whole and part will no longer suffice to cover the relation of the conscious subject to its various states or modes.

In working out his theory of monads, Leibniz made it his aim to rescue philosophy from that destruction of individual existence which seemed to him to be involved in the metaphysic of Spinoza. As against Spinoza, he took his stand upon the position that the individual as such was alone the truly real. But if one scrutinises more closely the conception of individuality, as it was developed by Leibniz, one will soon have reasons for suspecting that the conception will not bear the weight he was wishful to impose upon it. The one characteristic absolutely essential to individuality, as he regarded it, was the characteristic of limitation, negation, passivity. Pure unbounded energy or activity seemed, as I have said, to Leibniz incompatible with the notion of real being. Whatever is must be limited. The monad's character is determined by its " point of view " ; and that " point of view " is dependent upon the passive, privative, negative element in the monad. In truth, that which renders the monads mutually impenetrable or exclusive is matter ; without the element of materiality they would be absorbed in the being of God, the supreme Substance. Now, matter is, in fact, passivity ; matter is the correlative of confused ideas. And with the clearing up of knowledge, matter must tend to disappear ; just as, according to Spinoza, that which marks off one thing from another tends to disappear as we pass from imagination to rational knowledge. It becomes, however, straightway apparent that if limitation be essential to individuality, then God is not an individual, not a monad in the sense in which a monad had been originally defined.

We are here face to face once more with the two totally distinct ideas of what constitutes real existence,[1] but the point I want now to emphasise is the predicament in which Leibniz is thereby landed when he comes to deal with the relation in which God stands to the world of monads. On the one hand, when Leibniz permits the qualifying terms

[1] *supra*, pp. 316-9.

" necessary " and " contingent " to affect the very nature of
the existence qualified, he is led to describe the relation in
terms that are practically identical with those of Spinoza.
The monads are not to be regarded as distinct from God, nor
is it easy to see how they can be regarded as distinct from one
another. " Everything ", we are told, " is in God, as place is
in that which is placed " ; and, in a letter to Bayle, the
assertion is made that " from the creator of all things, all
actual forces or perfections emanate by a sort of continual
creation ". So, again, in the *Monadology* (§ 47), it is affirmed
that " God alone is the primary unity or original substance,
of which all created or derivative monads are products, and
have their birth, so to speak, through continual fulgurations
of the Divinity from moment to moment ". Once more, a
similar thought receives expression in the *Discours de
Métaphysique*. " Created substances depend on God, who
conserves them, and even produces them continually by a
kind of emanation, as we produce our thoughts." " From
God all individuals emanate continually, and he sees the universe not only as they see it, but besides in a very different
way from them." These passages, and there are many others
to a like effect, might easily have been written by Spinoza
himself. On the other hand, when Leibniz is concerned to
emphasise the independence of the monad, he is forced to
ascribe to the divine being a position of transcendence. The
world of monads is metaphysically contingent, he argues ;
its notion does not involve its existence. It springs from a
choice on the part of God. God therefore stands to the
system of monads in the external relation of cause to effect.
That is to say, it is through the very notion of external relation, which had been dismissed as illegitimate when applied
to the world of monads, that Leibniz is now compelled to
represent the relation between God and the whole system of
monads. No ingenuity can help him out of the contradiction
into which he has thus fallen. No method is open to him of
accommodating within the scope of one and the same view

both the completeness of God *and* the quasi-independence
which is claimed for the world of monads. He appeals, for
instance, to the vague principle of the choice of the best, or
the tendency of the Divine activity towards perfection. But
the difficulties of the situation are rather increased than
diminished thereby. For perfection or the good, as Leibniz
understands it, is equivalent to the greatest sum of reality,
so that God thus becomes once more the *ens realissimum*.
Not only is it impossible to effect in this manner a connexion
between God and the world of monads, but the notion of God
at once begins to fluctuate between that of a totality of
positive qualities and that of an indeterminate ground destitute of any distinguishing mark. In short, Spinoza's dilemma
reappears again with all its former acuteness. Whichever
way be taken, it is impossible for Leibniz to explain, as he
desired to do, the limited, passive, negative factor ; the conception of the choice of the best avails him not at all to bring
into conjunction the infinite ground and the diversity of
finite monads.

It is worth while, perhaps, referring to another point. The
life of the monad, the perceptions or phases of consciousness
through which it passes, are the ways in which it expresses the
universe. But Leibniz insisted upon ascribing to the higher
monads the power of forming ideas of the Divine nature—
ideas, that is to say, of that which stands to the monads in a
relation very different from the relation in which they stand
to one another. He is frequently to be found asserting that
the development of each of these monads takes place as
though only that monad and God existed. While, then, such
monad excludes from itself all influence from the other
monads, it is, notwithstanding, susceptible to influences from
God. Yet, how is it possible for the monad thus to transcend
its isolation in the one case and to be incapable of doing so in
the other ? And how are we to reconcile with the finitude and
limited character of the monad the possession on its part of
ideas of an infinite reality—of a reality, that is, which is not

only other than itself but which is other than the whole world of monads? The considerations I am urging are sufficient to show how hopeless it was for Leibniz to preserve such a conception of God as is involved in the two or three passages in which God is described by him as a monad. As *actus purus* without any passivity, God would be what Leibniz once said a monad without matter would be, namely, " a deserter from the general order "; and how, in that case, God could be in communication with monads who are not deserters is one of the many enigmas Leibniz has left unsolved.

5

Conclusion

The discussion in which we have been engaged is by no means one of merely historical interest. At the present time the questions at issue between Spinoza and Leibniz are reasserting themselves afresh, and in such reference it is not unimportant to inquire how far, as a matter of fact, Leibniz succeeded in surmounting difficulties that Spinoza could not resolve. When it is asked, for example, "whether finite individuals possess a substantive or an adjectival mode of being", the issue, I take it, is once again being raised whether the finite individual is to be regarded as a " mode " or as, in some sense at least, a "monad". What it is now customary to call the Absolute retains in essential respects the meaning which Spinoza assigned to Substance, and to a large extent F. H. Bradley's philosophy is the philosophy of Spinoza worked over anew in the light of subsequent science and reflexion. " The positive relation of every appearance as an adjective to Reality, and the presence of Reality among its appearances in different degrees and with diverse values "— this, Bradley tells us, is the "double truth" which he has found to be the " centre of philosophy". That the position is beset with difficulties has been made evident enough by recent criticism. If, however, any conclusion can be drawn from the comparison I have been instituting, it is most assuredly this —that there is no way out of those difficulties by the simple device of claiming some special efficacy for the notion of "Activity" or "Life" in conceiving of one ultimate all-embracing ground of things. When so used, the notion in question loses the significance it possesses as applied to concrete individual existents, and becomes at once infected with all the ambiguity of meaning which attaches to the term Absolute itself. We shall seek in vain to form any intelligible conception of how the Whole of things can be said either to live or to act.

One consideration alone I will allow myself at the end. Leibniz's fundamental mistake, as I conceive it, lay not in his insisting upon the active character of all finite existences, but in his attempting to exhibit this activity of theirs as a "fulguration" of, or detachment from, one ultimate source of activity. To postulate a source of that description seems to me to be a contradiction in terms. We can form, of course, a general notion of activity, as of other things ; but if we suppose that precisely answering to the notion there is an actually existent reality, we are illegitimately hypostasising the said notion and making an entity of an abstraction. Just as there is no such thing as feeling in general but only specific states of feeling, just as there is no such thing as willing in general but only specific processes of willing, so there is no such thing as activity in general but only specific modes of activity. On the other hand, activity, as specifically exercised by particular concrete individuals, does appear to me to be a characteristic so essential that any metaphysical interpretation of them which ignores it is bound to result in failure. Whether, following Leibniz, we are entitled to affirm that everything which exists is active, we need not now stay to inquire ; our concern, for the moment, is with some existents that admittedly are active. An individual mind, for example, whatever else it may be, is, at least, a continuous succession of acts or processes of the kind called mental ; it is only in and through such acts or processes that there is for it awareness of " connexions of content " at all. To assert, therefore, that all finite individual subjects " are in ultimate analysis connexions of content within the real individual to which they belong " [1] seems to me tantamount to saying that these finite individual subjects *are* what they are aware of, and to leaving completely out of account the acts or processes of being aware. Doubtless *then* that which alone is peculiar to individuals so regarded—their specific " points of view," namely—is matter of little or no moment ; what is of moment is the connexion of content viewed *sub specie aeternitatis*. Accordingly, the contention that in the Absolute these limited, imperfect, fragmentary " points of view " must be transformed, transmuted, merged and dissolved becomes explicable ; and " because I cannot spread out my window until all is transparent, and all windows disappear," I am clearly not justified in insisting on " my window-frame's rigidity ".[2] But what vitiates the whole argument is, I submit, the unwarranted assumption made at the start. As an *existing* entity, the finite individual subject *is not* what it is aware of. In its regard, as in regard to other matters of inquiry, it is necessary to distinguish that which is important from that which is fundamental. The " connexions of content " are certainly of supreme importance ; they give to a mental life meaning, value and significance. Yet, all the same, its acts or processes, its temporal states and modes of being aware, are for it fundamental ; apart from them, it would have no place at all in the realm of existence, let alone a claim to any independence of its own. And I confess I am baffled when I am bidden to conceive of my individuality, in the latter sense, as included within a wider individuality to which I and other finite individuals belong. I do not, that is to say, see in what conceivable way a state or act of my mind can be part of a state or act of an infinite mind, or the latter

---

[1] Bosanquet : *Logic*, 2 ed., vol. ii, p. 258.

[2] Bradley : *Appearance and Reality*, p. 253.

Y

state or act be " immanent " in my state or act. I can understand what is meant by "immanence" when that term is used with respect to values in their relation to finite consciousnesses ; I cannot understand what is meant by it if it has reference to the relation between one existent individual mind and another.

INDEX

Abercrombie, John, 107-8

Absolute and relative Truth, according to Bradley, 172-4

" Abstracta " and " existents ", 77

Abstraction, involved in conceptual thinking, 125

" Acquaintance, knowledge by " and " knowledge by description ", the antithesis of, 17 *sqq.* ; calls to be rejected, 24

Activity, according to Spinoza and Leibniz, constitutes the individuality of determinate existences, 321-5 ; mental activity, not the kind of activity ascribable to material things, 183 ; no such thing as activity in general, 336 ; activity of finite existents, according to Leibniz, " fulgurations " of one ultimate source, 336-8 ; involves " passivity ", according to him, 320-1

Act of apprehending, from the first a process of discriminating and comparing, 73

Adamson, Robert, xiv *sqq.*, 124

Alexander, Samuel, his view of the life of mind as a system of " conations ", 33 *sqq.* ; referred to, xiii, 90, 135

Ameseder, Rudolf, 298, 299

Animata, different grades of, according to Spinoza, 327-9

Appearance and Reality, according to Bradley, 169 *sqq.* ; two conflicting views in his treatment of their relation to one another, 171-2

" Appearance ", or phenomenon, carries with it the significance of fragmentariness, of incompleteness, as contrasts with the existing object, 75

" Appearances ", nature of, 45 *sqq.* ; not existents, 77-8 ; under certain circumstances inevitable that a thing should seem to have characteristics other than those which it really does have, 76-7

" Appearing ", the characteristic of, in large measure explicable from the nature of perceptive activity, 74 *sqq.*

Aristotle, his doctrine of μοναί, 88 *n.* ; his view of " substance ", 308-10 ; referred to, 111 *n.*

Association, not the main function involved in abstraction and generalisation, 279-81.

Atomic structure, according to modern science, 193-4

Atomic theories and the concept of energy, 193 *sqq.*

" Attributes ", Spinoza's doctrine of, 307-8

Auditory imagery of the objective type, 105 *sqq.*

Awareness, no such thing as awareness in general, 15

Barrie, J. M., his picture of a child's mind, 98

Bartlett, F. C., 102-3

Being, different senses of the term, according to Meinong, 301-3.

Belief in the existence of an independent external world depends, according to Stace, on our belief in the existence of other minds, 255 *sqq.*

Bergson, Henri, his explanation of the consciousness of a flash of light, 31 *sqq.* ; his indictment of conceptual thought, 143 *sqq.* ; his view of intuition, 144-5 ; referred to, 86, 110 *n*., 113, 147, 148, 311 *n*.

Berkeley, George, his theory of the *esse* of sensible things, 44 ; his treatment of abstract ideas, 275 *sqq*. ; referred to, 6, 9, 44, 53, 90, 136, 137, 158, 275, 277, 281

Bifurcation of Nature, 158

Biran, Maine de, 181, 182 *n*.

Bosanquet, Bernard, xix *n*., 29, 41, 97, 157, 337.

Boscovich, Roger Joseph, 188

Bradley, F. H., his philosophy largely the philosophy of Spinoza worked over again, 325-6 ; his treatment of Nature, 156 *sqq*. ; his view of the nature of judgment, 149 *sqq*. ; what he designated " floating adjectives ", 143 ; referred to, 16 *sqq*., 57, 88, 130, 139, 182, 183, 186, 191

Brentano, Franz, 270

Broad, C. D., his reason for holding that the " objective constituent " of a perceptual situation is not a spatio-temporal part of a physical object, 51 *sqq*. ; his theory of " sensa ", 48 *sqq*. ; his theory of the mind as a compound substance, 229 *sqq*. ; comparison of this theory with Kant's doctrine of the " empirical subject ", 231-2 ; what is it that according to Broad we perceive? 58 ; referred to, 32, 75, 140, 177 *sqq*., 187 *n*.

Caird, Edward, 266

Causal laws, natural and mnemic, according to Russell, 247

Causality, physical and psychical, according to Wundt, 247

Causal relation, Meinong's analysis of, 286

" Choice of the best ", according to Leibniz, 318

Clifford, W. K., his view of " mind-stuff ", 224-5, referred to, 226, 227

Cognition, the nature of, 1 *sqq*.

Cognitive act, nature of, 12 *sqq*.

Coleridge, S. T., 105

Conatus, Spinoza's conception of, 323

Concepts and universals, 135

Concepts, not pictures or copies of universals, 141-3 ; concepts of likeness or difference, not part of the datum immediately given, 71 *sqq*.

Conceptual thinking and perceptive activity, 146 *sqq*.

Conceptual thinking, cannot be identified with that which it essays to know, 151 ; characteristic of it that its contents are regarded as necessarily connected, 131 *sqq*. ; in its regard the threefold distinction of act, content, and objective reality, holds, 134-5 ; invariably refers to the objective order of real existent entities, 130 *sqq*. ; involves both analysis and synthesis, 125 *sqq*. ; its inwardness or reflective character, 122 *sqq*.

Conceptual thought and real existence, 121 *sqq*.

Consciousness, as an " existent " and as a " knowing ", 10 ; Holt's view of, 37 *sqq*. ; the view of it as " diaphanous ", 41 *sqq*.

Conscious subject, the unity and continuity of, 240-3

" Content apprehended " and " content of the act of apprehension ", 92-4

" Content " of an act of apprehension and the " object " of that act, distinction of, according to Meinong, 289 *sqq*.

Continuity, the principle of, according to Leibniz, 325-7

Critical Realism, the Basis of, 1 *sqq*.

Discrimination, the essence of every act of apprehending and virtually the very act of knowing, 74 ; in its primitive stages does not involve abstract ideas of comparison and relation, 14

" Description, knowledge by " and " knowledge by acquaintance ", 17 *sqq*.

" Desideratives ", according to Meinong, 303-4

" Dignitatives ", according to Meinong, 303-4

Dillmann, Eduard, 320

" Dogmatism ", as Kant viewed it, xx

Dream-experiences only to be understood by reference to what takes place in normal perception, 114

Dream-imagery, 109 *sqq.*

Dream-images, influence of attention upon, 115-6

Dreams, a very large number at least originate in consequence of actual perception, 110 ; some, initiated through " organic sensations ", 111

Dualism, 43

Duff, Robert A., 323

Eddington, Sir Arthur, his conception of the mind, 214-6 ; his philosophy of nature, 204 *sqq.* ; his illustration of the relativity of velocity, 207-8

Effort, feeling of, composite in character, 182-3

Ehrenfels, Christian v., his view of *Gestaltqualitäten*, 291-2

Eigenlicht, influence of, upon visual dream-images, 112

Einfühlung, 117-9

Einstein, A., his principle of equivalence, 200, referred to, 212

Ellis, Havelock, 110 *n.*, 113

" Emergence ", the notion of, 232-3

Energy and force, in the physical world, 187 *sqq.*

Energy, concept of, and modern atomic theories, 193 *sqq.* ; concept of energy as an entity *per se* leads to inconsistency, 198-9 ; development of the doctrine of energy, 189 *sqq.*

" Entelechies " and " psychic factors ", 249-50

Epistemology, subject-matter of, xix *sqq.*

Esse essentiae and *esse existentiae*, according to Spinoza and Leibniz, 308 *sqq.*

Existence and essence or content, according to Bradley, 92

Existence and subsistence, 294-5

Existence, the term, 139-40 ; twofold significance of, according to Spinoza, 310-2

Experientia vaga, according to Spinoza, 327-8

External world, belief in the existence of, according to Stace, 261-2

" Factuality " (*Tatsächlichkeit*), according to Meinong, 302-3

Falsehoods, not subsistents, according to Meinong, 141

Faraday, Michael, his conception of " lines of force ", 188-9, referred to, 190

Fechner, G. Th., 179, 293 *n*

Feeling, Broad's use of the term, 62 *sqq.*

Finite minds, not included in an infinite Mind, 337-8

Force, the term, 175 ; does not denote a " subjective " interpretation of ours, 201-3 ; denotes something of which we are conscious and not something inherent in the mental life itself, 184 *sqq.* ; is it possible to adhere to the use of the term as signifying " the rate of change of momentum " ? 176-7 ; force has its being in the physical world, 187 *sqq.* ; inseparable from matter, 192-3

Fullerton, G. Stuart, xvi

Fundamentum relationis, according to Meinong, 282-3

Galton, Sir Francis, 100-1

Gegenstände, four classes of, according to Meinong, 297 *sqq.*

Gegenstandstheorie, Meinong's, 8 *sqq.* ; 271, 293 *sqq.* ; Meinong's wide use of the term *Gegenstand*, 9

Generalising, as a feature of conceptual thinking, 124 *sqq.*

Gestaltqualitäten, 291-2

God, relation of, to finite individuals, according to Spinoza and Leibniz, 329 *sqq.* ; inconsistencies in Leibniz's notion of God, 334-5

Gravitation, new conception of, 213-4

Green, Thomas Hill, xvii, 275
Grote, John, 124

Haldane, J. S., 185, 187
Hamilton, Sir W., 62, 118
Hammond, 111 n.
Hardy, Thomas, illustration from
  Tess, 98-9, 119
Hegel, G. W. F., xiv, xvii, 39, 40, 45,
  146, 156, 232, 305
Helmholtz, Hermann L. F., 112,
  189, 191, 192-3
Hering, H. E., 86
Hobhouse, L. T., on " the fallacy
  of the supersensual ", 129-30 ;
  his Theory of Knowledge, xvi
Hodgson, Shadworth H., xvi, 10
Holt, Edwin B., his conception of
  " mental entities ", 35 sqq. ; his
  view of consciousness, 37 sqq.; re-
  ferred to, 15, 16, 44
Hume, David, his negative arguments in support of nomenalism,
  276-7 ; his positive line of argument in support thereof, 277-9 ;
  referred to, 6, 50, 72, 85, 90 n.,
  136, 252, 275, 281 sqq., 285.
Hume-Studien of Meinong, 275 sqq.
Husserl, Edmund, 141, 273

Ideating activity, Lotze's view of,
  281-2
" Ideas of relation ", the origin of,
  inexplicable on the basis of the
  empirical theory of Locke and
  Hume, 71 sqq.
Imagination, continuous with perception and growing out of it, 89 ;
  how in the process of imagination
  subjective factors affect the " content apprehended ", 116
Imaginative activity, clearly limited, 90
" Images ", ambiguity in the use of
  the term, 100-1 ; nature of, 85
  sqq. ; images of taste, smell,
  touch and vision, 103 sqq. ; the
  nucleus and penumbra of, 101 sqq.
Indeterminancy, the so-called principle of, 227-8
Individual things, stages in the development of, according to Spinoza and Leibniz, 325 sqq.

James, William, 34, 103, 120
Jeans, Sir J. H., 200 sqq.
Joachim, H., 313 n., 315
Johnson, W. E., 94-5, 183
Jones, Sir Henry, xvii sqq.
Judgment, nature of, according to
  Bradley, 149 sqq.

Kant, Immanuel, xix sqq. ; his critical method, xxi sqq. ; his analysis of the act of perceiving an object, 1 sqq. ; difficulties in that
  analysis, 3 sqq. ; his view of sense-
  impressions, 6 sqq. ; the term
  " object ", according to Kant, 9 ;
  matter, according to Kant, must
  be endowed with the two forces
  of attraction and repulsion, 192-
  3 ; referred to, 10, 19, 21, 23, 24,
  25, 26, 28, 40, 74, 231-2
Kinaesthetic imagery, 103 sqq.
Knowing and the known, an antithesis in the very notion of
  knowledge itself, 43, 166
Knowing process, subjectivity of,
  not a vitiating influence in respect
  to knowledge, 152 sqq.
Knowing, the act of, not an act of
  synthesising in Kant's sense, but
  an act of discriminating, 7 ; the
  fundamental characteristic of
  mental life, 42 sqq.
Knowledge, a realistic theory of,
  rests on the distinction between
  the act of knowing and the object
  known, 40 sqq. ; " representative theory " of, 41

Ladd, G. T., 112
Laguna, Grace A. de, 19
Laird, J., 99
Language and the use of signs in
  conceptual thinking, 130
Latta, R., 318
Leibniz, G. W., his conception of
  " monads " and Spinoza's conception of " nodes ", 305 sqq. ;
  according to his view the " existence " of monads implies something over and above " essence ",
  317-9 ; his distinction between
  " primary substance " and
  " created substances ", 316-7 ;

reverts to the Aristotelian definition of " substance ", 315 ; but regards each " monad " as a " substance ", 316 ; referred to, 199, 305 *sqq.*

Liebmann, Otto, 23

" Lines of force ", Faraday's conception of, 188-9

Locke, John, xxi, 71, 121, 136, 175, 275, 281, 282, 283, 285, 319

Lossky, N. O., xvi, 13 *sqq.*

Lotze, Hermann, on the logical notion, 142-3 ; his view of an ideating activity, 281-2 ; referred to, xiv, 72, 74, 97, 130, 219, 242, 265-6, 288, 295 *n.*

" Mass " and its relation to " energy ", Eddington's conception of, 209-11 ; two kinds of " mass ", according to the relativity theory, " invariant " and " relative ", 211-12

Material things and sensible appearances, 68

Matter and force, duality of, and inseparability of, 192-3

Matter, conceived as non-Euclidean in character, 199 *sqq.*

Martineau, James, 181

Marvin, Walter T., xviii *sqq.*

Maxwell, J. Clerk, his contention that energy is only to be found in connexion with matter, 194 ; referred to, 189, 190

Meinong, Alexius, the philosophical researches of, 259 *sqq.* ; biographical details, 269-71 ; referred to, 7 *sqq.*, 12, 138, 141

" Mental reaction ", the notion of, does not render explicable the qualitative differences of nature,33

Meyer, G. H., 103, 108

Mill, James, 89 *n.*

Mill, John Stuart, 89

Mind, the, as conceived by Eddington, 214-6 ; conceived as a compound substance, 229 *sqq.* ; the " bodily " and the " psychic " factors of, according to Broad, 233-7; what does Broad mean by the term " mind " ? 239-40

Minds and things, 26 *sqq.*

" Monads ", finite, their relation to God, according to Leibniz, 332-4

" Modes ", the, of Spinoza and the " monads " of Leibniz, 305 *sqq.*

" Modes ", two ways of regarding them, according to Spinoza, 312-3

Moore, G. E., xiii, 68 *sqq.*, 79-80

Müller, Johannes, 111 *sqq.*

Multiple Personality, 243

" Multiple relation theory " of perception, according to Broad, 64 *sqq.*

Muscae volitantes, 112

Myers, C. S., 108

Nature, F. H. Bradley's treatment of, 156 *sqq.*, regarded by Bradley as but " one part of the feeling whole ", 159 *sqq.* ; dynamic aspect of, 175 *sqq.*

" Neo-realism ", xiii *sqq.* ; neo-realistic conceptions of the mental life, 32 *sqq.*

Nettleship, R. Lewis, 130

" Neutral entities ", Holt's conception of, 35 *sqq.*

Newton, Sir Isaac, 134, 192, 253

Nicholson, J. W., 197

Nominalism, Hume's, examination of, 276 *sqq.*

Numbers, not mental entities, 139

" Objectives ", Meinong's view of, 300-1

Objectivity, characteristic of, the central problem of the theory of knowledge, according to Kant, and his solution of the problem, 1 *sqq.*

Object, the, according to Kant a construction on the part of the mind itself, 5

" Objects of higher order ", according to Meinong, 293-4

" Objects " (*Objekte*), various species of, according to Meinong, 297

" Organic habits ", 87

Organisms, finite, and physical nature, 162-4

Other Minds, Stace's account of the way in which the individual comes to discover their existence, 259-61

Pains and pleasures, according to Holt, 39

Passivity, elements of, in the development of individual experience, according to Spinoza, 324-5; Leibniz's notion of, 320-1

Pear, T. H., 110

Perceiving and thinking, not disparate faculties of mind, 132

Perceiving, the two-fold character of the act of, 8 *sqq*; conditions giving rise to the act of, 11 *sqq*.

Perception and introspection, according to Broad, 68 *sqq*.

Perception, becomes less and less dependent upon what at the time is actually given, 97; is enormously facilitated by the operation of retention or revival, 95; what Broad means by the term, 80-2

" Perceptional situations ", 49 *sqq*.

Perry, R. B., xiii, xxiii

Philosophical inquiry, nature and aims of, according to Meinong, 272 *sqq*.

Physical entities, conceived as " only an extract of pointer readings ", 223-4

Physical nature and finite organisms, 162-4; Bradley's position that no element of physical nature probably " falls outside the experience of finite centres ", 164 *sqq*.

Physical object, and sensible object, 30 *sqq*.; " brickbat " theory of a physical object, 46-7

Plato, 140, 179

Planck's constant, 197

Presentations, a chaos of, not the starting-point of knowledge, 258-9; Meinong's view of, 288

Podmore, Frank, 231 *n*.

Pringle-Pattison, A. Seth, 308

Psychical research, 230-1

" Psychic factor ", the hypothesis that this is a universal factor, 237

Psychologism, 273

Radestock of Krauss, 114

Rankine, W. J. Macquorn, 189

Ratio, the grade of, according to Spinoza, 328

Reid, L. Arnaud, 101 *n*.

Reid, Thomas, and the Scotch Common-sense School, xiv

Realism, meaning of the term, xiii *sqq*.; no new departure in philosophical speculation, xiv; can it dispense with a theory of knowledge? xviii *sqq*.

Reality and appearance, according to Bradley, 169 *sqq*.

Relations, Hume's theory of, 281 *sqq*.; how ideas of relation come to be formed, 72 *sqq*.; relations of comparison and of compatibility, 283-5; " real " and " ideal " relations, according to Meinong, 285-7; subjectivist interpretation of, 291-3; relations and concepts, 137-8

Relative and Absolute Truth, according to Bradley, 172-4

Relativity, general theory of, and the forces of nature, 199 *sqq*.

" Residua " and " traces ", misleading terms, 88

Resistance, experience of, 186

Retention and revival, for psychology an ultimate condition of mental life, 86 *sqq*.

Revived experiences, do not necessarily falsify perception, 120

Ruskin, John, 117

Russell, Bertrand, his doctrine of a " thing " as being identical with the " class of its appearances ", 26 *sqq*.; his use of the term " appearance ", 28 *sqq*.; referred to, xiii, 19 *sqq*., 20 *sqq*., 24, 33, 44 *sqq*., 53, 78, 139, 216, 247, 291, 292 *n*., 298 *n*., 306

Scientia intuitiva, according to Spinoza, 328

Scott, J. W., his view that " appearances " constitute the content of reality, 45

Secondary qualities, conceived as " inhering in " sensa, 82-4

Self-consciousness, Spinoza's failure to do justice to the facts involved in, 330-1; the transcendental unity of, according to Kant, 3

Self, the, not subject to strain as physical things are, nor to be thought of as putting forth energy, 180 *sqq.*

Sensa, as Broad conceives them, are they rightly regarded as "appearances of" material things? 53 *sqq.* ; 79-80 ; said to serve as "signs" of physical objects, 56 ; described as "existents", although neither physical nor mental, 78-9

Sense-apprehension, even in a crude form, an act of discriminating and comparing, 24 *sqq.*

"Sense-fields" and "sense-histories", as conceived by Broad, 60 *sqq.*

Sense-perception, development of, 25

Sensibility and understanding, according to Kant, 3 *sqq.*

"Sensible appearance", true meaning of the term, 69 *sqq.*

"Sensible appearances" and material things, 68 *sqq.*

"Sensible object", what Russell means by the term, 21 *sqq.*

Sensing, Broad's theory of a general process of, 64 *sqq.*

Sensory appearances, not existents, 71 *sqq.*

Sensum theory, the, 48 *sqq.*

Sheldon, W. H., 196

Sidgwick, Henry, xiv

Solipsism, can be logically refuted, 262 *sqq.*

Sommerfeld, 194

Sorley, W. R., xv

"Soul-substance", the notion of, 47

Spencer, Herbert, 176, 178

Spinoza's conception of "modes" and Leibniz's conception of "monads", 305 *sqq.*

Stace, W. T., his theory of knowledge and existence, 251 *sqq.*

Stirling, J. Hutcheson, 96, 152

Stout, G. F., 96, 243

Strain, the act of perceiving a strain different from the strain perceived, 179

Stricker, 104-5

Stumpf's case, 59

Subjectivism, the refutation of, 251 *sqq.*

Subsistence (*Bestehen*), 138 *sqq.* ; and existence, 294-5

Subsistent entities, enumeration of, 140

"Substance", according to Aristotle, 308-10 ; according to Spinoza, 307 ; two inconsistent notions of, in Spinoza's *Ethics*, 329-31

Sully, James, 108

Synthesis, the act of, according to Kant, 2 *sqq.* ; nature of, as involved in conceptual thinking, 126 *sqq.*, 145-6

Taine, H., views perception as a process of imagining, 91 ; referred to, 105, 107-8

Tait, P. G., 175, 177

Tension or strain, not identical with the consciousness of it, 179

Things and Minds, 26 *sqq.*

Things of nature, not psychical in character, 158-9

Thinking and perceiving, not disparate faculties of mind, 132

Thomson, Sir J. J., his hypothesis of a mass-producing material, 198

Thought, viewed as mediate knowledge, 123

Tissié, P., 110 *n.*, 111, 113

"Traces" and "dispositions", so called, the doctrine of, 235-7, 243 *sqq.*

Twardowski, K., his treatise on Content and Object of Presentations, 289

Understanding and sensibility, according to Kant, 3 *sqq.*

Universals and concepts, 135 ; universals not existents, 138-9

Visual imagery, its prevailingly objective character, 106 *sqq.*

"Vital force", the notion of, 186-7

Volkelt, Johannes, 265-6

Ward, James, emphasised the difference between a succession of presentations and the presentation of succession, 148 ; referred to, 61, 66, 69, 88, 92-3, 105, 117, 135

Watson, J. B., 105

Weygandt, W., 110 *n.*

Weyl, Hermann, his contention that matter is an offspring of the electro-magnetic field, 195-7 ; referred to, 188, 200

Whitehead, A. N., his rendering of the theory of relativity, 202-3 ; referred to, 22 *sqq.*, 216

Windelband, Wilhelm, 3

Winslow, Forbes, 111 *n.*

Witasek, S., 118

" World-building ", according to Eddington, 217-23

Wordsworth, W., 117

World, the, conceived as consisting of " mind-stuff ", 224 *sqq.*

Wundt, Wilhelm, 110 *n.*, 247

PRINTED IN GREAT BRITAIN BY ROBERT MACLEHOSE AND CO. LTD.
THE UNIVERSITY PRESS, GLASGOW

NEW WORKS ON PHILOSOPHY

PSYCHOLOGY DOWN THE AGES. By Prof. C. SPEAR-
MAN, Ph.D., F.R.S. 2 Vols. 30s. net.

STUDIES IN THE PHILOSOPHY OF RELIGION. By
Prof. ARCHIBALD A. BOWMAN. 2 Vols.

THE FAITH OF A MORALIST: GIFFORD LECTURES,
1926-1928. Series I. The Theological Implications of
Morality. Series II. Natural Theology and the Positive
Religions. By Prof. A. E. TAYLOR, D.Litt. New Edition
in one volume. 18s. net.

THE CONCEPT OF MORALS. By Prof. W. T. STACE.
8s. 6d. net.

A BASIS OF OPINION. By ADRIAN COATES, M.A.

DIVINE CAUSATION: A CRITICAL STUDY CONCERNING
" INTERMEDIARIES ". By W. J. BEALE, M.A., B.D.,
D.Phil. 7s. 6d. net.

RELIGION AND REALITY : AN ESSAY IN THE CHRISTIAN
COORDINATION OF CONTRARIES. By MELVILLE CHANING-
PEARCE. 7s. 6d. net.

PLATO'S CONCEPTION OF PHILOSOPHY. By H. GAUSS,
Ph.D. 6s. net.

HUME'S THEORY OF KNOWLEDGE: A CRITICAL
EXAMINATION. By CONSTANCE MAUND. 12s. 6d. net.

MACMILLAN AND CO. LTD. LONDON

OTHER WORKS ON PHILOSOPHY

By Prof. S. ALEXANDER

SPACE, TIME, AND DEITY : GIFFORD LECTURES, 1916-1918. 2 Vols. 25s. net.

BEAUTY AND OTHER FORMS OF VALUE. 10s. 6d. net.

By Prof. HENRI BERGSON

CREATIVE EVOLUTION. Translated by ARTHUR MITCHELL, Ph.D. 12s. 6d. net.

THE TWO SOURCES OF MORALITY AND RELIGION. Translated by R. A. AUDRA, C. BRERETON, and W. H. CARTER. 10s. net.

LAUGHTER : AN ESSAY ON THE MEANING OF THE COMIC. Translated by CLOUDESLEY BRERETON, M.A., and FRED. ROTHWELL, B.A. 3s. 6d. net.

———

NATURE, MAN AND GOD : GIFFORD LECTURES, 1932-1933 and 1933-1934. By Dr. WILLIAM TEMPLE, Archbishop of York. 18s. net.

PHILOSOPHICAL STUDIES. By Prof. A. E. TAYLOR, D.Litt. 15s. net.

PERSONAL REALISM. By Prof. J. B. PRATT, Ph.D. 15s. net.

CRITIQUE OF PURE REASON, Translated by Prof. NORMAN KEMP SMITH, D.Phil. Abridged Edition. 10s. 6d. net.

HOLISM AND EVOLUTION. By General the Rt. Hon. J. C. SMUTS. Third Edition (1936). 12s. 6d. net.

MACMILLAN AND CO. LTD. LONDON

Date Due			
Dec 12'41			
May 11'43			
Jun 14'46			
May 21 '48			
Jan 4 '50			
Nov 11'52			
Jan 21 '53			
DEC 23 1955			
14 FEB 1972			
1 3 MAR 1972			
1 1 MAR 1973			
7 FEB 1974			
2 2 MAR 1979			
MAY 1 0 1984			
RETURNED MAY 1 4 1984			